World Food Aid

The photograph on the front cover
shows people on a food for work programme
supported by WFP and other donors
WFP/Fiona McDougall

WFP deliveries (*clockwise*)
1. Maize by rail from Zimbabwe for shipment from Mozambique to 16 African countries
2. by air to Somalia
3. by truck to Sudan
4. by river to Sudan
5. by river to Cambodia

World Food Aid

Experiences of Recipients & Donors

Edited by
JOHN SHAW & EDWARD CLAY

World Food Programme
ROME
in association with
James Currey
LONDON
Heinemann
PORTSMOUTH (N.H.)

James Currey Ltd
54b Thornhill Square
Islington
London N1 1BE

Heinemann
A Division of Reed Publishing (USA) Inc
361 Hanover Street
Portsmouth N.H. 03801, USA

British Library Cataloguing in Publication Data
World Food Aid: Experiences of Recipients
and Donors
  I. Shaw, John   II. Clay, Edward J.
  338.91

ISBN 0-85255-146-0   (cloth)
     0-85255-145-2   (paper)

ISBN 0-435-08097-0 (Heinemann Cloth)

Library of Congress Cataloging-in-Publication Data
Shaw, John & Clay, Edward
World food aid : experiences of recipients & donors.
     p.   cm.
  Includes bibliographical references and index.
  ISBN 0-435-08097-0 (cloth)
  1. Food relief. 2. International relief. I. Shaw, John.
II. Clay, Edward J.
HV696.F6W678   1994
363.8'83--dc20
                              93-38251
                              CIP

Typeset by Colset Pte. Ltd., Singapore
Printed in Britain by Villiers Publications London N3

Contents

v

Acknowledgements

The editors alone are responsible for the contents of this volume on the experiences of recipient countries and donors. The views expressed are not necessarily those of the countries and donors concerned, or of the World Food Programme. The editors are, however, indebted to a large number of people who provided information and data for the various case studies and commented on drafts prepared. First and foremost are the government officials dealing with food aid in the respective countries and staff of aid agencies as well as representatives of non-governmental organizations. WFP country officers also played a crucial role in the assembling of material. At WFP headquarters in Rome, the country desk officers in the Operations Department checked the text and provided updated information. Jean-Marie Boucher, Chief of the Policy and Data Analysis Branch, and his staff responsible for managing the WFP International Food Aid Information System (INTERFAIS) provided data on which most of the statistical tables are based. Special thanks are due to Gian Piero Lucarini who compiled the data and supervised the production of the tables. Diana Dixon arranged the photographs and captions. The arduous task of checking the first draft was diligently carried out by Judy Pickford. Typing was done in WFP's Documentation Production Unit by Debbie Reid, Cynthia Panlilio, Daniela Giannangeli, Liliana D'Aniello and Anne Walder under the supervision of Norma Peverell. Charlotte Benson of the Overseas Development Institute provided valuable assistance in bringing diverse material together and James Daglish undertook the first editing of the case studies. We are also grateful to Margaret Cornell for her editing skills, and to James Currey, Keith Sambrook, Clare Currey and Lynn Taylor for the professional way in which they have published this volume.

John Shaw
Edward Clay
Editors

Foreword

This book is a distinctive contribution to the considerable literature on food aid in that it provides an account of the practical experience of donors and recipient countries with food aid. As such, I believe that it makes an important contribution to a better understanding of food aid and to the international discussion concerning its future use.

All indications are that food aid will be needed on an increasing scale during the 1990s and beyond. In many developing countries there are growing numbers of malnourished people, rising food imports, a diminishing capacity to pay for them and a high level of debt servicing. These negative developments have been made worse by large-scale and often protracted emergency situations caused by man and by nature, particularly in sub-Saharan Africa.

Food aid is a controversial form of development assistance. Both donor and recipient governments have displayed an ambivalent attitude to it that has undermined its usefulness. Detractors point to the political and commercial motives that have sustained food aid flows, to their disincentive effects and to the risk they carry of creating dependence. However, these criticisms apply equally to other forms of aid. There is nothing inherently wrong with food aid. As with all external assistance, its effectiveness depends on the ways in which it is provided and used.

Food aid plays a vital role in emergencies in feeding the poor and saving lives. A recent joint study by the World Bank and the World Food Programme on food aid in Africa, which reflects the shared belief of the two organizations that food aid is an important and undervalued resource for development, has shown that food aid also has a special advantage in sustaining a poverty focus, supporting food security and attenuating the social costs of economic adjustment programmes that many developing countries must undertake. The world food crisis of the early 1970s and the African food crises of the 1980s have brought about a fundamental rethinking of food aid policies and programmes in donor and recipient countries. Once primarily a mechanism for disposal of food surpluses, food aid has increasingly come to be considered as an important resource to promote economic growth and enhance food security in recipient countries.

At the World Food Conference in Rome in 1974 delegates were concerned not only to provide an adequate level of food aid – a minimum annual target of 10 million tons of aid in cereals was established – but to ensure that the food aid policies and programmes of donors were well co-ordinated to achieve maximum benefit for developing countries. As a result, one of the resolutions of the Conference was to restructure the governing body of the World Food Programme into the Committee on Food Aid Policies and Programmes (CFA) and to enlarge its mandate. Thereby it became a forum for intergovernmental consultations on national and international food aid policies and programmes and for formulating proposals for more effective co-ordination of multilateral, bilateral and non-governmental food aid programmes, including emergency food aid.

Thus the CFA has become the world focus for discussion on all aspects of food aid from all sources. In order to assist it in carrying out these wide-ranging functions, I suggested at its Session in May 1983 that one approach to achieving a common understanding of food aid policies and programmes, of the problems encountered in implementing them and of the most appropriate uses of food aid would be to review the national experiences of donor and recipient countries on a selective basis. The reviews were not to constitute an in-depth evaluation but would present an overview of the food aid policies and programmes in the context of the country concerned. The basic objective of examining and discussing these reviews in the CFA was to share understanding and appreciation of the important issues surrounding food aid and its utilization. I felt that such discussion could help in the development of agreed policies arising out of more specific knowledge of the practical experience of individual donor and recipient countries.

The CFA agreed to my proposal. It stressed, however, that the reviews should be entirely voluntary and should be undertaken by the WFP Secretariat with the active participation of the governments concerned. Since its approval, the CFA has conducted sixteen reviews, eight of donors and eight of recipients. In selecting the countries for reviews, an attempt has been made to cover recipients from each of the developing regions and a range of large and small donors, and to show how food aid has been used to address a variety of developmental problems.

Summaries of the national review papers submitted to the CFA are included in this volume, supplemented, where necessary, by additional information to bring them up to date. A synthesis of the major issues they have raised is presented by way of introduction. These national reviews have proved to be useful for the countries concerned. They have also been instructive for other food aid donors and recipient countries, for other aid organizations – multilateral, bilateral and non-governmental – and for the general public, fostering a better understanding of how food aid can contribute to sustained and equitable development, as well as of the difficulties it faces in the process. The reviews also indicate the importance of integrating food aid into the national development plans and programmes of recipient countries and co-ordinating it with financial and technical assistance. If development assistance is planned and processed within a common policy framework and a common set of programmes and projects, the cost-effectiveness and efficiency of all aid transfers would be increased.

For these reasons it was decided to publish the national reviews and to make them more widely available. I commend this publication in the hope that it will make an important contribution to constructive discussion of the effective use of food aid in the future for the benefit of all recipient countries and people in need.

James Ingram
Executive Director
World Food Programme
Rome

Glossary

General notes, acronyms and abbreviations
1. All monetary values are in United States dollars ($), unless otherwise stated.
2. One billion equals 1,000 million.
3. All quantities are in metric tons, unless otherwise specified.
4. All statistical tables have been produced from the WFP INTERFAIS database, unless otherwise stated.
5. Low-income food-deficit countries include all food-deficit (i.e., net cereal-importing) countries with per capita GNP not exceeding the level used by the World Bank to determine eligibility for IDA assistance ($1,195 in 1990).
6. The category of least developed countries was established by the United Nations General Assembly in its resolution 2768 (XXVI) of 18 November 1991. New criteria established in 1991 defined LDCs as 'those low-income countries that are suffering from long-term handicaps to growth, in particular low levels of human resource development and/or severe structural weaknesses'.
7. Geographic regions referred to in this study are as follows: Africa, comprising all the countries of Africa, including the African islands; sub-Saharan Africa, comprising all African countries south of the Sahara except South Africa; North Africa and the Middle East, comprising the African countries north of the Sahara, the countries of the Middle East, Turkey and Afghanistan; Asia and the Pacific, comprising the countries between the Mediterranean Sea and the Pacific Ocean, South East Asia and the Pacific Ocean islands; Latin America and the Caribbean – or the Americas – comprising all American and Caribbean countries south of the United States of America; Eastern Europe, including the former Soviet Republics.

Common acronyms

AID	Agency for International Development (United States)		comprising UNDP, UNFPA, UNICEF, IFAD and WFP
CARE	Cooperative for American Relief Everywhere	M&E	Monitoring and evaluation
		MCH	Mother and child health
CRS	Catholic Relief Services	NGO	Non-governmental organization
CIDA	Canadian International Development Agency	NORAD	Norwegian Agency for Development
		ODA	Official Development Assistance
CFA	Committee on Food Aid Policies and Programmes	OECD	Organisation for Economic Co-operation and Development
CSD	Consultative Subcommittee on Surplus Disposal (FAO)		(comprising Australia, Austria, Belgium, Canada, Denmark,
CEC	Commission of the European Communities (excludes national actions of EC member countries: Belgium, Denmark, France, Germany, Greece, Ireland, Italy, Luxembourg, the Netherlands, Portugal, Spain and the United Kingdom)		Finland, France, Germany, Greece, Iceland, Ireland, Italy, Japan, Luxembourg, the Netherlands, New Zealand, Norway, Portugal, Spain, Sweden, Switzerland, Turkey, the United Kingdom and the United States of America)
		PRO	Protracted refugee and displaced person operations (WFP)
EC	European Community		
FAC	Food Aid Convention	UN	United Nations
FAO	Food and Agriculture Organization of the United Nations	UNBRO	United Nations Border Relief Operations (Thai/Kampuchea)
FFW	Food-for-work	UNCDF	United Nations Capital Development Fund
GATT	General Agreement on Tariffs and Trade	UNDP	United Nations Development Programme
GDP	Gross Domestic Product		
GNP	Gross National Product	UNDRO	Office of the United Nations Disaster Relief Co-ordinator
IDA	International Development Association (World Bank)	UNFPA	United Nations Population Fund
IEFR	International Emergency Food Reserve (WFP)	UNHCR	United Nations High Commissioner for Refugees
IFAD	International Fund for Agricultural Development	UMR	Usual marketing requirement
		UNESCO	United Nations Educational, Scientific and Cultural Organization
ILO	International Labour Organization		
IMF	International Monetary Fund	UNICEF	United Nations Children's Fund
INTERFAIS	International Food Aid Information System (WFP)	UNIDO	United Nations Industrial Development Organization
IRA	Immediate Response Account (of the IEFR)	UNRRA	United Nations Relief and Rehabilitation Administration
LDC	Least developed country	WFP	World Food Programme
JCGP	Joint Consultative Group on Policy,	WHO	World Health Organization

1 Convergence & Diversity

Evolution of Food Aid Policies & Programmes

Introduction: Many Donors and Many Recipients

Food aid is aid supplied as food commodities on grant or concessional terms. It includes donations of food commodities by governments, intergovernmental organizations (particularly the World Food Programme), and private voluntary or non-governmental organizations; monetary grants tied to food purchases; and sales and loans of food commodities on credit terms with a repayment period of three years or more (FAO, 1980). It does not include the larger transactions in the 'grey area' between aid and trade of export enhancement and subsidy programmes.

Food aid comes in different forms and is used in different ways. The mechanisms by which it contributes to development vary accordingly. Food aid is categorized into three types: programme (non-project), project, and emergency, although the difference between them has become increasingly blurred (see Box 1).

Certain facilities have been established with the aim of ensuring an adequate and assured supply of food aid both for development and in times of emergency (Box 2). Increasingly, although still only a small proportion of total food aid, food produced in developing countries is being used as food aid through various arrangements (Box 3). More attention has also been given to using food aid constructively to assist the development process in developing countries rather than merely as a stopgap and as a means of disposing of surpluses in donor countries.

While the greater part of food aid is provided bilaterally on a government-to-government basis, the creation of the World Food Programme in 1961 added an important multilateral dimension. WFP has grown significantly since its beginnings as a small, experimental programme. It is now the primary international provider of food aid for development and disaster relief and is the largest source of grant resources for developing countries in the United Nations system (Box 4). Its governing body, the Committee on Food Aid Policies and Programmes (CFA), is also an intergovernmental forum for consultation on all food aid (Box 5).

Food aid is a controversial form of development assistance. Its detractors have pointed to the political and commercial motives that have sustained food aid flows. They have emphasized the possible disincentive effect food aid can have on local food production and the disruption to trade, as well as the problem of creating dependence on the part of both governments and beneficiary groups. These dangers should not be

1

BOX 1. TYPES OF FOOD AID AND INTENDED USES

Food aid has traditionally been classified into three broad types – programme, project, and emergency – each with its own set of donor legislation, procedures, sources of financing, and methods of operation.

Programme food aid. Programme food aid is provided as a grant or on soft repayment terms. It helps to fill the gap – at given prices in normal years – between demand at existing income levels and the supply of food from domestic production and commercial imports thus obviating pressure on food prices or additional demand for imports. It is provided exclusively on a bilateral, government-to-government basis. By replacing commercial imports, it provides balance of payments support as the foreign exchange that would have been used to pay for those imports is saved. When it is sold in the recipient country, which is usually the case, it provides additional local currency for the government. It is therefore a macroeconomic resource that allows recipient countries to increase development expenditures without inflation or balance of payments problems. During economic crises or periods of structural adjustment, it helps to shield development expenditures that would otherwise be cut.

Project food aid. Project food aid is usually aimed at transferring income to the poor or satisfying their minimum nutritional needs in normal years. This food aid is provided on a grant basis for specific beneficiaries and development objectives. It helps to meet the additional demand for food generated by its support for development projects. Although the World Food Programme is the major provider of such aid, other international organizations and national governments and some non-governmental organizations also provide project food aid.

WFP project food aid supports a wide range of development projects for the poor, mainly in rural areas, and has:
- improved the nutrition and health of mothers and pre-school children by offering supplementary food at mother and child health care centres;
- supported education, especially primary schools, and training programmes;
- transferred additional income to poor households through food-for-work programmes, principally labour-intensive infrastructure, community development and self-help projects;
- provided help to poor households during periods of land settlement or transition to new farming systems;
- supported market reform and price stabilization measures through the establishment of food reserves.

Funds saved from governments' budgets have been used to expand or improve existing development projects or to invest in social services. Project food aid commodities are sold in three ways: first, to designated beneficiaries (project workers or members of co-operatives, often at subsidized prices); second, as part of a project (for instance, reconstituted milk produced with food aid commodities in dairy development schemes); and third, a small amount, on the local market. Some project food aid is sold to buy local materials, tools, or equipment for the food-aided project, thus generating more employment and higher incomes.

In practice, the division between programme and project food aid has become increasingly blurred. Funds from programme food aid sales are being targeted for project-type activities, and project food aid may be used to support sector-wide programmes.

Emergency food aid. Emergency food aid is a response to sudden natural disasters, war or civil strife, and shortfalls in production caused by drought or pest and disease attacks. During the 1980s, emergency food aid took up an increasing proportion of food aid, primarily for victims of famine caused by drought and war in Africa. Emergency food aid is provided bilaterally and multilaterally, mainly by the World Food Programme. Non-governmental organizations have also played a major role. Almost all emergency food aid is free. A growing problem is the need for food for refugees and displaced people in protracted relief situations. As their numbers have grown, an increasing proportion of what is designated as 'emergency' food aid has been allocated to them. International and national tensions suggest that special efforts will continue to be required to ensure an adequate level of emergency food aid that can be deployed rapidly.

BOX 2. FOOD AID FACILITIES

A floor of 7.5 million tons of cereal food aid (in wheat equivalent) is guaranteed under the **Food Aid Convention** of 1986, which is related to the Wheat Trade Convention. Signatories to the Convention are Argentina (35,000 tons), Australia (300,000 tons), Austria (20,000 tons) Canada (600,000 tons), European Community (1,670,000 tons), Finland (25,000 tons), Japan (300,000 tons), Norway (30,000 tons), Sweden (40,000 tons), Switzerland (27,000 tons), United States (4,470,000 tons). The figures in brackets are the minimum annual contributions of each signatory in wheat equivalent. The cereal commodities provided are converted into their equivalent amount in wheat using standard conversion factors. The signatories have undertaken to provide their minimum contributions irrespective of food stock, production, and price fluctuations. In most years they have exceeded their obligations.

Pledges to the **World Food Programme** are voluntary and are made biennially in commodities and cash. WFP's regular resources are used mainly for development projects. A small amount is used for emergency food aid. A separate account was created in 1989 for long-term refugees and displaced people. WFP does not provide programme food aid.

The **International Emergency Food Reserve**, a facility intended to respond rapidly to emergency situations, was established in 1975 and is administered by WFP. It has an annual target for voluntary contributions of 500,000 tons of cereals. Its resources have not always proved sufficient or flexible enough to respond to emergencies in recent years. An Immediate Response Account of cash was established as an integral part of the Reserve in 1991 for the purchase and delivery of food to enable the fastest possible response to emergencies prior to the arrival of donor food aid commodities.

BOX 3. USING FOOD FROM DEVELOPING COUNTRIES

Food produced in the developing countries is used as food aid through a variety of arrangements.

Under **triangular transactions** a donor purchases food in one developing country for use as food aid in another developing country. In **trilateral operations**, a donor commodity is exchanged for a different one in a developing country, which is then used as food aid in another developing country. Donors also make **local purchases** in a developing country for use as food aid in the same country. Finally, **exchange arrangements** involve swaps of a commodity, such as wheat, provided by a donor, for use in urban areas, for a local commodity, such as maize, which is then used as food aid.

These mechanisms provide a relatively small, but growing, proportion of food aid. There are many constraints to larger-scale operations. These efforts are aimed at increasing cost effectiveness and timeliness, and stimulating increased agricultural production and trade in developing countries. They can also help ensure that the commodities provided are acceptable to the recipients.

(Relief and Development Institute, London, 1987 and 1990; Food Studies Group, 1989; Ronco Consulting Corporation, 1988)

BOX 4. WORLD FOOD PROGRAMME

The World Food Programme (WFP) is the food aid organization of the United Nations system. It was established in 1961 by parallel resolutions of the UN General Assembly and the FAO Conference. It has evolved from an initial experimental programme of about US$100 million for the three-year period 1963–65 to what is now the largest source of grant aid to developing countries in the United Nations system, with an annual expenditure of US$1.6 billion in 1991.

WFP is the primary source of international food aid for development and for disaster relief. Its activities take three main forms: assistance to development projects; food emergency operations; and, more recently, support to protracted operations involving refugees and displaced people. Development assistance is provided for government projects that benefit poor people, mainly in rural areas, with priority given to low-income, food-deficit countries. About two-thirds of this development assistance has been provided for agricultural and rural development and one-third for human resource development. In 1992, WFP assisted over 270 on-going development projects with a commitment of US$3 billion of aid; over the life of these projects of three to five years, an estimated 52 million people will receive WFP assistance. In 1992 alone, it is estimated that 15 million people received WFP food through these projects.

The simultaneous outbreak of large-scale natural and man-made emergencies has created a major upsurge in the need for disaster relief. Over half of all WFP assistance now goes for relief, compared to about one-third in previous years. In 1992, some 26 million people, including 14 million refugees and displaced people, received WFP relief food.

The WFP Secretariat, with its headquarters in Rome, is headed by an Executive Director appointed for a term of five years by the Secretary-General of the United Nations and the Director-General of FAO, after consultation with the Committee on Food Aid Policies and Programmes. The Secretariat comprises about 1,600 staff, three-quarters of whom are assigned to country offices in 82 countries that serve 92 developing countries in all developing regions. This global network is more extensive than that of any other food aid organization.

In addition to its own programme, WFP has been called upon increasingly by donors to assist them in the execution of their own bilateral food aid programmes. WFP's expertise and experience have been provided for the purchase and transport of bilateral food aid as well as for the monitoring of its distribution. WFP has also been asked to co-ordinate large-scale international food aid operations, particularly in emergencies and for refugees and displaced people. In the process, WFP has become a major transport and logistics agent in the service of bilateral donors, other UN organizations and NGOs.

---

ignored. But many of the criticisms levelled at food aid are equally – and in some cases more – applicable to other forms of aid. Its value also deserves equal prominence. Food aid plays a vital role in saving lives in emergencies. Properly applied, it can assist countries in achieving more rapid and more equitable development (Singer *et al*, 1987; Clay and Stokke, 1991; Ruttan, 1993). The case studies in this volume provide illustrations of both the benefits and problems of using food aid, based on practical experience.

It is also necessary to adopt a proper perspective on food aid. It represents a very

---

BOX 5. COMMITTEE ON FOOD AID POLICIES AND PROGRAMMES

The Committee was jointly established by the United Nations and FAO and is composed of 42 member states or nations of the United Nations or of FAO, 27 from developing countries and 15 from more economically developed nations.

The Committee is authorized, within the framework of WFP's Basic Texts, to exercise the responsibility for the intergovernmental supervision and direction of the Programme, including food aid policy, administration, operations, funds and finances, and to carry out such other responsibilities as are conferred upon it in the present General Regulations.

The Committee also helps evolve and co-ordinate short-term and longer-term food aid policies recommended by the World Food Conference (of 1974); in particular:

(i) it provides a forum for intergovernmental consultation on national and international food aid programmes and policies;

(ii) it reviews periodically general trends in food aid requirements and food aid availabilities;

(iii) it recommends to governments, through the World Food Council, improvements in food aid policies and programmes on such matters as programme priorities, the commodity composition of food aid and other related subjects;

(iv) it formulates proposals for more effective co-ordination of multilateral, bilateral and non-governmental food aid programmes, including emergency food aid;

(v) it reviews periodically the implementation of the recommendations made by the World Food Conference on food aid policies.

WFP, *General Regulations for the World Food Programme.* Rome, 1992.

---

modest proportion of global cereal production and of cereal production in developing countries. It accounts for about 9% of the cereal imports of developing countries and some 7% of cereal stocks in developed countries. Its importance in the cereal imports of least developed countries and in sub-Saharan Africa is growing, however, as their food gap increases and their ability to import food commercially declines (see Table 1.1).

The ideas or perceptions of what food aid is have changed considerably. Until the early 1960s, food aid was (correctly) seen as almost synonymous with US food aid. The issues that dominated professional and policy discussions on food aid focused on India, the largest recipient, and the problems of drought, the disincentives to agricultural production and the often awkward policy relationships between donors and recipients, plus the programmes of, largely US, voluntary agencies and the nascent, still experimental, venture of WFP.

In retrospect, the first Food Aid Convention of 1967 can be seen as a watershed; more donors with commitment to provide food were brought in, reinforced by an international agreement. The 1970s was a decade of international food crisis, with many developing countries confronting what had come to be known as problems of food insecurity. The United Nations World Food Conference held in Rome in November 1974 called for an improved policy for food aid (see Appendix 1.1). The problems of food insecurity and poverty in Asia still dominated the international agenda, with famine in Bangladesh in 1974 and severe distress elsewhere in the region. But the food crises in Africa also caught the attention of the world community. The

Table 1.1 *Global food aid profile 1988–91*

	1988	*1989*	*1990*	*1991*[a]
Total food aid ($ million) of which (%):	3,798.0	3,224.0	3,151.0	3,558.0
Bilateral food aid	75.4	82.2	81.1	77.0
Multilateral food aid	24.6	17.8	18.9	23.0
Food aid grants	82.9	84.2	83.1	79.9
Food aid loans	17.1	15.8	16.9	20.1
Proportion of total ODA	7.9	6.9	5.8	6.1
Cereal food aid deliveries (million tons)	13.1	10.4	12.9	13.2
% of world cereal production	0.8	0.6	0.7	0.7
% of cereal production by developing countries	1.6	1.0	1.2	1.3
% of world imports of cereals[b]	6.6	5.1	6.2	7.1
% of developing countries' cereal imports[b]	11.3	8.8	8.7	10.1
% of developed countries' cereal stocks[c]	4.7	5.6	7.8	6.9
Food aid cetegories (% of total)				
Cereals				
Programme/non-project food aid	51.2	55.6	61.3	50.8
Emergency food aid	22.2	20.7	18.9	27.6
Project food aid	26.6	23.7	19.8	21.6
Non-cereals				
Programme/non-project food aid	46.3	41.5	46.5	33.3
Emergency food aid	21.4	20.8	26.2	36.0
Project food aid	32.3	37.7	27.3	30.7
Regional and country group distribution (% of total cereals)				
Sub-Saharan Africa	31.4	24.8	22.5	30.6
North Africa and Middle East	18.4	25.5	23.4	24.4
Asia and Pacific	33.1	29.0	19.6	23.4
Latin America and Caribbean	17.1	18.0	16.5	14.1
Eastern Europe and former USSR	0.0	2.7	18.0	7.5
Low-income food-deficit countries	87.9	81.6	66.8	80.5
Least developed countries	46.4	39.1	29.4	39.5
Non-cereal food aid ('000 tons)	1,692.4	1,990.0	1,183.9	1,137.1
Vegetable oils and fats	881.7	520.9	553.5	344.5
Dairy products	339.9	156.0	137.0	233.9
Pulses	201.3	148.2	182.0	295.4
Other commodities	269.5	164.9	311.4	263.3

[a] Provisional.

[b] Import statistics refer to July/June periods ending during the reported year except for rice which refers to the calendar year shown.

[c] For crop years ending in reported calendar years.

Source: WFP, INTERFAIS and OECD, Development Assistance Committee.

international aspect of food aid was further enhanced with the continued growth of WFP, the establishment of the International Emergency Food Reserve (see Appendix 1.2) and agreement on guidelines and criteria governing all food aid (Appendix 1.3).

The 1980s have been described as the lost decade of development for many developing countries, a situation exacerbated by food crisis and hunger in Africa. By this time developments in telecommunications had created a 'global village' so that the interactions of drought and civil war provided headlines and television pictures worldwide, resulting in the BandAid phenomenon of massive public support for help to developing countries. These events also provoked a considerable amount of policy analysis on how to make food aid more effective in providing relief and in strengthening food security. The 1980s also became the decade of structural adjustment as developing economies hard hit by international recession and debt struggled to cope with the economic and human consequences of what increasingly came to be seen as unavoidable national and sectoral adjustment.

Poverty alleviation in developing countries was once again prominent on the international agenda at the beginning of the 1990s. The simultaneous outbreak of large-scale natural and man-made disasters, particularly, though not exclusively, in Africa, has come to dominate the work of donors and aid agencies, resulting in a shift of effort from development activities to emergency relief, and a search for ways to strengthen the interrelation between the two. At the same time, there has been the almost entirely unanticipated problem of financing the large-scale development needs, including the food deficits, of the republics of the former Soviet Union and several countries of Eastern Europe. Food aid is therefore more needed now than it was three decades ago when WFP first began operations. The United States continues to be the largest donor, but the European Community has emerged, especially in response to the problems of the former Soviet Union and Eastern Europe, as another major source of food aid. The role of WFP has an even higher profile than a decade ago, particularly in providing assistance to famine-threatened populations and in feeding the ever-growing number of refugees and displaced people, as well as in helping to co-ordinate food aid from all sources.

This then might be the widely accepted, albeit highly summarized, account of the evolution of food aid over the past three decades that provides the backdrop to this book. The reality, while not inconsistent with this broad sketch of developments, is considerably more complex. In recent years, WFP alone has assisted development projects and supported emergency and protracted refugee and displaced people operations in 93 countries, including 44 in sub-Saharan Africa, 26 in the Latin American and Caribbean region, 12 in North Africa and the Middle East, and 11 in Asia and the Pacific. Including Eastern Europe and the republics of the former Soviet Union and emergency operations in Afghanistan, Iraq and Kampuchea, over 100 countries, or about two-thirds of UN member states, have recently been food aid recipients. The distribution of food aid amongst these recipient countries is highly skewed. In terms of total food aid, there has been a small number of large recipients, including Bangladesh, Egypt and, during emergencies, Ethiopia, Mozambique and Sudan. There have been large-scale relief operations for Afghan, Cambodian, Kurd and, increasingly, displaced African populations. There is a large number of diverse recipient country situations in terms of quantities, commodities, uses and sources of food aid.

The food aid system has also become complex on the donor side. While the United States remains the largest single donor, the European Community operates a Community-wide programme organized by the EC Commission in addition to 11 separate national programmes. Austria, Australia, Canada, Finland, Japan, Norway,

Sweden, Switzerland amongst member countries of the Organisation for Economic
Co-operation and Development, as well as Argentina, China, India, Saudi Arabia and
the former Soviet Union provided substantial quantities during the 1980s. A number
of other recipient countries also contribute to international food aid programmes and
occasionally provide aid bilaterally to disaster-affected countries, as well as supporting food aided activities in their own countries.

The provision of food aid by donors has been similarly highly skewed, with the US,
the EC and its member states and Canada being the major providers. Donors provide
different resources, money as well as commodities, on different terms, and different
types of commodities, allocate their resources differently, and accord different
priorities to humanitarian relief and economic and social development.

The conventional conception of food aid has been one of grants or concessional sales
by food-exporting or surplus-producing countries to developing nations with deficits
and either structural problems of under-consumption or immediate problems of
distress. The first FAC in 1967 involved non-exporters in financing food aid. Then the
1980s witnessed the growth of non-conventional forms of aid involving triangular
transactions (food acquired in one developing country to be used as food aid in
another developing country), local purchases for food-assisted operations in the same
country and commodity exchanges that together now account for around 10% of the
total volume of food aid. Developing countries have been involved as suppliers of food
aid commodities, for example India and Pakistan (wheat), China, Thailand and
Indonesia (rice) and Kenya and Zimbabwe (white maize). The reality of food aid in
the early 1990s is of a highly complex system of transactions and transfers involving
at any one time some 120 countries as donors, recipients and sources of supply. At
the same time, food aid has declined relatively in importance as a share of agricultural
trade and as part of Official Development Assistance (ODA), from 20% of total ODA
in 1972 to 12% in 1981 and 6% in 1990.

All these developments make it increasingly difficult to generalize about policies and
practices of donors and recipients, and about the impact and effectiveness of food aid
transfers. The complex system of relationships has been further complicated by international institutional arrangements through the FAC, WFP as a multilateral agency,
and the sequence of Lomé Conventions between the EC and developing countries in
Africa, the Caribbean and the Pacific that have led to there being many, small food
aid recipients. Attempts to achieve co-operation and consistency in food aid policy,
programming and use of resources involving both donors and recipients have been
given impetus through the Committee on Food Aid Policies and Programmes (CFA).

Since the early 1980s, substantive thematic initiatives, such as poverty alleviation,
structural adjustment, food security strategies, human resources development, women
in development and environmental protection, have impinged on development,
including food aid. Similarly, the modalities whereby food aid is delivered, including
direct distribution of food aid commodities, monetization, triangular transactions,
local purchases and exchange arrangements, have come under increasing scrutiny. To
obtain a sense of the evolution of food aid policies and programmes in recipient as well
as donor countries, even to generalize on the impact and effectiveness of food aid, and
then to use these policy analyses as a basis for devising appropriate policies and
resource requirements, involves taking account of this diversity.

It was partly with the growing complexity of the world food aid system as its context
that the CFA began in 1983 to review the experience of recipient and donor countries,
as part of its mandate to co-ordinate food aid policies and programmes globally. To
assist the CFA in this task, the WFP Secretariat prepared review papers with the

co-operation of food aid officers in the countries concerned. Sixteen papers, relating to eight recipient countries and eight donors, have been produced and are brought together in this volume. They represent a substantial body of case evidence on food aid policy and practice, and how these have evolved. Three broad criteria were used to select the countries to be reviewed. First, recipients should be included from each of the developing regions. Second, a range of large and small donors should be covered. Third, a variety of developmental and emergency uses should be described. In all cases, the studies were undertaken with the co-operation of the country concerned.

Recipient Country Experience

The eight recipient countries included in this book cover a wide range of situations in terms of geographical size and population, the volume of food aid provided, the proportion of ODA accounted for by food aid, and different uses of food aid for development and relief purposes. They are all countries in which project food aid in support of development projects has been a relatively important part of overall food aid.

Table 1.2 *Food aid by recipient country and category of use: 1987–91 (annual average, '000 tons, cereals in grain equivalent)*

Recipient	Relief	Project	Programme	Total
Bangladesh	101.3	702.2	620.7	1,435.7
India	9.7	375.5	52.5	437.7
Pakistan	467.1	24.8	169.8	661.7
Honduras	7.0	33.7	111.9	152.6
Tunisia	17.3	56.8	276.7	352.7
Benin	0.4	10.5	3.2	14.1
Lesotho	–	28.4	12.5	40.9
Tanzania	11.6	11.7	21.7	45.0
World total	2,829.2	3,336.9	7,530.2	13,696.3
Case studies as % of world total	21.7	37.3	16.9	22.9

They represent the more constructive cases; countries in which civil war and the collapse of social order have disrupted developmental programmes and projects with economic or social goals are not included. These cases should be considered as illustrating the possibilities of food aid and indicating generic problems. They show the wide variety of uses of food aid in Africa, Asia and Latin America, and the various ways in which it can be provided to poor, food-insecure people. They show, too, that there have been substantial constraints on the donor side.

The changing geographical focus of food aid   The substantial shift in focus from South Asia to Africa is illustrated by the experiences of the three South Asian countries of Bangladesh, India and Pakistan in contrast to those of other recipient countries. Whereas in the early 1970s there were thought to be problems of burgeoning global food deficits, the successes of agricultural growth and food policy in the Asian region make for a more diverse picture, as reflected in these case studies. Many of the Asian countries have been moving towards self-sufficiency in basic food staples, exploiting the technological opportunities of the Green Revolution, but they are progressing at a varying pace, and so are at different stages in the transformation process.

In contrast, no general trends are observable for food aid in the middle-income countries of Latin America or the Middle East and North Africa. A number of countries, such as Tunisia, have structural deficits in food that have increased with population and income growth. Many countries in these regions, such as Honduras, have also been severely affected by economic recession.

Much of sub-Saharan Africa, however, has experienced increasing food deficits with high population growth and urbanization but low *per capita* economic growth rates exacerbated by drought and other disasters. Variability in food production has resulted in acute problems of food insecurity. The three country experiences documented in this book are drawn from different parts of Africa, and different agro-ecological zones. They illustrate a more diverse, and occasionally more positive, reality than pessimistic, generalized analyses of sub-Saharan Africa might imply. Even within one country, such as Tanzania, there are contrasting experiences. Zanzibar, as a declining export-oriented primary commodity producer, has faced difficulties in financing its traditionally imported food staple, rice. Mainland Tanzania, on the other hand, after economic difficulties exacerbated by drought that led to food crisis and increased imports in the early 1980s, has again re-established itself as broadly self-sufficient in basic staples, particularly maize. But the demand for rice or wheat for largely urban markets continues to create import problems, while periodic variability in agricultural production also remains a continuing threat to food security in rural areas. The experience of Benin is broadly similar; it is self-sufficient in basic staples but remains vulnerable to some variability in production, with a need for imports of wheat to meet urban demand. Lesotho illustrates an aspect of the special problems of southern Africa, with the politically related risks to food security during the *apartheid* era and also the large-scale out-migration of male labour, which leaves a rural economy of potentially vulnerable female-headed households.

Food aid and poverty alleviation   The history and inherent nature of food aid demonstrate its special advantages in sustaining a poverty focus, supporting food security programmes and attenuating the social costs of adjustment (World Bank/ WFP, 1991). The experiences of Bangladesh, India and Pakistan illustrate the ways in which food aid can be used to sustain poverty-focused interventions that provide a food security net. In the sub-continental proportions of India, there are large internal food transfers through the public distribution and logistics system of the Food Corporation of India, as well as externally supplied food aid. To date, African experience illustrates the opportunity rather than widespread achievements, but there are small, in population terms, relative successes, as illustrated in this volume by Lesotho. The experience of Honduras is a reminder that within the Americas there are still countries that are relatively poor by global standards, and where food aid can have an important role in combating structural poverty.

Changing food aid uses   The eight recipient countries reflect the considerable diversity in food aid uses, and the changing patterns of use, amongst developing countries. In Asia the trend has been more toward project food aid, with a decline in the proportion of programme aid. In contrast, Honduras, under the impact of severe economic recession, has been one of the Central American economies, in a region of increased insecurity, more dependent on programme food aid for sale on local markets. In sub-Saharan Africa, there has been a considerable increase in emergency food aid. The relative importance of different channels for the supply of food aid is related in a complex way to changes in its uses. Historical factors, and the specifics of country situations, explain why certain donors are more prominent in some developing regions and countries than others, and whether WFP or NGOs are relatively more important in providing project or relief food aid. For example, NGOs have provided more project food aid in India and Honduras, whereas WFP is a major source in Africa.

Programme food aid: As noted in Box 1, food commodities supplied as programme aid are normally sold in the urban markets of recipient countries. This category of food aid can make a positive contribution to food security and long-term development. The case studies illustrate how programme aid can be an efficient way of transferring resources to meet balance of payments and budget support objectives. With some notable exceptions (as in India), however, it has seldom made a major direct contribution to the alleviation of poverty and hunger because deliveries have been irregular, funds have not been targeted and the benefits have often been dissipated in general food subsidies in urban areas. Donors have increasingly directed the funds generated to development projects which they support with financial and technical assistance in order to help meet local costs. The funds realized may not reflect the real value of the food aid commodities provided, however, because of over-valued exchange rates or subsidized food prices in the urban markets in which they are sold. It has often been difficult to assess the amount of local currency generated because of inadequate accounting systems.

Project food aid: This type of food aid has been mainly used in food-for-work (FFW) programmes and for human resource development.
FFW programmes: Labour-intensive infrastructure works have been undertaken by poor households and communities, with food provided as part of their wages. The rationale behind these programmes lies in the concept of additionality. They provide additional consumption for people whose incomes are too low for them to buy sufficient food for a healthy and productive life. The food supplied can also result in a substantial addition to their income; additional employment can be created and construction work extended. The multi-faceted additionality of FFW programmes can permit the extension of consumption, income, employment and investment beyond what would have been possible without food aid.

FFW programmes have resulted in substantial benefits, as in the national programme of construction and rehabilitation of irrigation and drainage channels and flood protection embankments in Bangladesh, the rural road network in Lesotho, and the multi-purpose community development works programme in Benin. FFW programmes have been expanded during emergencies, thereby avoiding the mass exodus from rural areas that would otherwise have occurred. These programmes have reached the poorest groups and women have particularly benefited. This is not surprising. The structure of the regular labour market often excludes women. Usually only the very poor work for food: women, especially when they are single heads of households, are often in this category. FFW is flexible and women find its timing, particularly when it can be organized outside the period of agricultural work, compatible with their domestic and other responsibilities. Payment in food is also attractive in situations where women have more command over food than cash.

However, FFW programmes have their problems. They often lack the necessary financial, technical and administrative resources to carry them out effectively. Money may not be available to pay the cash component of the wage; part of the food provided could be sold for that purpose. FFW has been used as a relief measure during and after emergencies. In many instances the activities undertaken have been designed to provide food to poor people rather than as an integral part of a development programme.

Controversy, therefore, still surrounds FFW. Three issues have been identified in the wide-ranging debate (Clay, 1986; Maxwell, 1978; Bryson et al, 1991). First, there is the tension between short-run employment creation and income generation and the size and distribution of longer-term income and assets. Secondly, there is the use of food, as opposed to cash, as a wage good. Thirdly, the relative success of major FFW programmes in Asia justifies their assessment both as food security mechanisms and in expanding employment to disadvantaged groups in situations of widespread structural underemployment as well as during the process of economic adjustment. Experience has shown, however, that FFW raises special problems in Africa. Nevertheless, scope exists for flexible and innovative uses of FFW.

Human resource development: Project food aid has also been used in support of different kinds of development programmes designed to assist the development of human resources. These programmes include supplementary food for pregnant and lactating women and pre-school children and feeding at schools and training centres. They have a welfare function but are primarily designed to improve maternal and child nutrition, to encourage attendance at mother and child health centres, schools and training institutions where the food aid commodities are provided, and to give budgetary support for basic health, education and training services.

Experience has shown that supplementary feeding can be effective if it is well-managed and carried out in well-financed and adequately staffed programmes. Where these conditions do not exist, benefits are likely to be reduced. Other factors contributing to success include careful targeting, nutrition surveillance and growth monitoring, community involvement, links between feeding programmes and the use of local foods, and attention to planning and administrative concerns (Mora et al., 1990).

School feeding programmes can help to improve the health and nutrition of children and increase their physical energy and alertness. Provision of school meals can also help increase school enrolment and contribute to reduced absenteeism and lower drop-out rates. But inadequate transport and logistics systems have resulted in food supplies being irregular. It is difficult to assess objectively the nutritional and educational impact of school feeding programmes as few studies have been carried out. Such programmes may not reach the poorest and most undernourished children, as they often do not attend school. They may also reach children whose undernourishment is difficult to repair because they were inadequately fed in their pre-school years (WFP, 1991).

Food aid has supported training programmes that enhance skills and productivity, thereby contributing to raising the incomes of poor households. Food enables the trainees, including women, to benefit from training programmes often for the first time, as it offsets the earnings forgone during the training period (Hay and Clay, 1986).

Emergency food aid: The emergency uses of food aid have loomed even larger since the early 1980s. This volume does not include examples from the war and drought-affected Horn of Africa that has been the focus of much recent attention. Rather, what the case studies show is that, where there is political stability, food security is achievable in low-income countries, and food aid can play a useful role in reaching this goal as well as in supporting relief, disaster mitigation and rehabilitation activities.

Poverty-focused development projects have become increasingly important, but in somewhat different ways, providing the programmatic and logistical capacity to cope with the effects of natural and even man-made disasters. The precise mechanisms, such as multi-purpose projects in countries with relatively small populations, as in Benin, and the large poverty-focused programmes in Bangladesh and India which can be expanded during emergencies and provide guaranteed employment for the very poor, illustrate how this basic concept can be institutionalized in different ways.

Refugees and displaced people: Globally, emergency and subsequently protracted relief operations for refugees and displaced persons (PROs) have become a larger part of international food aid operations. Bangladesh, Honduras, Pakistan and Tanzania have experience of food aid to cope with these problems.

PROs are not like conventional emergency relief situations. Refugees and displaced people depend almost exclusively on international and host government assistance. They may find it difficult to obtain employment and may receive little or no cash to supplement their food rations or to cover their basic requirements other than food. They may also have difficulty obtaining access to land.

Refugees and displaced people require a food ration that is not only adequate for good health, but is also sufficiently varied. A review by WFP in 1989 (WFP, 1989) found that these requirements were often not met. Nor was assistance flexible enough to meet changing needs. The demand for assistance had also grown to such an extent (over 70% of IEFR resources were going to the victims of man-made emergencies) that emergency resources to meet other kinds of natural disasters were being seriously reduced.

But problems were not restricted to resources. In the past, refugees and displaced people were regarded as temporarily in need of relief; little consideration was given to their longer-term needs. Food aid was often criticized as merely providing a hand-out and creating disincentives and dependence. Given the length of time involved (some refugees and displaced people have been isolated from their homes for many years), it became evident that assistance was needed not only for sub-sistence and survival, but also in terms of developing individual capacities for growth and independence. Some situations are so protracted that children are born and grow up in feeding camps. In these situations, there are possibilities for educating and training people to prepare them to earn a living in the future. Employment might also be provided in building and improving the infrastructure and, where land is available, in producing food. A developmental rather than an emergency approach is called for, which often requires financial and technical assistance as well as food aid.

Faced with these problems, WFP established a subset of its regular resources for refugees and displaced people in protracted situations of more than one year rather than from the IEFR, in order to ensure a stable and varied resource base to meet their food requirements. An agreement was reached with UNHCR, whereby WFP became the co-ordinator of food aid to refugees. And co-operation is sought with financial and technical assistance agencies in order to provide nutrition, health, education and train-ing to refugees and displaced people and also, where feasible, employment.

The WFP study also highlighted the problems of the host populations who receive refugees and displaced people. They are often themselves poor and malnourished and they bear a considerable burden in supporting these transient people, for which they receive no assistance. They may also be disadvantaged, in that emergency assistance is concentrated on the refugees. This points to the need for the provision of assistance for all concerned in an integrated area developmental approach. The case study of Tanzania shows what is possible when the host government allows refugees to settle and take up agricultural production. The case study of Pakistan shows what is required when faced with a large refugee population over a long period of time.

Integrating food aid with financial and technical assistance   Another area of consensus reached in the 1980s has been the need to integrate food aid more closely with financial and technical assistance. From a macroeconomic perspective, the balance of payments or budgetary support that can be provided by food aid, particularly in the context of structural adjustment, requires its integration into overall financial planning. The development effectiveness of project food aid has been limited by lack of complementary local currency and foreign exchange as well as human resources in planning, management and implementation. The eight cases in this volume variously show general recognition of this requirement. Programming and planning structures are needed in both donor agencies (see below) and recipient countries to encourage this integration. These are only partially in place, for example in Bangladesh, Benin and Honduras. The studies illustrate the need for strengthening project design and administrative and managerial capacity for food-assisted projects. Project evaluations, as in Bangladesh and India, have regularly pointed to the importance of complementing food aid with financial and technical assistance, and have shown the benefits where this has been done.

Non-conventional food aid supply   During the 1980s there was increased recognition of the advantages of greater flexibility in supplying food aid commodities rather than providing them only from donor countries. These advantages included reducing transport and other costs, speeding up delivery and providing commodities more in keeping with the food habits of recipients. Food aid commodities have been acquired in the same region or country of operations. In Africa, for example, white maize and other coarse grains predominate in rural consumption. Commodity exchanges can be especially useful in countries that are periodically, or more or less continuously, self-sufficient in certain food staples. In South Asia, imported cereal food aid is channelled into the public distribution systems. In Pakistan, this arrangement has played a crucial role in providing relief food to the large Afghan refugee population. In Bangladesh, the use of public stocks, to be replenished later by food aid supplies, has been a crucial aspect of food security during and immediately after major natural disasters. Imported food aid commodities have been exchanged for locally produced foods. Local purchases of foodstuffs to be used as food aid in the same country now take place, as in the German-funded food-aided projects in Honduras. Food aid commodities, mainly cereals, have been obtained in one developing country for use as food aid in another through what are referred to as 'triangular transactions' (see Box 3, p. 3), but logistical and quality control problems, among others, have impeded these transactions.

Disincentives   A widespread criticism of food aid is that it creates disincentive effects by:

- lowering local food prices, thereby discouraging local production;
- enabling recipient governments to neglect local agriculture and long-term food security;
- attracting workers away from vital activities during the agricultural year;
- creating a dependency mentality; and
- changing food habits.

The experiences of the three Asian countries described in this volume, in moving towards self-sufficiency, are consistent with the widespread professional view of practitioners and economists that disincentive effects are avoidable (Cathie, 1991; Maxwell, 1991; Clay and Stokke 1991; Singer *et al*, 1987). Nevertheless, as the Bangladesh case illustrates, there are potential problems in making the transition to self-sufficiency in an economy where food aid has an important role in sustaining anti-poverty and food security programmes. Scrutinized more closely, however, the eight studies of recipient countries included in this book suggest collectively that there is little evidence of strong negative impacts. The three African cases illustrate how modest levels of project food aid have contributed to the development of infrastructure that would support rural development, had problems of effective implementation not limited the developmental impact. These varied country experiences also illustrate the need for systematic sectoral analysis, particularly where food imports are large relative to domestic production of particular commodities, or as a share of the urban market, as in Honduras for maize and rice, Tunisia for cereals and vegetables, and Tanzania for rice and wheat.

Food aid that is not converted into money may have positive or negative effects on consumption. It could lead to a taste for expensive foods that cost more per unit of energy and that cannot be produced locally. Conversely, a change in commodity could lead to a more efficient diet. Food habits are not immutable. They can be changed by many factors, such as government import and pricing policies, changes in the relative prices of food commodities, increasing income, transport and logistical improvements, migration to urban areas, changes in fuel costs and changes when women participate in income-earning activities outside the home. To the extent that food aid substitutes for imports which would have occurred in any case, the causes of changes in demand must lie elsewhere (Cassen, 1986).

Food aid management   The case studies illustrate the variety of ways in which food aid is managed in recipient countries. Where cereals are integrated into the public distribution system, as in the three South Asian countries, or are handled by the government food authority, as in Tunisia, significant savings in cost and time in the delivery of the aid can result both for development and in times of emergency. Similarly, where the government has set up a special food aid management unit, common logistics and delivery systems and procedures have resulted in economies of scale and increased efficiency.

The complexity of food aid deliveries facing recipient countries is shown in Table 1.3. Food aid is provided bilaterally, either directly on a government-to-government basis or through NGOs on behalf of the bilateral food aid programme; multilaterally, mainly by WFP; or by NGOs financially from their own resources. The proportion of food aid provided through these different channels varies among the eight recipient countries. The number of donors ranges from 4 in the case of Lesotho to 17 in Bangladesh, each with their own procedures, schedules and requirements.

Overview   The recipient case studies underscore the need for realism in terms of what can be done with food aid. Food aid is not a panacea. It is less flexible than financial assistance for a variety of reasons that relate to constraints on the donor, as well as on the recipient, side. The resources made available continue to a large extent to reflect supply considerations in donor countries, and also, where alternative triangular transactions and local purchases are attempted, what food is available regionally and locally. There are continuing budgetary constraints on food aid, with annual

Table 1.3 *Food aid channels by recipient countries: 1987–91 (annual average, '000 tons, cereals in grain equivalent)*

Recipient	Bilateral		Multilateral	NGOs	Total
	Govt-to-Govt	Through NGOs			
Bangladesh	1,057.3	75.2	302.2	1.1	1,435.7
India	80.0	241.7	94.6	0.4	437.7
Pakistan	391.7	2.1	267.8	–	661.7
Honduras	122.9	10.6	19.2	–	152.6
Tunisia	301.8	13.1	37.7	–	352.7
Benin	7.2	2.6	4.2	–	14.1
Lesotho	17.0	4.0	20.0	–	40.9
Tanzania	28.3	1.3	15.3	–	45.0
World total	9,583.7	1,446.8	2,585.0	80.8	13,696.3
Case studies as % of world total	20.9	24.2	29.4	1.9	22.9

programming that relates to the budgetary cycles in donor countries. The separate programming of food aid from other forms of aid continues in both recipient and donor countries. In recipient countries, food aid programmes often continue to be handled by separate administrative entities with responsibilities for poverty alleviation, social welfare or food distribution and subsidies. The multiplicity of donors is a potentially more severe constraint, because integration of food aid requires more complex logistical management arrangements than financial assistance. The experiences during the 1980s in these countries which have been economically and politically more stable than many others, underscore how much still has to be achieved if the gap is to be narrowed between potential and practice in using food aid to assist development.

Changing Donor Policies and Practice

The juxtaposition of donor experiences provided by this volume offers an opportunity to identify common and differing elements of policy and practice in donor countries. The eight donors reviewed cover the greater part of food aid. They are also broadly representative of the different donor situations. There are agricultural exporters – the United States, Canada, Australia and the European Community – that became food aid providers as a way of utilizing surpluses for a mixture of developmental, humanitarian, foreign policy and domestic agricultural policy and trade objectives. Other donors, that are not major agricultural exporters, have historically seen themselves as providing finance for food as part of the international commitment to humanitarian relief and developmental assistance under the FAC or to multilateral programmes and the work of voluntary agencies. Japan and Sweden, as well as Germany and the Netherlands, are representative of this second group of medium-sized and smaller donors. Historically, the latter group has shown more flexibility in resourcing, contributing relatively more to meeting the non-commodity costs of food aid.

Donors have handled food aid separately from financial and technical assistance. Food aid has, therefore, acquired its own institutions, procedures and legislation. This

Table 1.4 *Food aid deliveries: 1987–91 (annual average, '000 tons, cereals in grain equivalent)*

Donor	Cereals	Non-cereals
Australia	333	5
Canada	1,122	97
EC Community Action	1,695	250
Germany	250	49
Netherlands	113	23
Japan	485	8
Sweden	114	30
United States	7,158	664
World total	12,422	1,274
Case studies as % of world total	90.7	88.4

has imposed a different mind-set, has led to difficulties in co-ordinating food with other aid, and has made transfers unacceptably rigid. If assistance were planned and implemented within a common policy framework and a common set of programmes and projects, the effectiveness and efficiency of all aid transfers would be enhanced (World Bank/WFP, 1991).

Since the beginning of the 1980s, however, most donors have entered into a phase of extensive reassessment of their food aid policies and programmes (Clay, 1985). Has this process resulted in greater convergence or increased diversity in donor policy and practice? In a comparative analysis of the evolution of policies and programmes, it is useful to distinguish between:

a) legislative and other formal, regulatory changes in the way food aid programmes are organized and operated;
b) qualitative or quantitative changes in the character of donor programmes that *de facto* have resulted in policy changes (budgetary allocation, selection of commodities, etc.); and
c) a thematic restatement of policy that implies a change of objectives, or an intention to change procedures. The most recent example would be the declaration by many donors that food aid should be used to support structural adjustment programmes in developing countries.

Donor diversity: regulatory and administrative frameworks   The legal and administrative arrangements for food aid are more elaborate and diverse than for other types of development assistance. The framework within which development co-operation is organized is complex, reflecting distinctive legal and constitutional arrangements and the particular history of aid in individual donor countries. Five ministries and agencies are directly involved in the financing and administration of German food aid and four in the case of Japan. The additional complexity of food aid involves links to ministries and governmental bodies responsible for domestic agricultural policy and trade. The US food aid programme was initiated under legislation for managing agricultural trade surpluses and continues as part of the farm bill and not under the foreign assistance legislation governing other types of US aid. Until recently US food aid was managed by an inter-departmental committee. The 1990 farm bill legislation divided responsibility between the Department of Agriculture for bilateral programme food aid credits, and the Agency for International Development (AID) for wholly grant developmental and humanitarian food aid.

Agricultural ministries and agencies have also been involved, for practical reasons, in the management, procurement and transporting of food aid commodities, even when the programmes, as in the EC and German cases, were financed under the developmental co-operation budget. Historically, aid ministries and departments worked closely with agricultural agencies to acquire food even when this was undertaken internationally, as in the case of Japan and EC member states with commitments to provide food aid, but with no available domestic surpluses.

This close association of food aid with agricultural policy and trade agencies has been seen increasingly as a constraint on organizing food aid to serve developmental and humanitarian objectives. The response to this critique of aid compromised by trade linkages and unhelpful, often too complex, inter-agency responsibilities, has been to organize and also increasingly to finance the management of food aid as part of mainstream development co-operation. For example, the EC explicitly transferred responsibility for the procurement and transport of food aid within the EC Commission from the Directorate General VI (Agriculture) to Directorate General VIII (Development Co-operation) in the 1986 and 1987 regulations concerning food aid. The re-allocation of responsibilities to AID for wholly grant programmes under US food aid also involves an explicit separation of developmental and trade promotion goals.

A reduction in the role of agricultural agencies in food aid may also be a *de facto* consequence of changes in the types of assistance provided. For example, in the Japanese case, this was a result of the phasing-out after 1983 of so-called 'rice loans' administered by the Food Agency in the Ministry of Agriculture, Forestry and Fisheries. The drive to privatize government functions in the 1980s has involved close scrutiny of activities, such as procurement, purely on the basis of efficient management criteria. This emphasis on efficiency appears also to be resulting in a rationalization of responsibilities in ways that are more likely to integrate food aid procurement with other development co-operation management activities, as in the case of Australia.

A second aspect of administrative complexity in food aid decision-making and budgeting arises in part because of the humanitarian impulse behind food aid and the fact that a significant part of it is provided for humanitarian relief. Historically, ministries of foreign affairs have tended to have responsibility for this aspect of international co-operation with its high profile and political sensitivity. This may involve the co-ordination of emergency food aid and other emergency assistance within agencies, as in the case of the Netherlands or Sweden, or inter-agency co-operation even over emergency food aid, as in the case of Germany or Japan. There have been similar attempts to rationalize humanitarian relief, including food aid, in response to large, difficult, and often extended emergency operations during the 1980s. This has led in the case of the EC, for example, to the proposed integration of all emergency aid functions within a new European Community Humanitarian Office (ECHO). Alternatively, rationalization may be attempted not through institutional arrangements but through policy on the allocation of food. For example, Sweden has historically confined its bilateral food aid to the provision of emergency support, while allocating food aid multilaterally to support developmental objectives.

It would be naive, even incorrect, to present developments in food aid regulatory and administrative frameworks in terms of linear, irreversible trends – as an attempt to de-link developmental and domestic agricultural policy concerns that is reinforced by a drive for increased management efficiency. For example, when the EC wanted to initiate food aid to Eastern Europe, initially to Poland, in 1989, it was found expedient to establish a special unit in the Directorate General for Foreign Affairs (DGI) using food funded out of the EC's agricultural budget. It is also conceivable, that, in the harsher budgetary climate for aid during the 1990s, the pressure of domestic interests could involve a reversal of, or at least a halt to, the tendency of the 1980s formally to de-link the administration of development aid from domestic agricultural support and trade policy.

As in the case of financial and technical assistance, domestic interests have found other ways of influencing food aid policy, for example, through legal requirements that favour particular producer and trader interests. In the Canadian case, for example, a requirement was introduced that 25% of food aid in value terms should be in non-cereals. Since 1986, three-quarters of all US Title II project and emergency food aid commodities must be in the form of bagged or processed products, and, under cargo preference legislation, 75% of US food aid commodities must be shipped in US vessels. A systematic examination of aid programmes would be required to establish whether such restrictive practices of tying and designating aid are increasing or declining, and whether they are more or less prevalent in food aid. The growth during the late 1980s in the acquisition of food produced in developing countries for use as food aid is a practical consequence of de-linking it from domestic concerns in donor countries. But, significantly, internal pressures have often set upper limits on developing country purchases. The introduction of a single EC market in 1993 may involve a greater reduction in restrictions on supply or the accumulation of restrictions achieved by domestic lobbies in the various member states to favour supply interests.

Policy and policy changes Considered in terms of food aid policy and trends towards policy change, the donor community is still highly diverse. There are obviously larger and smaller donors. The US is still dominant in terms of either the volume or the value of global food aid resources (56% and 53% respectively in 1989): no single donor is as dominant in other forms of aid. There are also substantial differences among donors in the share of ODA provided as food aid, as high as 21% for the US and 24% for the EC in 1989, but overall only 6–7% for all Development Assistance Committee (DAC) countries of the OECD.

Table 1.5 *Food aid, volume and value by donor and as a percentage of ODA, 1989*

Donor	Volume			Value	
	'000 tons	As % of world total	$m	As % of world total	Food aid as % of total ODA
Australia	322	2.9	96	3.1	9.4
Canada	835	7.5	276	8.8	11.9
EC Community Action	1,605	14.5	640	20.5	23.8
Germany	270	2.4	289[a]	9.3[a]	5.8[a]
Netherlands	115	1.0	102[a]	3.3[a]	4.9[a]
Japan	478	4.3	95	3.0	1.1
Sweden	144	1.3	49	1.6	2.7
United States	6,227	56.3	1,637	52.5	21.3
World total	11,062	100.0	3,119	100.0	6.7

[a] Some EC member states include their share of the financing of Community Action as part of national ODA.

Source: Data in volume terms from WFP INTERFAIS Dababase. Data in value terms from OECD, *Development Co-operation: 1990 Report*, Paris, December 1990.

Table 1.6 *Food aid by donor and channel: 1987–91 (annual average, '000 tons, cereals in grain equivalent)*

Donor	Bilateral		Multilateral	Total
	Govt-to-Govt	Through NGOs		
Australia	162	19	157	337
Canada	614	37	569	1,219
EC Community Action	1,315	251	379	1,945
Germany	121	53	125	299
Netherlands	57	4	75	136
Japan	436	2	55	493
Sweden	37	3	103	144
United States	6,089	1,030	703	7,822
World total[a]	9,584	1,447	2,585	13,616
Case studies as % of world total	92.1	96.7	83.8	90.5

[a] Excluding NGOs.

Donors are highly diverse in important aspects of their food aid policy. For example, Australia, Canada, the Netherlands and Sweden contribute more than half of their food aid to multilateral programmes, whereas the US and the EC allocate their food aid primarily on a bilateral basis. There are also wide differences in the extent to which bilateral aid is channelled directly to governments, multilaterally or through NGOs.

The US, EC and Germany make greater use of NGOs. Although there has been a widespread tendency in this direction during the 1980s, particularly in emergencies in Africa, these differences are more long-standing, being based on legislative requirements in the case of the US and reflected in, for example, the organization of project aid in many countries. These substantial differences in allocative policy and practices have also made some of the medium and smaller donors, for example Canada, the Netherlands and Sweden, relatively more important in supporting WFP or relief efforts than their share of global food aid might indicate.

There are also large differences among donors in the uses of food aid. In particular, the medium and small donors, as well as supporting multilateral programmes for a mixture of general policy and management cost-effectiveness reasons, tend to allocate their bilateral aid largely to relief and in support of development projects. The US and the EC stand apart in being the major providers of bilateral programme food aid to governments for sale on local markets.

There is a continuing large geopolitical dimension to donor food aid allocations. The US is the overwhelmingly dominant provider of food aid to Latin America. The EC is now providing large-scale food aid to Eastern Europe and the former Soviet republics. Similarly, Australia and Japan concentrate their assistance on the geographically closer countries in the Asia and Pacific region. Canada, the EC and its member countries give relatively higher priority to sub-Saharan Africa. By way of comparison, three-quarters of the activities of WFP have been in sub-Saharan Africa, especially because of the large relief effort, and in Asia because of a large project portfolio and the two major relief operations for the Afghans in Pakistan and the Kampucheans on the border of Thailand. This recent pattern of allocations is in marked contrast to that of the 1960s and early 1970s, when large-scale programme aid to Asia

Table 1.7 *Food aid by donor and category of use: 1987–91 (annual average, '000 tons, cereals in grain equivalent)*

Donor	Relief	Project	Programme	Total
Australia	83	185	70	337
Canada	277	752	190	1,219
EC Community Action	601	325	102	1,945
Germany	170	101	28	299
Netherlands	58	65	13	136
Japan	238	17	239	493
Sweden	69	64	11	144
United States	774	1,519	5,530	7,822
World total	2,829	3,337	7,530	13,696
Case studies as % of world total	80.2	90.7	82.1	90.5

Table 1.8 *Food aid by donor and recipient region: 1987–91 (annual average, '000 tons, cereals in grain equivalent)*

Donor	Sub-Saharan Africa	North Africa & Near East	Asia & Pacific	Latin America & Caribbean	Europe	Total
Australia	85	59	187	4	4	337
Canada	323	178	602	108	8	1,219
EC Community Action	706	304	433	97	405	1,945
Germany	176	16	86	23	0.6	299
Netherlands	82	5	43	6	–	136
Japan	152	21	268	21	31	493
Sweden	78	22	41	3	–	144
United States	1,463	2,232	1,865	1,952	311	7,822
World total	3,689	3,087	3,801	2,329	794	13,696
Case studies as % of world total	83.1	91.9	92.7	95.0	95.5	90.5

dominated bilateral food aid flows. The shift, particularly to Africa, reflects a significant element of donor response to changing requirements, while continuing to be sensitive to regional, geopolitical interests.

Supply factors: The kind of commodities provided as food aid and the balance of acquisition from domestic production in the donor countries or in developing countries continue strongly to reflect supplier considerations. The US, Australia, Canada and the EC, as major wheat exporters, continue to make the bulk of their food aid available in the form of wheat and wheatflour. The US and the EC provide rice from exportable surpluses, while Japan acquires rice externally. The US draws on its exportable surpluses of vegetable oils and pulses, while the EC is the main provider of dairy products. The commodity composition of WFP's multilateral food aid also reflects what food resources are available in major donor countries. However, the range of donors, some providing finance rather than commodities, has made it possible for WFP to provide a more balanced basket of appropriate commodities than any one bilateral donor.

Table 1.9 *Food aid by donor and commodity type, 1989–91 (annual average, '000 tons, cereals in grain equivalent)*

Donor	Cereals			Non-cereals			
	Wheat & wheat flour	Coarse grains	Other	Dairy products	Veg. oil & fats	Pulses	Other
Australia	133.0	16.2	7.7	0.7	0.2	1.1	0
Canada	492.2	30.1	0	1.3	25.5	7.9	4.9
EC Community Action	1,070.7	345.9	53.3	83.7	45.1	24.5	52.6
Germany	107.8	40.1	6.7	1.6	2.8	8.5	6.5
Netherlands	13.7	26.5	10.7	1.2	3.6	2.8	2.7
Japan	220.7	21.4	167.5	1.3	0	0	1.1
Sweden	10.3	0.1	3.2	0	1.6	0.1	5.2
United States	3,381.1	1,585.7	585.1	12.6	276.9	58.8	77.4
WFP-supplied	1,311.4	396.5	260.3	50.3	77.9	75.4	39.0
World total	7,157.1	2,549.2	1,160.7	157.9	460.0	188.6	212.5
Case studies as % of world total	75.9	81.0	71.9	64.9	77.3	55.0	70.8

Table 1.10 *Food aid procurement in developing countries by donor, 1989–90 (annual average, '000 tons, cereals in grain equivalent)*

Donor	Cereals		Non-cereals		Triangular transactions & local purchases as % of total food aid
	Triangular transactions	Local purchases	Triangular transactions	Local purchases	
Australia	20.1	–	–	–	10.2
Canada	20.8	5.2	1.2	1.5	6.1
EC Community Action	116.0	21.3	5.5	10.5	8.4
Germany	25.4	15.6	1.9	4.7	21.5
Netherlands	32.8	3.0	0.5	–	47.4
Japan	203.0	99.8	0.4	–	65.6
Sweden	12.8	–	7.1	–	72.5
United States	9.1	7.5	–	–	0.3
WFP supplies	93.3	101.7	6.7	27.2	11.4
World total	606.9	268.8	26.7	49.5	7.6
Case studies as % of world total	72.5	56.7	62.2	33.7	2.8

The issue of policy change, given the problems of matching supplies with require-ments, particularly of coarse grains in sub-Saharan Africa, gained in importance dur-ing the 1980s. Several of the donor case studies describe the modification of legislative and administrative regulations to enable triangular transactions or local purchases in developing countries. These policy changes have resulted in the procurement of about one million tons of food aid a year in developing countries in the late 1980s. However, the policy impact shows some divergence between the actual practice of traditional agricultural exporters and that of other donors. The US is hardly involved in hard-currency acquisition of food in developing countries and instead has preferred to enter into 'trilateral transactions', which have involved, for example, the provision of wheat to Zimbabwe in exchange for white maize which has been shipped as aid to Mozambique. In contrast, the EC and member states such as Germany and the Netherlands, as well as other non-agricultural exporting donors, provide a substantial part of their food aid through triangular transactions and local purchases.

Additionality: Another 'structural' difference among donors relates to the circumstances that have given rise to food aid programmes and which, during the 1980s, have influenced their continuation. There appears to be an element of 'additionality' (i.e. aid that would not otherwise be available if it were not provided as food aid) in the case of donors that are traditional agricultural exporters. *Prima facie*, there would seem to be some element of additionality because the major agricultural exporting countries give a higher proportion of their total aid as food aid, thus reflecting their comparative advantage as food producers and their policy of maintaining a domestic component in their aid resources. But closer analysis of individual countries suggests a much more complex relationship between food aid and overall aid budgeting (Ram and Konandreas, 1991).

Aid represents a relatively lower proportion of GDP in the case of the US than of other DAC/OECD members. Its overall food aid budget appears to be fixed in financial terms. The volume and commodity composition thus reflects the interaction of factors determining that overall budget in financial terms and the commodities that the Department of Agriculture decides are in surplus and available for export. Since the mid-1980s the element of additionality would appear to be reflected, most obviously, in the periodic provision of surplus commodities under Section 416 of the 1949 Agricultural Trade Act.

Australia reduced its minimum contribution to the FAC during the 1980s when it was confronted with a tighter wheat export position and competition from other programmes for aid funds in a period of financial retrenchment. The Netherlands and Sweden establish overall aid allocations and meet their share of contributions under the FAC and two multilateral programmes out of the overall budget. These three cases suggest little evidence of additionality. From 1989, the EC began to provide substantial bilateral food aid to Eastern Europe and subsequently to republics of the former Soviet Union, financing these actions through its agricultural, rather than aid, budget. The Community might have found it difficult to react so promptly if financial transfers had had to be funded out of other budgets.

Taken together, the eight case studies underscore the real diversity that exists in donor practice, the influences that lie behind particular features of these programmes, and their partial and complex relationship to domestic agriculture and export trade policy.

Integrating food aid: A theme common to virtually all donor food aid programmes is the need to integrate food aid more closely with other forms of development assistance. This, in part, reflects efforts within most donor agencies to make more effective use of resources under tighter budgetary constraints. It also suggests that analysis of policy problems is becoming increasingly international, working through the fora of the Committee on Food Aid Policies and Programmes (CFA) regarding food aid and the Development Assistance Committee (DAC) of the OECD for aid generally. Several donors have sought to provide their bilateral programme food aid on a multi-annual rather than a year-by-year basis, or to achieve this through increased development programmes and projects in some countries for a number of years. Apart from acquisition in developing countries, changes in regulations to allow increased monetization and substitution of financial for food aid would seem to be part of an overall policy to make food aid a more flexible and better integrated element of aid overall. There has undoubtedly been progress in this direction, as the various donor case studies in this volume indicate. A careful reading of the recipient country case studies, however, brings out constraints on the donor side that indicate the considerable scope for further progress in this direction.

Until relatively recently, food aid was handled separately in donor aid administrations from financial and technical assistance. Food aid staff often worked under different rules and procedures, with different budgets. They were fewer in number and often managed larger resources than their counterparts in other sections of aid administrations. Deliberate measures are now being taken to integrate food aid and funds accruing from food aid sales into country aid programmes along with financial and technical assistance in a common set of programmes and projects. But the historical legacy of separation still remains and staff unused to the intricacies of food aid and the modalities of its use need to be fully familiarized with its potential as a broad-based and versatile resource for development as well as in emergencies.

Policy initiatives: Another aspect of the policy changes identified above is thematic. The integration of food aid with other development assistance is one such theme. Others that were echoed in most donor programmes during the 1980s have been: relating food aid to food strategies and food security; and supporting the process of structural and sectoral adjustment. These themes illustrate the ways in which recipient governments and donors have, in some cases, attempted to improve the overall planning and programming of food aid.

Food strategies and food security: Donors endorsed the international initiative of food strategies that originated in the World Food Council in the late 1970s. They also formulated the policy that food aid should be programmed to support more effectively countries promoting agricultural development and food security for all. Several donors attempted to implement this policy initiative through discussions with recipient governments on priorities for the use of food aid and by providing multi-year commitments. Australia, Canada, the EC and its member states, as well as the US under the modified Title III legislation of the late 1970s, attempted this integration of food aid with recipient governments' agricultural development strategies. The results of these initiatives are seen in some of the recipient country experiences. The overall impression is, however, that the effect has so far been relatively restricted and only a small proportion of bilateral food aid programmes is provided on a multi-year basis.

Supporting structural and sectoral adjustment: Since the late 1980s, an increasingly dominant policy theme has been the integration of food aid into overall support for structural and sectoral adjustment (Shaw and Singer, 1988). A further refinement has been to use food aid in compensatory programmes to mitigate the short-term adverse social impact of structural adjustment measures on the poor. These themes have been reiterated in the policy statements of most donors. Structural adjustment programmes provide an overall framework for financial and commodity assistance, and also involve domestic budgetary as well as sector reform targets. There is a discernible associated increase in donor interest in the way funds from the sale of programme food aid commodities may be used – for example, the new US Title III food aid programme and the EC's fourth Lomé Convention of 1989. Structural and sectoral adjustment programmes, where these involve co-ordination of multilateral and bilateral financial and commodity assistance within a precisely specified policy framework, could prove to be one of the main vehicles through which a greater part of food aid becomes better integrated into the mainstream of development assistance during the 1990s. The diversity of institutional and legal arrangements and interests that influence donor food aid policy suggest, however, that such a process of convergence around a structural adjustment agenda may prove to be only partial.

Emergency food aid   While a number of donors have set up special procedures and supply provisions to respond quickly to emergencies, many have not contributed to the International Emergency Food Reserve in accordance with its approved modalities (Appendix 1.2). Established in 1975 as a multilateral facility, administered by WFP, the IEFR was never intended to cover all emergency food needs but was meant to enable a quick and effective first-line response until other complementary resources from the international community could be mobilized. A review of IEFR modalities conducted by WFP (1991) revealed serious weaknesses in its operation. Special restrictions have been applied by donors to their IEFR contributions. Most donors require that they be used in the fiscal or budgetary year and cannot be carried forward. Specific prior clearance for their allocation to a given emergency must be obtained, and may take time to obtain, often without assurance of a positive response. The effect has been to limit the flexibility of the Reserve and delays in its operation have been considerable.

Another serious limitation has been the extensive donor practice of directing pledges by country destination and end use as well as designating the source of purchase and the type of commodity to be provided. It was estimated that by 1990 close to 70% of IEFR contributions were restricted in one way or another, thereby depriving the IEFR of most of its multilateral character and placing severe restrictions on the flexibility of resource allocations. In situations where speedy response was essential, the practice by donors of directing contributions became a serious obstacle to WFP's management of international emergency resources. In addition, untied cash resources in the IEFR have never been sufficient to enable adequate, immediate food purchases close to where emergencies occur.

The WFP review showed the clear need for a minimum core of untied pledges to be available for emergency use. The WFP Secretariat therefore proposed the creation of a cash facility as an integral part of the Reserve for the purchase and delivery of food to enable the fastest possible response to emergency situations prior to the arrival of emergency food supplies from donors. The CFA approved the establishment of this Immediate Response Account, which came into effect in 1992. It is to be funded from amounts set aside from WFP's regular resources each year and by voluntary contributions in convertible currencies free of restriction as to their use, with the aim of assuring at least US$30 million annually.

The CFA has confirmed that the minimum annual target of 500,000 tons for the IEFR should be maintained. It has also confirmed that the Executive Director of WFP has the authority to reimburse up to 100% of the internal transport, storage and handling costs of emergency food aid. Donors have also expressed their willingness to review their procedures, to make known in advance their pledges to the IEFR, and to release the aid they supply more rapidly. They have also undertaken to notify WFP as far in advance as possible of their overall emergency food aid allocations and to provide it with full information on all bilateral emergency allocations.

Future roles of food aid   In reviewing these 16 experiences of recipient and donor countries, a shift of emphasis can be detected in food aid policy analysis. The early literature and official statements emphasized the role of food in directly supporting development by:

a) programme food aid releasing balance of payments constraints and providing budgetary support for development plans with ambitious growth targets; and
b) project food aid being used to create infrastructure and develop human capital.

Humanitarian assistance, while mentioned, was a modest footnote.

The food aid of virtually all donors did not expand markedly during the 1980s. Instead, this significant but small part of overall ODA was increasingly seen as being particularly effective in providing relief, contributing to food security, and assisting projects to alleviate poverty and, most recently, to preserve the environment. The links to structural adjustment have often emphasized ameliorating the short-term social pressures created by restructuring and economic reform. Recipient country experiences all stress the constraints in terms of programming and management and the provision of complementary resources that is required to make food aid more effective in also contributing directly to development. Will the humanitarian relief, food security and poverty alleviation goals for food aid become even more dominant during the 1990s or will there be other efforts to emphasize the direct contribution of food aid to development?

Appendix 1.1 World Food Conference 1974 Resolution XVIII

AN IMPROVED POLICY FOR FOOD AID*

The World Food Conference,

Recognizing that, while the ultimate solution to the problem of food shortages in developing countries lies in increased production in these countries, during the interim period food aid on a grant basis and any additional food transfers on concessional or agreed-upon terms to developing countries will continue to be needed, primarily for meeting emergency and nutritional needs, as well as for stimulating rural employment through development projects,

Stressing the importance of evolving a longer-term food aid policy to ensure a reasonable degree of continuity in physical supplies,

Noting that, contrary to earlier expectations, the year 1974 has failed to bring the good harvest needed for the replenishment of stocks and the re-establishment of a reasonable degree of security in world food supplies, and expressing concern that most developing countries will not be able to finance their increased food import bills in the immediate period ahead,

Stressing that food aid should be provided in forms consonant with the sovereign rights of nations, neither interfering with the development objectives of recipient countries nor imposing the political objectives of donor countries upon them,

Emphasising further the paramount importance of ensuring that food aid is provided in forms which are voluntary in nature and are consistent with the agricultural development plans of recipient countries, with the ultimate aim of promoting their long-term development efforts and ensuring that it does not act as a disincentive to local production and cause adverse repercussions on the domestic market or international trade, in particular of developing countries,

Taking note with interest of the work of the General Assembly at its twenty-ninth session on the subject of strengthening the Office of the United Nations Disaster Relief Co-ordinator, in particular in relation to disaster preparedness and pre-disaster planning,

Recognizing the need to increase the resources of the World Food Programme, so as to enable it to play a greater and more effective role in rendering development assistance to developing countries in promoting food security and in emergency operations, and also recognizing the need to increase the resources of the United Nations Children's Fund, to enable it to play a greater role in meeting the food needs of children in emergency operations,

1. *Affirms* the need for continuity of a minimum level of food aid in physical terms, in order to insulate food aid programmes from the effects of excessive fluctuations in production and prices;

2. *Recommends* that all donor countries accept and implement the concept of forward planning of 'food aid', make all efforts to provide commodities and/or financial assistance that will ensure in physical terms at least 10 million tons of grains as food aid a year, starting from 1975, and also to provide adequate quantities of other food commodities;

3. *Requests* that interested cereals-exporting and importing countries as well as current and potential financial contributors meet as soon as possible to take cognizance of the needs and to consider ways and means to increase food availability and financing facilities during 1975 and 1976 for the affected developing countries and, in particular, for those most seriously affected by the current food problem;

4. *Urges* all donor countries to (a) channel a more significant proportion of food aid through the World Food Programme, (b) consider increasing progressively the grant component in their bilateral food aid programmes, (c) consider contributing part of any food aid repayments to supplementary nutrition programmes and emergency relief, and (d) provide, as appropriate, to food aid programmes additional cash resources for commodity purchases from developing countries to the maximum extent possible;

5. *Recommends* that the Intergovernmental Committee of the World Food Programme, reconstituted as recommended in Conference resolution XXII on arrangements for follow-up action, be entrusted with the task of formulating proposals for more effective co-ordination of multilateral, bilateral and non-governmental food aid programmes and of co-ordinating emergency food aid;**

6. *Recommends* that Governments, where possible, earmark stocks or funds for meeting international emergency requirements, as envisaged in the proposed International Undertaking on World Food Security, and further recommends that international guidelines for such emergency stocks be developed as a part of the proposed

Undertaking to provide for an effective co-ordination of emergency stocks and to ensure that food relief reaches the neediest and most vulnerable groups in developing countries;

7. *Recommends* that a part of the proposed emergency stocks be placed at the disposal of the World Food Programme on a voluntary basis, in order to increase its capacity to render speedy assistance in emergency situations.

---

* United Nations, *Report of the World Food Conference*, Rome, 5–16 November 1974. E/CONF.65/20. New York, 1975. pp. 15–16.
** Resolution XXII states:
The World Food Conference,
Recommends further that the Intergovernmental Committee of the World Food Programme be reconstituted so as to enable it to help evolve and co-ordinate short-term and longer-term food aid policies recommended by the Conference, in addition to discharging its existing functions. The reconstituted Committee should be called, and function as, the Committee on Food Aid Policies and Programmes. The Committee should submit periodical and special reports to the World Food Council. The functions of the Committee on Food Aid Policies and Programmes should include the following:
a) To provide a forum for intergovernmental consultations on national and international food aid programmes and policies, with particular reference to possibilities of securing improved co-ordination between bilateral and multilateral food aid;
b) To review periodically general trends in food aid requirements and food aid availabilities;
c) To recommend to Governments, through the World Food Council, improvements in food aid policies and programmes on such matters as programme priorities, composition of food aid commodities and other related subjects.

ibid. p. 18.

Appendix 1.2 Modalities of Operation of the International Emergency Food Reserve*

(a) The CFA agreed to consider ways and means of implementing resolution 3362 (S-VII) of the United Nations General Assembly, which urged all countries to build up and maintain food grain reserves in accordance with the International Undertaking on World Food Security, and that, pending their establishment 'developed countries and developing countries in a position to do so should earmark stocks and/or funds to be placed at the disposal of the World Food Programme as an emergency reserve to strengthen the capacity of the Programme to deal with crisis situations in developing countries. The aim should be a target of not less than 500,000 tons'.

(b) The International Emergency Food Reserve of 500,000 tons should be a continuing reserve with yearly replenishments determined by the Committee on Food Aid Policies and Programmes and placed at the disposal of the World Food Programme. The Reserve should be in the nature of a standby arrangement; it would not necessarily entail the holding by WFP of physically separate stocks in specified localities.

(c) Participating countries should, over and above their regular pledges to WFP, indicate to WFP at the beginning of each calendar year or other appropriate 12-month period, availabilities of primarily foodgrains from stocks held in these countries, or cash contributions, which might be called upon for emergency food aid purposes. For that purpose the definition of emergencies adopted by the Intergovernmental Committee of the World Food Programme remained a valid guideline.**

(d) WFP should direct requests to draw upon such availabilities or funds to the participating governments. Reserves not called upon in any one year will be carried over into the next year.

(e) Insofar as possible, all availabilities or funds should be placed at the disposal of WFP and contributing countries should preferably indicate their allocations to the Reserve for more than one year in advance. In cases where the availabilities or funds were not placed directly at the disposal of WFP, the participating countries should keep WFP informed about their use in order to achieve effective co-ordination of the food assistance under the emergency reserve.

(f) The present procedures of WFP for the approval of emergency food aid should also be applied to operations under the reserve. The CFA might consider changes in the existing procedures at a later date in the light of experience.

(g) Developing countries not in a position to make contributions in cash or in kind to the Reserve should, where possible, make interest-free loans of commodities to be used by WFP in the initial stages of emergencies especially where such arrangements would speed up delivery of commodities.

(h) The governments contributing food to the IEFR should also assume responsibility for meeting the expenses of its transport and other related costs. When food contributions come from developing countries unable to finance such expenses, the Programme will explore the possibility of meeting such costs with other donors.

(i) When resources allocated by contributing governments to the IEFR are placed at the disposal of WFP, such governments shall take all possible measures to see that food is shipped in the most expeditious manner.

(j) Part of the contributions to the IEFR should be made in commodities such as rice and white sorghum to take account of the food habits of afflicted peoples.

---

* Approved by the CFA at the Sixth Session in October 1978. At its Thirty-second Session in December 1991, the CFA agreed to establish an Immediate Response Account as an integral part of the IEFR for the purpose of purchase and delivery of emergency food aid for food shortage situations of at least US$30 million annually.

** For purposes of WFP emergency operations, emergencies are defined as 'urgent situations in which there is clear evidence that an event has occurred which causes human suffering or loss of livestock and which the government concerned has not the means to remedy; and it is a demonstrably abnormal event which produces dislocation in the life of a community on an exceptional scale. This definition covers (a) sudden calamities such as earthquakes, floods, locust infestations and similar unforeseen disasters; (b) man-made emergencies like an influx of refugees; and (c) food scarcity conditions owing to drought crop failures, pests and 'diseases'. Reconfirmed at the Twenty-eighth Session of the Intergovernmental Committee in October 1975.

Appendix 1.3 Guidelines and Criteria for Food Aid*

The Committee on Food Aid Policies and Programmes (CFA) recommends the following guidelines and criteria for bilateral and multilateral food aid programmes so that food aid can make a more effective contribution to the solution of the food problem of developing countries. As agreed by the World Food Conference (in 1974) and subsequently endorsed by the United Nations General Assembly, the longer-term solution to the problem of food shortages in the developing countries lay in increased production in those countries. In the interim, food aid would continue to be needed for providing emergency relief, combatting hunger and malnutrition, promoting economic and social development, and food security.

(a) Food aid should be provided in forms consistent with the development objectives of recipient countries, with the aim of promoting their long-term development efforts and ensuring that it neither acted as a disincentive to local food production nor had adverse effects on the domestic market and international trade, in particular of developing countries. For maximum effectiveness, project food aid should be co-ordinated, to the fullest extent possible, with financial aid and other forms of development assistance.

(b) In order to facilitate effective planning and implementation of development and nutrition programmes, governments of recipient countries needed to have assurance of adequate food supplies over a sufficiently long period. To that end, all donor countries should make every effort to accept and implement forward planning, preferably on a multi-annual basis, in physical terms as appropriate, so as to ensure continuity of food aid. Periodic assessments of food aid needs should be undertaken with a view to assisting planning and programming of its provision and use in donor and recipient countries respectively.

(c) Food aid in support of economic and social development projects should be programmed on a multi-annual basis, taking full account of the special needs and priorities of recipient countries and the nature of the projects themselves. Such multi-annual commitments could be subject to periodic revisions by mutual agreement as regards commodities to be supplied and the use of counterpart funds for various development activities in recipient countries.

(d) In the allocation of food aid resources, donor countries should give priority to low-income, food-deficit countries.[1] Due attention should also be given to the food aid needs of other developing countries in support of projects specifically designed to benefit the poorest segments of their populations. An important consideration in allocating food aid to the eligible countries should be a strong commitment on the part of their governments to development policies for achieving self-reliance, reducing poverty and improving nutritional status particularly in rural areas.

(e) For the poorest countries, donors should undertake to finance, to the maximum extent possible, transport and storage costs, as appropriate, of donated food commodities, for emergencies and for use in developmental projects, including special feeding projects, in food-for-work schemes and for other specified target groups in those countries.

(f) Food aid should be provided essentially on a grant basis to developing countries, in particular to the least developed and most seriously affected among them.

(g) Donor countries should channel a more significant proportion of food aid through the World Food Programme and other multilateral institutions.

(h) Donor countries should make efforts to provide wherever possible cash resources with a view to financing food aid through triangular transactions between themselves, developing food exporting countries and recipient countries, including coverage of shipping costs wherever applicable, and further diversifying the varieties of food provided as aid. Such arrangements would increase the participation of developing exporting countries in providing food aid.

(i) In allocating and utilizing food aid, donor and recipient countries should give priority to:
  - Meeting emergency requirements. To that end, countries in a position to do so should earmark part of their national grain stocks or funds for emergency purposes as envisaged in the International Undertaking on World Food Security. Wherever possible, arrangements should be made to increase food aid levels to meet the needs of large-scale emergencies. Among other steps, countries which have not yet contributed to the International Emergency Food Reserve should do so, and other donors should make additional contributions so as to meet the minimum target, as established from time to time,[2] on a continuing basis with yearly replenishments.
  - Activities designed to increase agricultural, and especially food, production, to raise incomes, to meet basic needs and stimulate self-reliance and to create opportunities for employment for the populations of developing countries, particularly in rural areas, including education and training geared to the achievement of these objectives.
  - Nutrition intervention programmes, with special emphasis on projects for improving the nutritional status of the vulnerable groups of pre-school children and expectant and nursing mothers.

(j) Donor and recipient countries should also, wherever appropriate, use food, financial and technical assistance for the creation and maintenance of food reserves, including storage and transport facilities in developing countries.

---

[1] The Committee considered that the term 'low-income' covered countries eligible for concessional assistance by the International Development Association. The poorest countries within this group should receive special attention.

* Approved by the CFA at its Seventh Session in May 1979.

References

Bryson, Judy. C. *et al.* (1991). *Food for Work: A Review of the 1980s with Recommendations for the 1990s*. Washington, D.C., Agency for International Development.

Cassen, R.H. and Associates (1986). *Does Aid Work?* Oxford, Oxford University Press.

Cathie, John (1991). 'Modelling the Role of Food Imports, Food Aid and Food Security in Africa: The Case of Botswana' in Clay and Stokke, pp. 91–117.

Clay, E.J. (1985). *Review of Food Aid Policy Changes since 1978*. WFP Occasional Paper no. 1, Rome.

Clay, E.J. (1986). 'Rural public works and food-for-work: a survey', *World Development*, Vol. 14, no. 10/11, October/November, pp. 1237–52.

Clay, Edward and Stokke, O. (eds) (1991). *Food Aid Reconsidered: Assessing the Impact on Third World Countries*. London, Frank Cass.

---

[2] Currently 500,000 metric tons.

Cornia, Giovanni Andrea, Jolly, Richard, and Stewart, Frances (1987). *Adjustment with a Human Face*, Vol. 1 *Protecting the Vulnerable and Promoting Growth*. Oxford, Clarendon Press.

FAO (1980). *Principles of Surplus Disposal and Consultative Obligations of Member Countries*. Rome.

Food Studies Group (1989) *European Community Triangular Food Aid: An Evaluation*. Synthesis Report. Oxford, Queen Elizabeth House.

Hay, R. and Clay, E.J. (1986). *Food Aid and the Development of Human Resources*. WFP Occasional Paper No. 7, Rome.

Maxwell, Simon (1978). 'Food Aid, Food for Work and Public Works', *IDS Discussion Paper* no. 127. Brighton, University of Sussex.

Maxwell, Simon (1991). 'The Disincentive Effect of Food Aid: A Pragmatic Approach' in Clay and Stokke, pp. 66–90.

Mora, Jose, O. *et al.* (1990). *The Effectiveness of Maternal and Child Health (MCH) Supplementary Feeding Programs. An Analysis of Performance in the 1980s and Potential Role in the 1990s*. Washington, D.C., Logical Technical Services Corporation for A.I.D., September.

Ram, Saran and Konandreas, Panos (1991). 'An Additional Resource? A Global Perspective on Food Aid Flows in Relation to Development Assistance', in Clay and Stokke, pp. 37–66.

Relief and Development Institute, London (1987). *A Study of Triangular Transactions and Local Purchases in Food Aid*. WFP Occasional Paper No. 11, Rome.

Relief and Development Institute, London (1990). *A Study of Commodity Exchanges in WFP and other Food Aid Operations*. WFP Occasional Paper No. 12, Rome.

Ronco Consulting Corporation (1988). *Trilateral Food Aid Transactions: USG Experience in the 1980s*. Washington, D.C., March.

Ruttan, Vernon, W. (ed.) (1993). *Why Food Aid?* Baltimore, MD, Johns Hopkins University Press.

Shaw, John and Singer, Hans (1988). 'Food Policy, Food Aid and Economic Adjustment', Special Issue *Food Policy*, Vol. 13, No. 1, pp. 2–9.

Singer, Hans, Wood, John and Jennings, Tony (1987). *Food Aid. The Challenge and The Opportunity*. Oxford, Clarendon Press.

World Bank and World Food Programme (1991). *Food Aid in Africa: An Agenda for the 1990s*. Washington, D.C. and Rome, August.

WFP (1989) *Review of Protracted Emergency Operations for Refugees and Displaced Persons*, document WFP/CFA:27/P/7, Rome, April.

WFP (1991). *Review of IEFR Modalities*, document CFA:31/P/7, Rome, April (see also document CFA:32/P/5, Rome, October).

Appendix Table 1.1 Global non-cereal food aid deliveries ('000 tons)

	1987	1988	1989	1990	1991	1987–91 Average
Total:	1364.7	1695.3	1006.5	1183.7	1120.9	1274.2
By food aid channel:						
– Bilateral	1029.2	1346.3	713.1	866.6	763.6	943.8
– Gvt-to-Gvt	841.8	1125.6	576.9	633.9	462.3	728.1
– through NGOs	187.4	220.7	136.2	232.7	301.3	215.7
– Multilateral	329.5	343.0	288.9	299.0	348.3	321.7
– NGOs	6.0	6.1	4.4	18.1	9.0	8.7
By food aid category:						
– Emergency Relief	223.7	360.9	213.5	311.5	423.4	306.6
– Project	533.3	550.0	382.1	321.1	328.2	422.9
– Agr./Rural Development	183.6	228.7	158.3	108.9	119.0	159.7
– Nutrition Intervention	213.8	207.6	77.3	71.9	79.4	130.0
– Food Reserve	5.2	8.6	6.0	2.9	0.3	4.6
– Other Development Project	130.7	105.1	140.5	137.4	129.5	128.6
– Non-project (Programme)	607.8	784.3	410.9	551.1	369.3	544.7
By region:						
– Sub-Saharan Africa	348.3	422.6	295.6	347.1	404.9	363.7
– North Africa/Mid-East	186.6	256.8	184.0	134.4	149.1	182.2
– Asia and Pacific	452.8	691.3	336.6	348.6	185.3	402.9
– Latin America and Caribbean	375.7	324.6	173.3	207.5	188.4	253.9
– Europe	1.2	–	17.0	146.2	192.1	71.3
By Donor [a]:						
– USA	725.8	885.6	484.2	582.1	352.6	606.1
– WFP	296.0	303.9	260.6	235.2	303.8	279.9
– EC Community Action	107.7	214.6	143.4	190.1	333.1	197.8
– Canada	99.2	116.7	20.8	56.0	17.7	62.1
– Italy	43.1	45.4	12.2	17.9	32.0	30.1
– Germany	23.1	39.5	25.6	29.9	21.4	27.9
– Sweden	19.9	20.1	16.0	2.5	2.0	12.1
– Netherlands	9.5	23.7	2.5	7.9	14.8	11.7
– Saudi Arabia	1.3	21.1	6.1	–	0.2	5.7
– Switzerland	4.2	1.4	0.7	7.9	10.6	5.0
– USSR	2.3	–	5.8	10.0	–	3.6
– Norway	0.9	4.4	0.9	9.5	–	3.1
– Finland	4.5	1.7	6.0	1.6	0.7	2.8
– France	0.2	0.7	3.8	4.8	4.3	2.7
– UK	–	1.2	5.7	1.4	4.9	2.6
– Japan	0.9	2.1	2.0	1.6	3.5	2.0
– Australia	1.5	–	2.3	1.0	2.9	1.5
– NGOs	6.0	6.1	4.4	17.2	6.8	8.1
– Others	18.6	7.1	3.5	7.1	9.6	9.2

[a] Multilateral food aid provided through WFP appears under WFP as donor.

Source: WFP/INTERFAIS Database

Appendix Table 1.2 *Global cereal food aid deliveries ('000 tons – in grain equivalent)*

	1987	1988	1989	1990	1991	1987–91 Average
Total:	13039.5	13155.7	10452.3	12902.3	12560.1	12422.1
By food aid channel:						
– Bilateral	10937.9	10449.2	8579.1	10786.0	9681.7	10086.7
– Gvt-to-Gvt	10239.2	9244.8	7498.6	9152.5	8143.5	8855.6
– through NGOs	698.7	1204.4	1080.5	1633.5	1538.2	1231.3
– Multilateral	2057.0	2630.1	1821.8	2014.4	2793.2	2263.3
– NGOs	44.5	76.4	52.0	101.9	85.0	72.1
By food aid category:						
– Emergency Relief	1751.9	2917.7	2162.7	2476.0	3304.8	2522.6
– Project	3405.5	3510.0	2495.8	2515.3	2643.3	2914.0
– Agr./Rural Development	1765.2	1706.7	1076.3	1199.0	1400.2	1429.5
– Nutrition Intervention	899.0	1055.6	460.5	354.4	463.9	646.7
– Food Reserve	22.9	34.7	27.9	39.1	14.4	27.8
– Other Development Project	718.4	713.0	931.1	922.8	764.8	810.0
– Non-project (Programme)	7882.1	6728.0	5794.4	7911.0	6611.9	6985.5
By region:						
– Sub-Saharan Africa	3155.3	4126.5	2594.3	2921.7	3826.3	3324.8
– North Africa/Mid-East	3314.2	2414.9	2660.9	3021.7	3110.2	2904.4
– Asia and Pacific	4210.9	4364.2	3031.1	2540.5	2844.7	3398.3
– Latin America and Caribbean	2358.4	2250.1	1880.7	2091.7	1796.1	2075.4
– Europe	0.7	–	285.9	2326.4	1002.4	723.1
By donor[a]:						
– USA	7107.7	6592.0	5502.1	7051.7	6371.1	6524.9
– WFP	1855.6	2464.5	1695.2	1873.8	2673.9	2112.6
– EC Community Action	1199.1	1294.2	1285.7	2026.7	1464.7	1454.1
– Canada	767.0	616.8	399.6	529.2	628.2	588.2
– Japan	543.6	509.2	428.4	440.9	258.0	436.0
– France	145.2	253.3	281.9	97.7	252.3	206.1
– Germany	182.1	247.7	173.6	213.2	128.4	189.0
– Australia	186.0	219.3	178.3	221.7	90.8	179.2
– USSR	183.3	317.2	94.3	60.0	–	131.0
– Italy	153.7	167.8	76.5	46.9	116.0	112.2
– UK	94.3	136.7	66.4	13.5	117.9	85.7
– Saudi Arabia	207.2	17.4	16.1	1.7	10.0	50.5
– Netherlands	47.5	35.0	12.2	73.9	76.6	49.0
– Switzerland	21.4	25.5	24.6	37.4	43.7	30.5
– Sweden	71.1	31.3	25.4	10.3	5.0	28.6
– Belgium	18.2	17.9	25.3	45.7	26.5	26.7
– Spain	23.6	19.4	23.6	16.6	23.2	21.3
– Austria	12.7	9.2	21.0	13.1	28.8	17.0
– India	48.6	–	–	5.0	25.2	15.8
– Denmark	43.0	9.5	24.3	0.2	0.3	15.5
– Norway	3.2	13.6	13.6	0.1	30.8	12.3
– Argentina	28.6	3.0	5.0	2.5	7.0	9.2
– Pakistan	6.4	3.0	2.0	–	25.4	7.3

Appendix Table 1.2 *(continued)*

	1987	1988	1989	1990	1991	1987–91 Average
– Turkey	–	–	–	0.4	35.8	7.2
– China	4.5	3.9	–	–	11.5	4.0
– Greece	–	17.0	2.5	–	–	3.9
– Finland	0.1	0.1	1.4	13.2	–	3.0
– Taiwan	–	10.0	5.0	–	–	3.0
– Libya	–	–	–	–	10.6	2.1
– Thailand	–	1.7	0.1	–	5.0	1.4
– Kuwait	1.7	1.2	–	–	2.5	1.1
– NGOs	44.5	76.4	52.0	1.9	85.4	72.0
– Others	39.6	41.9	16.9	5.0	5.5	21.8

[a] Multilateral food aid provided through WFP appears under WFP as donor.

Source: ibid.

Appendix Table 1.3 *Cereal food aid by recipient – 1970–92 ('000 tons – in grain equivalent)*

Year July–June	Bangladesh	India	Pakistan	Honduras	Tunisia	Benin	Lesotho	Tanzania	World Total
1970/71	–	2384.2	1003.9	2.0	254.3	1.3	27.2	8.8	12357.3
1971/72	610.1	1776.6	1113.6	1.2	215.0	3.8	14.4	5.6	12512.8
1972/73	1272.0	461.0	1109.5	2.7	122.4	9.9	18.5	9.6	9964.1
1973/74	660.3	252.1	383.4	3.8	99.9	6.0	25.1	10.9	5818.7
1974/75	2076.0	1582.2	584.0	30.8	59.1	8.8	14.3	147.7	8399.4
1975/76	1186.9	1107.8	788.9	13.4	60.8	7.4	18.1	108.7	6847.0
1976/77	994.8	1176.3	336.2	30.5	107.0	7.4	10.6	134.5	9022.4
1977/78	1277.4	568.4	266.0	8.5	209.8	11.5	23.6	101.6	9215.5
1978/79	1496.6	386.2	370.6	13.2	157.2	5.0	37.8	53.6	9499.7
1979/80	1479.5	343.9	146.3	26.8	164.5	5.0	28.6	89.3	8887.0
1980/81	736.9	435.4	276.8	35.8	98.7	11.1	44.1	235.8	8941.6
1981/82	1005.5	337.6	347.4	33.8	96.0	8.3	34.2	307.5	9140.2
1982/83	1252.3	281.6	368.6	94.5	153.5	14.0	28.6	171.4	9238.0
1983/84	1162.7	371.3	394.9	98.8	146.0	5.7	50.2	141.4	9848.7
1984/85	1500.1	303.9	410.7	117.6	191.9	21.4	70.8	124.9	12510.7
1985/86	1300.3	257.4	383.8	135.0	79.7	10.8	40.4	65.8	10949.2
1986/87	1588.9	208.1	471.0	137.3	396.1	8.0	34.2	55.4	12599.0
1987/88	1567.7	373.1	649.1	180.9	303.1	10.7	42.8	42.4	13609.4
1988/89	1398.0	572.9	536.4	148.1	479.7	18.2	28.5	72.4	11326.3
1989/90	1058.5	355.4	430.5	116.2	433.7	10.0	30.6	26.2	10912.6
1990/91	1422.8	241.4	342.9	84.2	353.9	8.7	31.1	23.9	12542.7
1991/92	1466.3	318.6	336.6	156.1	87.6	2.4	28.5	14.6	13904.4

Sources: FAO, *Food Aid in Figures* and WFP INTERFAIS Database.

Appendix Figure 1.1 Cereal food aid by recipient – 1970–92 ('000 tons – in grain equivalent)

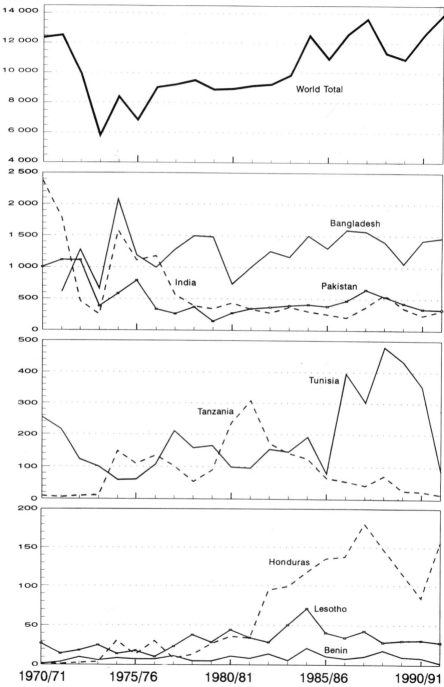

Sources: FAO, *Food Aid in Figures* and WFP INTERFAIS Database.

Appendix Figure 1.2 Cereal food aid by donor – 1970–92 ('000 tons – in grain equivalent)

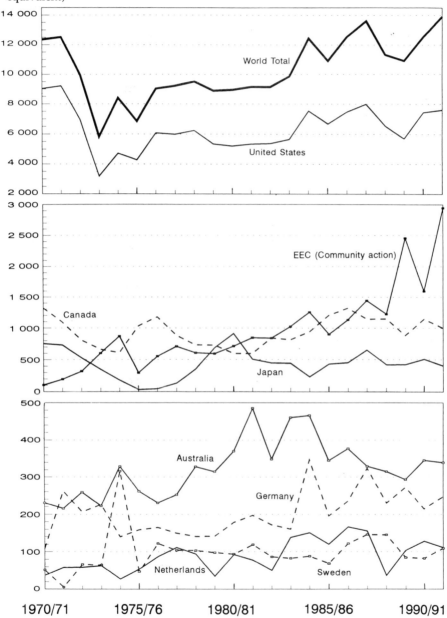

Sources: ibid.

Appendix Figure 1.3 Cereal food aid by donor (3-year averages: '000 tons – in grain equivalent and % of world total)

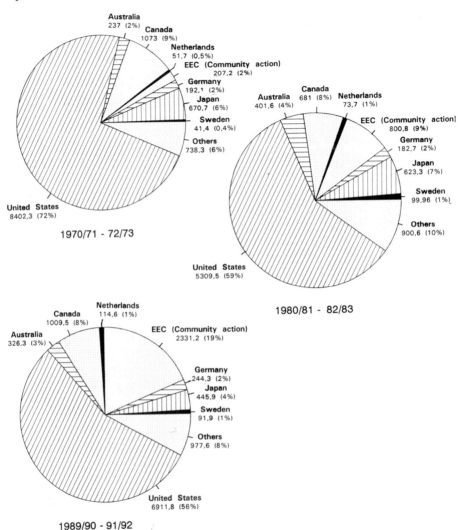

Sources: ibid.

Food distribution in Thailand to displaced people. WFP/Martin Becka

Food for displaced children in Somalia. WFP/Mitchell

Many women in Bangladesh have to support their families. Food-for-work programmes provide employment and food for them and their families. WFP/Trevor Page

Houses demolished by a tornado at Gopalganj in Faridpur District. WFP supplies food for the victims of tornadoes and flash floods. WFP/Trevor Page

2 Bangladesh

The Challenges
of Food Security & Development
in a Disaster-prone Economy

Bangladesh was one of the largest recipients of food aid during the 1970s and 1980s. Its experience is amongst the most important and interesting in reviewing the uses and impacts of food aid.

In few developing countries have the issues of food security and food aid taken on such importance as in the first two decades of independence for Bangladesh – a poor and heavily populated country with a history of oft-recurring natural disasters. Since independence in 1971 it has regularly suffered major floods, drought, devastating cyclones and tidal waves, and the influx of destitute refugees. Most of the poorest Bangladesh people face continuing problems of hunger, deprivation and seasonal food insecurity. By conventional anthropometric indicators the majority of children are chronically under-nourished; some children and many poor women, particularly those of child-bearing age, are at severe nutritional risk.

The average household spends 60% of its budget on food. Foodgrains account for 80% of the calorie intake and 60% of the protein. Food security has inevitably been given the highest priority in the development of national policy. Food imports, and in particular food aid, have played an important part in attempts to provide food security, combat wider problems of poverty, and foster development. Efforts have been increasingly effective in preventing famine.

Broadly, three phases in food security and food aid policy can be distinguished. First, there was the difficult period of post-independence reconstruction, which involved the return of refugees and then combating the devastating effects of drought followed by floods at a time of international food crisis. From independence until the late 1970s, large-scale food aid played a critical role. Programme food aid sustained public food distribution systems and provided considerable budgetary support. Targeted food aid programmes, food-for-work (FFW) and vulnerable group feeding were introduced as famine containment and relief measures, and were subsequently expanded as anti-poverty programmes.

The second phase, from about 1978 to 1988, was a period during which the role of food aid changed significantly. Public policy sought to achieve increased self-sufficiency in foodgrains through expanded cultivation of high-yielding varieties of rice and wheat. With growth in financial aid at around 10% a year, combined with growth in non-traditional export revenues and remittances from overseas workers,

41

food aid became relatively less important in macroeconomic terms, although levels increased from time to time in response to major natural disasters. Within food aid, targeted projects became a crucial element in the rural poverty alleviation strategy, whilst strengthening Bangladesh's capacity to cope with the effects of natural disasters. From around 5% of food aid at the time of the 1974 famine, targeted projects accounted for 50–60% of food aid during the late 1980s.

Despite devastating floods in 1988, the worst in recent times, it quickly became clear that Bangladesh was entering a new phase of food security and food aid policy. With rapid growth in rice production, Bangladesh at last seems to be close to self-sufficiency, albeit at low levels of food intake among the poorest 60% of the population. Requirements for commercial imports and for programme food aid have reduced greatly.

The relative success of targeted food aid projects in combating rural poverty and providing the major component of a food security net during the disasters of 1987 and 1988 and after the cyclone in 1991 leaves two major problems to be solved. First, there is the task of enhancing the developmental impact of project food aid through the development and maintenance of infrastructure, human resource development amongst the rural poor, and other possible new measures. The second is ensuring that the resourcing of what had become the world's largest rural poverty alleviation programme supported by food aid is consistent with the agricultural development objective, now within reach, of achieving and maintaining self-sufficiency in rice.

Background

With a population of 110 million people in an area of only 144,000 km, and a *per caput* GNP of around US$200, Bangladesh is the most densely settled and one of the poorest countries in the world. There are continuing severe problems of poverty, chronic malnutrition and vulnerability. More than half of all rural households are landless; and the labour force is still expanding at close to 3% a year, despite an encouraging decline in the population growth rate revealed by the 1991 census (from more than 3% to between 2.1 and 2.2%). With industrialization only now beginning to have a significant impact on income and employment generation, agriculture still dominates the economy. The recent expansion in rice production based on private investment in irrigation, more intensive fertilizer use and the adoption of high-yielding varieties has brought Bangladesh close to self-sufficiency in foodgrains. But agriculture can at best absorb 25% of future rural job seekers. As a result, there is a continuing problem of massive rural poverty, linked to unemployment and landlessness.

Although estimation of growth rates is especially difficult in such an economy, there seem to have been important, if modest, achievements since independence. During the 1980s rice production grew by 2.7%, exceeding the rate of population growth (2.2%). But average consumption levels remain low, with consumption and anthropometric evidence confirming widespread chronic undernutrition and the existence of highly vulnerable and acutely malnourished groups, especially amongst the poorest. The prices of staple cereals have remained a crucial factor in poverty and food insecurity. There has been a substantial reduction in the variability of average seasonal prices, which fluctuated by 30% in the 1960s and as much as 60% in the war and famine-affected 1970s, but by only 20% in the 1980s. This reduction is partly the result of a rapid increase in irrigated rice production in the dry

(*Boro*) season, which has smoothed out peaks and troughs in production, combined with public food distribution and anti-poverty programmes supported by food aid.

Two factors have dominated the agricultural and food strategy since independence. First, during the 1980s, self-sufficiency in cereals was promoted through the expansion of irrigation and the use of high-yielding varieties and fertilizers. This strategy was linked increasingly to promoting private sector activity, and reducing public sector regulations. Secondly, public food distribution channels have been used both to ensure that food is available to politically important groups in society at stable prices and, through anti-poverty programmes, to provide a food security net for poor rural households. As food aid has been a major source for public food distribution, it has made a vital contribution to the economy.

Food Aid Flows

Official Development Assistance (ODA) played a crucial role in providing resources first for the rehabilitation of a severely war-damaged economy, and then to sustain development. At first, food aid and other commodity assistance represented a large proportion of total ODA. By 1988–90, food aid had come to play a more modest role, averaging US$245 million out of total ODA of US$1483 million a year (US$2.25 *per caput* out of US$13). The United States, Canada, the European Community, Australia and WFP have typically accounted for around 90% of all food aid to Bangladesh. During the first decade after independence, about two-thirds of this aid was supplied bilaterally as programme assistance (bulk food aid), and one-third was directly targeted to poor groups through projects. The proportions have since reversed, with some 60% of food aid now being linked to targeted programmes. Donors have also entered into increasingly detailed agreements for the directing of cash generated by the sale of programme aid (counterpart funds) to specific development projects.

A trend towards multi-annual commitments, linked increasingly in the case of most donors to targeted projects, has also improved the continuity, and thus the predictability, of food aid resources. The United States, Canada, the EC and WFP now provide their assistance in this way, with annual food aid allocations recently averaging 1.4 million tons. Until recently, more than two-thirds of these allocations have been in the form of commitments in advance.

Non-cereals aid has usually been in the form of edible oils, with small quantities of dairy commodities. In terms of total food aid, consignments of such commodities are very small. They are mostly allocated for budgetary support activities and emergency relief.

Policy Framework and Sectoral Strategies

Concessional cereals aid and commercial inputs are either sold at partly subsidized prices, distributed free, or given as wages through the Public Food Distribution System (PFDS) under the Ministry of Food. Several parallel channels are involved, reflecting the multiple objectives of food policy. The relative importance of these various objectives has changed with time; and the overall levels of off-take and sources of supply have varied substantially, depending on the balance between food security and agricultural price support concerns, and the levels of carry-over stocks and commitments of aid.

Price stabilization The PFDS off-take has recently accounted for approximately one-eighth of total apparent consumption, and for a substantial proportion of marketed supply. Carry-over levels of stock in recent years have exceeded 1 million tons. Public storage capacity as a result of investments during the 1980s is close to 2 million tons. As a result, the government can significantly influence market prices, private production and stock-holding decisions.

Government policy has sought to prevent extreme price variations. Past experience has shown that even small reductions in expected or actual harvests, and the dislocation of communications by natural disasters, can have a marked effect on market prices. The high proportion of consumer expenditure that is devoted to food has made it imperative that intervention measures be taken as a food security measure to prevent sharp upward speculative movements in prices. On the other hand, an upsurge in production (which often occurs partly in reaction to previous losses and the higher relative prices of cereals associated with natural disasters and food crises) can lead to a sharp fall in prices to farmers. The government has used domestic procurement at pre-announced prices to try to sustain a floor price for domestic rice, and to a more limited extent wheat, producers. Rice is now being procured through open tender and the response is encouraging.

Open market sales through government-recognized grain dealers in all parts of the country have also been used to a limited extent since 1979 as a mechanism for stabilizing wheat prices. Here, the market triggers the release of government stocks, and the whole population benefits from more stable prices. Such operations have, however, remained small in comparison with public distribution operations and distributions of project food aid. The Ministry of Food has declared that OMS is to be given an increased role as a price stabilization mechanism.

The PFDS rationing system: The distribution of cereals and to a limited extent other commodities through the PFDS rationing system dates back to the colonial era (pre-1947). The eligible groups are concentrated mainly in urban areas and include those employed in state and nationalized institutions (civil service, the military, jute mills, hospitals, etc.). Smaller quantities have been made available in rural areas to benefit poorer groups of the population. Both urban and rural rationing distribution was sharply curtailed in the late 1970s and has subsequently remained broadly stable in quantities of grain off-take (see Figure 2.1). However, the balance between rice and wheat, imported and domestically procured commodities, and the element of subsidy, has fluctuated substantially over time. The government has taken increasing responsibility for supply from domestic procurement and from commercial imports. A stated longer-term policy objective has been gradually to reduce the scale of such operations, and to eliminate subsidies. In addition, flour mills are now encouraged to import wheat directly. The efficiency and cost-effectiveness of rationing and price stabilization interventions and stock-holding are currently the subject of a Ministry of Food/ International Food Policy Research Institute (IFPRI) research programme.

Local-cost financing: One result of PFDS marketing operations is the generation of core finance from the sale of bilaterally provided programme food aid. During the 1980s, about 750,000 tons of wheat and rice were imported under grant or loan agreements every year and sold, generating the equivalent in local currency of US$130 million. The cost of shipping, internal transport, storage, administration and distribution amounted to about US$50 million, but the remainder represented a significant contribution to the government's annual revenues. Bilateral donors have agreed with the government on the use of these funds to meet part of the local costs of development projects.

Figure 2.1 Bangladesh: public food distribution system, annual off-take by channel (wheat and rice)

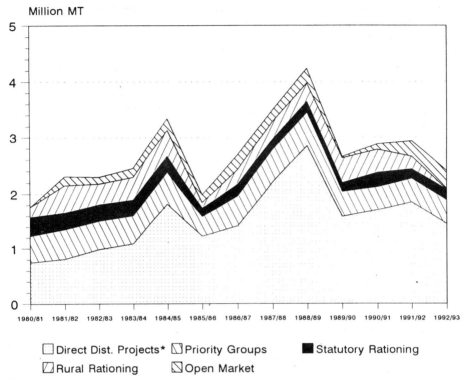

Million MT

☐ Direct Dist. Projects* ◪ Priority Groups   ■ Statutory Rationing
◩ Rural Rationing   ◪ Open Market

* Includes Food-for-Work, Vulnerable Group Development, Relief and Cluster Village Programmes

Source: WFP

In addition, a proportion of project food aid is being monetized to meet the transport and other complementary local cost elements of targeted food distribution programmes. Between 1988/89 and 1990/91, the quantities of wheat monetized increased from 55,000 to 82,000 tons, or from 8 to 11% of total project food aid.

Directly targeted distribution programmes Direct intervention through targeted project food aid has become an important aspect of the country's overall policy. Whereas in the mid-1970s only 5% of food distributed through government channels was handled in this way, by the late 1980s this proportion had increased to 45% of all food aid and to 60% of cereals food aid. Attention has been directed particularly at focusing such programmes on the poorest groups in the population and on those areas of the country where population density, landlessness, lack of job opportunities and susceptibility to natural disasters increase already high distress to critical levels.

Efforts have been made to design schemes to allocate food resources that take into account both the socio-economic situation and the geography of poverty. The difficulties experienced during the 1974 famine in targeting effectively and preventing leakages from the public food distribution system in rural areas were a major factor in shifting towards project food aid based on beneficiary self-selection. The initial priority was therefore to ensure that only the poor participated – as in employment generation through FFW programmes, which were considerably expanded from the mid-1970s onwards. The essential complementary feature of directly targeting food intervention has been a focus on development. FFW programmes currently absorb about 70% of all project food aid. They are geared to the construction or rehabilitation of drainage and irrigation channels, flood protection embankments, rural roads and, more recently, reforestation and fisheries development. During 1990–91, FFW was supported by WFP, Canada, Australia, the European Community, Germany, Austria, Belgium, and the United States (through the voluntary agency CARE), with the Government of Bangladesh contributing approximately 10% of the commodities.

Almost 30% of project food aid is distributed at present through the Vulnerable Group Development Programme (VGD). The main target group is poor women who are the principal or sole providers for their families. The cereals provided as income transfer also improve the nutritional status of such groups. Increasingly, VGD food distribution is linked to the provision of a package of services including health care, functional literacy and vocational training. During 1990–91 WFP, Canada, Australia, the European Community, Germany and Belgium supported this programme; the government also contributed approximately 10% of the food commodities provided.

Finally, emergency food relief is provided in disaster conditions where the need is urgent and substantial. Increasingly, such assistance has been provided through a temporary expansion in the scale of FFW and VGD activity, targeting additional resources to disaster-affected areas. The relief food is drawn directly from public stocks and is not dependent on the arrival of additional imports. This important development, sometimes referred to as the 'concertina' approach to emergencies (involving the expansion and contraction of existing anti-poverty programmes), enables a rapid response from stocks that are in turn usually replenished with additional emergency aid provided by many donors. This approach has evoked widespread international interest.

Cost-effectiveness   A number of in-depth studies have been undertaken in Bangladesh, looking at the efficiency of various aspects of public food distribution and the direct and indirect benefits of programme and project food aid. Studies such as that by the Bangladesh Institute of Development Studies and IFPRI in the early 1980s (IFPRI/ BIDS, 1989) and a survey of FFW in 1989 by the Bangladesh Bureau of Statistics have broadly confirmed the greater cost-effectiveness of targeted direct distribution interventions in reaching poorer households on a major scale. There has been a continuing evolution of policy with regard to the balance to be struck between monetized and directly distributed food aid and the scale and balance of commodities provided through each channel.

Major economies have been achieved by having a single operational system to deal with the storage, distribution and management of both food aid and commercial imports as well as domestically procured commodities. Direct handling and delivery costs, including bagging, are about US$40 per ton for bulk supply of project aid grain, equivalent to 25% of its market value (if full amortization of storage construction costs were taken into account, the cost would be higher). Government costs for handling programme food aid cereals are about 50% higher: although final delivery costs are lower, a much higher proportion of the shipping costs has to be borne by the recipient country than is the case with project food aid. Although such costs have seemed high, the establishment of a parallel delivery system to directly targeted programmes would be even more expensive, with no benefit to be gained from economies of scale in storage and transportation. The cost-effectiveness of such operations continues to be reviewed and, as the balance between procurement and distribution of domestically produced and imported grains changes, so may the appropriate modalities of operation.

By contrast, the costs of food aid administration are low, mainly because existing technicians, storage personnel and local government staff are used. The additional administrative costs seldom exceed 3% of market values, except where cooked meals are served. In this case, they might reach 10%.

Alternative approaches are continually being examined. Some are rejected because trained personnel are not available or because the schemes fail to reach the target group. An alternative such as school meals has been rejected in the past as being simply too expensive to operate, or because they would have to be restricted to very limited areas of the country where facilities or logistics costs were not a constraint. Replicability is probably almost as important as cost in determining strategy.

As Bangladesh is such a large recipient, the issues that have received most attention are precisely those of the major policy debate on food aid. First and foremost, the scale and programming of food aid should contribute to sustaining the overall development process. Bangladesh had unhappy experiences, particularly in the first five years following independence; the close consultation that now takes place between the government and the donor group on both the level and timing of food aid is intended to improve programming. More recently, the responses to the floods of 1987 and 1988 underscored the risk of over-reacting – programming too high a level of additional commercial imports, as well as aid, when confronted with a crisis of potentially severe dimensions.

The increasing attention now given to counterpart fund management, and the shift from programme to multi-year project assistance through FFW and VGD, reflect recognition by government and donors alike that the country is moving closer to self-sufficiency in basic cereals. However, because there is still massive poverty and under-employment, there is considerable scope for the use of food as an income transfer and nutritional support. As the joint government and donor task force on Strengthening Institutions for Food Assisted Development (SIFAD 1989) emphasized in its review of project food aid:

> Over the past 14 years approximately the humanitarian purposes of food aid have been well-served. Seasonal and year-round employment has been created for a very large number of people under the food-for-work programme and the rural maintenance programme. Income transfers in the form of wheat allowances have been made to very large numbers of women under the Vulnerable Group Development (VGD) programme. In other words, short-term benefits have been provided by the food itself for intended target groups.
>
> But the longer-term developmental impact of what is done with this targeted food has been short of expectations, short of the possibilities. The principal task, therefore, is to enhance the developmental impact of the food aid and to do this there must in the future be a new emphasis on the developmental *functions* (sic), including the development and maintenance of rural infrastructure, human resource development amongst the rural poor and a range of possible new development functions in the future.

Project Food Aid

WFP is a major contributor (40% in 1990/91) of project aid, assisting FFW and VGD (including small institutional feeding programmes). It also monitors the managerial and equity aspects of bilateral food aid provided by Canada, Australia, the EC and several EC member states, and Norway and Austria during 1990–92. The United States has concentrated its project food aid on FFW programmes (15% in 1990–1991). The voluntary agency CARE is contracted to monitor distribution and provide technical supervision for US-supported projects. CARE and WFP have co-ordinated their activities, working together to ensure that government priorities are met and that officials have data on which to evaluate project performance and take corrective action when necessary. The government itself is a major contributor of food (10% in 1990–91) to employment-generating and vulnerable group projects. These projects almost entirely distribute wheat, except for locally-procured rice, which is provided by the government on a modest scale.

Food-for-work (FFW)   The problem of rural poverty is closely linked to landlessness and the patterns of high seasonal underemployment. The national FFW programme has the objectives of:

- improving rural infrastructure (e.g., through the upgrading of rural roads);
- increasing the agricultural productivity of land;
- providing protection from natural disasters through a variety of earthworks;
- generating lean season employment opportunities for the rural poor.

It also has the effect of facilitating stabilization of the Bangladesh foodgrain market. In 1988–9 a total of 507,000 metric tons of wheat was made available for dry season FFW between December and May. Including the government's small test relief programme, some 522,000 tons of grain (largely wheat) was distributed to labourers, generating an estimated 130 million days of employment. That part of the programme monitored by WFP included over 320,000 tons of wheat allocated to more than 6,000 schemes. Until recently the largest part of the programme has been relatively small Local Initiative Schemes, primarily involving road construction and repairs (80.9 million cubic metres of earthwork and 14,000 km of roads and embankments in 1989–90). Progressively, a greater share of the FFW programme is being organized under the Bangladesh Water Development Board programme of coastal and river embankments, and on rivers and main canals, thereby covering a major proportion of the total cost of the main rural infrastructural development programme. In addition, building on earlier pilot projects, the programme now includes the construction of connecting roads between growth centres, excavation of fisheries tanks under the Ministry of Fisheries, reforestation under the Ministry of Environment and Forests, land preparation for clusters of villages for landless people, and a variety of pilot projects involving NGOs.

Programmes as large as this have created major problems of administration, planning, logistics and management. Given the financial and administrative constraints that exist, instances of inefficiency and improper use of resources have been inevitable. Government and donor concern over these issues has promoted several investigations and surveys. Studies have confirmed positive features of the programme, in particular considerable success in reaching the landless poor. FFW workers typically earn less than half the national average wage, and 75% have been found to be landless to all intents and purposes. Studies confirm increases in income, with many beneficiaries being able to reduce their indebtedness without resort to the sale of assets, particularly in periods of crisis. The powerful stabilizing impact of FFW programmes with high levels of activity after disasters have intensified the stress on the rural poor has been widely recognized. Nevertheless, problems of under-payment of workers and leakage of resources have been acknowledged. The difficulties of organizing poverty-oriented programmes on a massive scale should not be underestimated. In particular, the modest complementary financial resources available to administer the programmes place a constraint on absorptive capacity. Co-ordination between government and donors so that their resources complement each other is crucial for maximizing the value and impact of the inputs available. The increasing share of resources monetized to meet local costs (10.6% in 1990–91) is partly a recognition of these problems and one way of overcoming them.

The SIFAD review recommended institutional changes that took account of past weaknesses as well as indicating ways in which FFW might be strengthened. Historically, FFW and VGD grew out of relief programmes sponsored by the Ministry of Relief and Rehabilitation and were unrelated to the country's mainstream development planning process which involved the Ministry of Planning and line Ministries. From a developmental perspective, reconstruction and maintenance works were unplanned, resources for structures and earthworks were inadequate, and supervision was poor and understaffed. These shortcomings largely triggered the SIFAD exercise; and remedying these problems was a main focus of the recommendations of the SIFAD task force. FFW activities have been placed in a broader planning framework, complementary inputs have been provided and the programme has shifted increasingly towards road construction, controlled drainage irrigation, afforestation and fisheries activities which adopt a project approach working closely with line development ministries.

Vulnerable Group Development (VGD):   This anti-poverty programme with a human resource development dimension is seen as a crucial complement to the FFW programme. The self-selection aspect of FFW in practice screens out not only many of the less needy but also many who live on the margins of subsistence, for example, impoverished families which do not possess active workers capable of arduous earth-moving activities. For such families, food aid for the VGD programme provides limited, but important, food entitlements and, in effect, access to income transfer mechanisms. The selection of eligible women according to criteria such as landlessness, low irregular income and lack of assets is made by local committees. Those selected are eligible to receive a monthly take-home ration of 31.25 kg of wheat for two years, distributed at local centres and markets. Nationally, the programme is targeted at *upazilas* (sub-districts) in relatively more distressed areas. In 1989–90, 52% of all VGD cardholders were located in 100 heavily and moderately distressed *upazilas* representing 22% of the country.

The initial objective of the VGD programme was poverty alleviation, but its focus has gradually moved towards economic and social development. Local council centres received 95% of the resources that provide food entitlements to more than 450,000 women. In addition, Women's Training Centres involving more than 30,000 women have been included in the programme. Institutional feeding programmes focusing especially on children also provide for some 56,000 beneficiaries. Distribution centres have gradually increased their range of activities to include functional literacy, family planning and health programmes, as well as training in income-generation activities and saving schemes. Some, particularly the Women's Training Centres, combine a package of activities. However, such programmes continue to be constrained by the quantity of complementary financial inputs available and sometimes by lack of motivated and trained staff in the locality.

A number of surveys of the impact of VGD have confirmed that the beneficiaries are among the very poorest. Although there are administrative and logistical problems, as the programme was expanded rapidly, surveys also indicate that the amounts of food provided to beneficiaries and the regularity of rations had increased to 78 and 93% respectively of the planned levels by 1987. However, the impact of such development activities has remained modest. Recognition of the potential for complementing poverty alleviation with economic and social development has now begun to bring a substantial increase in complementary resources.

Emergency Relief Operations

Food aid has played a major role in relief operations. The major monetized distribution channels are intended to assure food supplies at stable prices to urban and other priority groups. In rural areas food distribution under the rationing system has proved to be an ineffective mechanism for extensive emergency relief because of problems of targeting the most vulnerable and of leakage. Major project food aid programmes have played an increasingly important role in limiting the impact of disasters on vulnerable groups. Some measure of the scale of the post-disaster response is shown in Table 2.1 by the amount of food distributed through the FFW and VGD programmes after the floods of 1984, 1987, 1988 and the cyclone of 1991.

Such interventions have two important disaster-mitigating features. First, large numbers of the unemployed and vulnerable groups have been provided with food, despite the limitations of targeting in a food crisis. Secondly, direct distribution programmes have ensured a large flow of food out of public stocks at a time when disruption of communications and marketing systems could have resulted in temporary large increases in prices and associated problems for the poorest and those most affected in gaining access to food. In addition, the use of vulnerability mapping has enabled improved geographical targeting of additional resources.

These programmes also clearly underscore the problematic nature of the formal distinction between emergency and developmental food aid, which obscures the

Table 2.1 Bangladesh: Public Food Distribution System, annual off-take by Channel (wheat and rice: '000 MT)

	Statutory Rationing	Priority Groups	Open Market & Other Sales	Rural Rationing	Direct Distribution Projects[a]
1980/81	349	484	0	182	745
1981/82	312	540	156	491	808
1982/83	308	519	118	368	984
1983/84	293	513	158	400	1,088
1984/85	282	564	209	465	1,818
1985/86	160	363	138	103	1,223
1986/87	210	545	257	257	1,415
1987/88	188	570	207	314	2,208
1988/89	202	599	263	326	2,844
1989/90	157	453	26	431	1,586
1990/91	260	414	99	400	1,706
1991/92	169	420	275	217	1,850
1992/93	189	438	330	0	1,450

[a] Includes Food-for-Work, Vulnerable Group Development, relief and cluster village projects.

Source: WFP, Dhaka.

underlying issue of the links between hunger, poverty and development. The provision of food entitlements, and the buffering effect of public distribution on local cereal markets, prevent disaster-induced crises from degenerating into famine. The same interventions may also prevent the sale of assets such as livestock by affected households in order to buy food, or the pawning of agricultural tools or other means of livelihood. FFW can also have an invaluable role in rehabilitation.

The disastrous cyclone of April 1991 is a prime example of the effective use of FFW in an emergency. WFP, in collaboration with the Bangladesh Water Development Board, was able to agree simplified procedures whereby temporary dwarf embankments were constructed over 400 kilometres of coastline in places where embankments preventing saline intrusion from tidal flow had been damaged or breached. Unprecedentedly, work was carried out during the monsoon. The distribution of some 35,000 tons of wheat protected the production of an estimated 200,000 tons of rice during the transplanting *aman* season (between July and December), as well as providing much needed employment for the unemployed in the cyclone-affected areas.

Future Development

The long-term prospects for development in Bangladesh remain uncertain. There are grounds for increased optimism – such as the declining population growth rate and the close approach to self-sufficiency in rice. Many now consider that Bangladesh has entered a new phase in its agricultural and rural development in which the challenge is to sustain food production at levels close to self-sufficiency while addressing more effectively the problems of malnutrition and poverty, not only in the countryside but also in the rapidly growing towns. The balance of efforts to provide assurance of food security will increasingly involve measures to enhance the food entitlements of the poorest and most vulnerable groups through employment creation and human resource development.

Policies are now generally well developed to support large-scale poverty alleviation programmes with a vital food security and disaster mitigation dimension. An increased level of monetization has made more complementary local currency resources available. A number of bilateral donors have also sought to improve the integration of the provision of food aid with complementary financial assistance.

But there are other challenges. In a country close to self-sufficiency in its staple food, rural poverty alleviation programmes that rely on large-scale importation and distribution of cereals will raise more complex problems of food management. Exchange arrangements involving imported wheat and domesticly produced rice may have a larger role to play in food-assisted projects, as they have done in some other Asian countries that have become regionally or nationally self-sufficient in basic staple production during the past decade. The US food aid programme managed by CARE is planning to switch in 1992–3 from supporting FFW to full monetization with the use of locally generated funds to finance rural works. But as pre-independence experience in Bangladesh demonstrated, cash wage programmes have both advantages and potentially severe problems of administration and leakage. The merits of different options should be compared to find appropriate solutions to providing resources for essential rural works and poverty alleviation programmes.

The SIFAD review has confirmed general acceptance of the necessity of such large-scale programmes, but also underlined the need to improve their developmental effectiveness. The following measures have been identified among the institutional developments and changes needed to achieve a greater emphasis on development:

- integration of food-assisted projects into the mainstream of development planning in the five-year plans and the sectoral programmes of development ministries;
- closer interaction of development ministries with the resource management agencies and donors;
- adopting a project-based approach to the use of food with funding, planning, definition of objectives and implementation as part of a coherent cycle in place of one-season schemes;
- strengthening the pre-assessment and feasibility aspects of food aid projects;
- improved monitoring and shifting attention to ensure the necessary follow-up to labour-intensive works and integration of food distribution with other resource development;
- ensuring a better balance of complementary resources, including finance, planning and other technical managerial inputs;
- diversification of rural works away from easy-to-implement road construction and repairs to water resources and directly productive, and environmental improvement, investments;
- more effective targeting in terms of groups and periods of greatest vulnerability, e.g., involving a higher proportion of female workers and increasing employment generation in the post-monsoon period of greatest stress when labour-intensive earthworks are difficult to organise;
- as the national review of Bangladesh's experience with food aid in 1982 concluded, 'If better ways can be found for sharing the costs of improved food entitlement programmes without slowing the progress of food production then some of the new approaches being tried today can be introduced on a wider scale tomorrow. Food aid policies are difficult to decide in isolation. Regular consultation between donors and recipients is likely to result in workable solutions for the most pressing food problems facing the world.'

The Bangladesh experience over the past 20 years has highlighted fundamental issues of food aid policy and management. It has also shown how feasible solutions can be found in difficult and challenging circumstances.

References

IFPRI/BIDS (1989). *Development impact of the food-for-work program in Bangladesh.* Final Report submitted to the World Food Programme.

Bangladesh Bureau of Statistics (1989). *Food-for-work: a Survey.* Dhaka.

SIFAD (1989). *Joint Government of Bangladesh/Donor Task Force on Strengthening the Institutions for Food Assisted Development.* Final Report. Dhaka: Ministry of Planning, July.

Appendix Table 2.1 *Bangladesh: Cereal food aid receipts ('000 tons – in grain equivalent)*

	1987	1988	1989	1990	1991	1987–91 Average
Total:	1806.3	1402.7	1299.1	1090.6	1489.5	1417.6
By food aid channel:						
– Bilateral	1483.2	1078.8	1023.8	881.8	1113.0	1116.2
– Gvt-to-Gvt	1391.6	992.2	1003.4	786.0	1032.1	1041.1
– through NGOs	91.6	86.6	20.4	95.8	80.9	75.1
– Multilateral	321.1	323.8	274.2	208.7	374.3	300.4
– NGOs	2.1	–	1.1	–	2.2	1.1
By food aid category:						
– Emergency Relief	84.9	95.2	235.6	–	88.1	100.7
– Project	895.0	690.8	412.2	587.4	914.0	699.9
– Agr./Rural Development	626.5	205.6	302.1	447.2	737.4	463.8
– Nutrition Intervention	217.5	343.3	–	28.7	98.1	137.5
– Other Development Project	51.0	141.9	110.1	111.5	78.5	98.6
– Non-project (Programme)	826.4	616.7	651.3	503.2	487.4	617.0
By donor[a]:						
– USA	522.9	344.9	389.7	433.0	455.8	429.3
– WFP	321.1	323.8	274.2	208.7	374.2	300.4
– Canada	326.2	152.2	120.0	204.6	333.9	227.4
– EC Community action	247.0	321.7	269.1	133.1	116.1	217.4
– Japan	181.3	78.1	55.0	32.9	54.4	80.3
– Australia	50.0	62.3	56.3	50.0	50.1	53.7
– France	–	28.0	44.0	–	37.0	21.8
– UK	38.5	49.9	9.8	–	–	19.6
– Germany	30.0	26.5	19.8	14.3	–	18.1
– Sweden	51.0	–	22.0	–	–	14.6
– Norway	–	9.8	11.9	–	30.5	10.4
– Denmark	20.0	–	20.0	–	–	8.0
– Pakistan	–	3.0	–	–	20.4	4.7
– Belgium	–	–	4.0	12.0	–	3.2
– Netherlands	12.5	–	–	–	–	2.5
– Thailand	–	1.5	–	–	5.0	1.3
– India	–	–	–	–	5.0	1.0
– NGOs	2.1	–	1.1	–	2.2	1.1
– Others	3.7	0.7	2.0	2.0	5.0	2.7

[a] Multilateral food aid provided through WFP appears under WFP as donor.

Source: WFP/INTERFAIS Database

Appendix Table 2.2 *Bangladesh: Non-cereal food aid receipts ('000 tons)*

	1987	1988	1989	1990	1991	1987–91 Average
Total:	41.1	22.4	11.1	12.1	3.8	18.1
By food aid channel:						
– Bilateral	36.5	21.1	9.0	11.3	3.8	16.3
– Gvt-to-Gvt	36.5	21.0	8.8	11.2	3.7	16.2
– through NGOs	–	0.1	0.2	0.1	0.1	0.1
– Multilateral	4.5	1.3	2.1	0.8	–	1.8
By food aid category:						
– Emergency Relief	–	–	3.0	–	–	0.6
– Project	4.6	3.4	6.1	0.9	0.1	3.0
– Agr./Rural Development	–	–	–	–	0.1	–
– Nutrition Intervention	4.6	3.4	1.1	0.9	–	2.0
– Other Development Project	–	–	5.0	–	–	1.0
– Non-project (Programme)	36.5	19.0	2.0	11.2	3.7	14.5
By donor[a]:						
– USA	26.0	19.0	–	9.0	–	10.8
– EC Community Action	1.0	2.1	3.8	2.3	3.8	2.6
– Canada	9.5	–	–	–	–	1.9
– WFP	4.6	1.3	2.1	0.8	–	1.8
– UK	–	–	5.0	–	–	1.0
– Germany	–	–	0.2	–	–	–

[a] Multilateral food aid provided through WFP appears under WFP as donor.

Source: ibid.

Women, helped by their daughters, bring milk from their cows to sell at a dairy centre. Operation Flood has increased the amount of milk available for consumption, as well as providing a source of income for poor rural families. Food aid, in the form of dried skimmed milk and butter oil, helped generate funds for investment in dairy development in India. WFP/Banoun-Caracciolo

The Indira Gandhi Canal has brought water to desert areas of Rajasthan and provided work and land for the poor who helped to build it. WFP/Trevor Page

3 India

Towards Cereal Self-sufficiency
& the Transformation of Food Aid

The experience of India, formerly the largest food aid recipient country, exemplifies the evolving uses of food aid as an effective resource for development. Large-scale programme food aid to India in the 1950s and 1960s served to meet a major food gap that was periodically exacerbated by serious drought and famine conditions. Funds generated from the sale of that programme food aid were invested in a national development programme that gave priority to increasing food and agricultural production, helping fuel the Green Revolution launched in the mid-1960s. As a result of the successes of this programme, India no longer receives a major share of food aid.

Since independence, India has recorded significant progress in the production of foodgrains. Total foodgrain production increased by 2.7% per annum during the period 1949/50 to 1988/89, significantly higher than the rate of population growth of about 2.3% per annum. As a result, per capita food availability increased from 395 grams per day in 1951 to 497 grams per day in 1989.

There has been a gradual transformation in the uses, commodity composition and modalities of food aid. Food aid to India is now project-oriented, focusing on groups of poor, food-insecure and disadvantaged people, and on specific development activities that are targeted directly on these groups. Cereals, other than wheat and rice, and non-cereals, particularly dairy products and vegetable oils, are now provided. There has also been a switch from the direct distribution of food aid provided by donors to local purchases, exchange arrangements and the specific use of funds generated from the sale of food aid commodities. At the same time, India has developed its own capacity to contend with large-scale emergency situations, and to conduct its own food aid programmes.

Background

Any study of India must take account of the size, diversity and complexity of a country that is sub-continental in scale, with an estimated population of 830 million people and a federal system of government and administration covering 25 states and 7 union territories.

India has made considerable economic and social progress since independence. The economy performed well in the 1980s, mainly as a result of increasing productivity, with a GNP growth rate of 4.8% a year. Progress in foodgrain production has been brought about mainly by the high priority given to agriculture by the central government, the spread of irrigation and the application of Green Revolution technology. From the late 1970s, India was able to accumulate large food stocks, which enabled it to withstand the severe drought of 1987, one of the worst this century, without interruption in food supply to even the most severely affected and remote regions.

Despite these considerable advances, doubt has been expressed as to whether the growth in food production can be sustained and whether future food security could be threatened. Production increases in crops other than rice and wheat have been less impressive; and rapid increases in personal incomes, coupled with a fairly low starting point in terms of per capita calorie consumption, could result in more rapid growth in demand for food than in the past. Recent experience has also shown that even large food stocks can be reduced quickly by a severe drought: two consecutive poor harvests could still have disastrous results.

Intensified agricultural production has resulted in environmental degradation in some areas, and has increased pressure on renewable rural energy resources. These factors have led to a call for a national strategy for conservation and sustainable development. It is now felt that future increases in agricultural production must come from better use of the infrastructure already created, as well as from the economically and ecologically disadvantaged rainfed areas that constitute 70% of India's cultivated areas.

There has also been a geographical imbalance in agricultural development due to concentration of production on the more favoured and irrigated areas. Although significant gains have been made, an estimated 200 million people (about a quarter of the total population and more than the total number of malnourished people in sub-Saharan Africa) are still undernourished and living in severe poverty. Lack of gainful employment in the rural areas is leading to an ever-increasing movement of resource-poor households to the towns, resulting in the emergence of mega-cities and the expansion of urban slums. There is need to accelerate economic growth in such a manner that the poor are the main beneficiaries.

A comprehensive system of food management aims to improve the access of the poor to the food they need. Foodgrains are supplied to all at subsidized prices through a non-discriminatory public distribution system of government-controlled fair-price shops. A scheme for the distribution of foodgrains at subsidized prices to over 57 million people living in the poorest areas was also initiated in 1985. At the same time, rural poverty and malnutrition are also being attacked through employment generation and poverty alleviation programmes. Meanwhile, the elimination of poverty has been, and remains, a primary objective of India's development efforts. Despite recent progress, however, poverty remains a massive problem, and a large proportion of India's population continue to be subject to malnutrition, ill health and poor life expectancy. They also lack access to education, training and the means of production that would enable them to participate fully in, and benefit from, the process of economic growth.

India is experiencing serious and growing balance of payments and budgetary deficits, exacerbated by a high level of debt servicing. These negative forces have a strong impact on the level of inflation, the allocation of resources and investment decisions. Recognizing the severity of these problems, India is now implementing far-reaching structural adjustment and stabilization programmes with IMF and World Bank assistance. The government's economic reform policies recognize the substantial scope for strengthening existing programmes without large increases in expenditure, and for adjusting public investment and expenditure flows to ensure that priority is given to the alleviation of hunger and poverty. In view of the magnitude of the problem, external assistance, including food aid, as well as better co-ordination of financial, technical and food assistance, will continue to be required.

Programme Food Aid

A distinctive feature of food aid to India in the past was the provision of large-scale programme food aid by the United States and Canada. Over a period of two decades (1956–76), the United States provided a total of more than 59 million tons of programme food aid, with a value at current prices equivalent to US$4.8 billion. Some US$4.1 bn of this was payable in Indian currency, mostly for use for grants and loans to the Indian Government for economic development activities. The remaining US$700 million were dollar credit sales repayable over 40 years at 2% interest for the first ten years, and 3% for the subsequent 30 years of the repayment period.

Table 3.1 India: Foodgrain production, procurement, imports, stocks, public distribution and programme food aid: 1956–76 (in million MT)

Year	Gross production	Internal procurement	Net imports	Total closing stocks[a]	Total public distribution	Programme food aid[b]	Value of programme food aid (Rs m.)	(7) as % of (4)	(7) as % of (6)
(1)	(2)	(3)	(4)	(5)	(6)	(7)	(8)	(9)	(10)
1956	66.9	0.037	1.400	0.319	2.082	0.147	57.2	10.5	7.1
1957	69.6	0.295	3.600	1.175	3.050	2.711	1,209.1	75.3	88.9
1958	66.6	0.526	3.210	0.906	3.980	2.009	741.2	62.6	50.5
1959	78.8	1.806	3.851	1.398	5.164	3.197	1,147.5	83.0	61.9
1960	77.1	1.275	5.119	2.801	4.937	4.349	1,620.3	85.0	88.1
1961	82.3	0.541	3.486	2.636	3.977	2.335	895.3	67.0	58.7
1962	82.4	0.479	3.029	2.281	4.365	2.887	1,134.3	95.3	66.1
1963	80.3	0.750	4.536	2.259	5.178	4.198	1,685.7	92.5	81.1
1964	80.7	1.430	6.252	1.016	8.665	5.586	2,366.1	89.3	64.5
1965	80.4	4.031	7.439	2.079	10.079	6.308	2,450.2	84.8	62.6
1966	72.3	4.009	10.311	2.216	14.085	8.214	3,861.0	79.7	58.3
1967	74.2	4.462	8.659	1.956	13.166	5.835	3,487.3	67.4	44.3
1968	95.1	6.805	5.676	3.991	10.221	4.097	2,433.0	72.2	40.1
1969	94.0	6.381	3.886	4.453	9.385	2.563	1,609.2	66.0	27.3
1970	99.5	6.714	3.579	5.569	8.841	2.452	1,370.4	68.5	27.7
1971	108.4	5.645	2.027	8.137	7.816	1.210	762.2	59.7	15.5
1975	99.8	9.563	7.241	8.289	11.253	0.791	1,102.0	10.9	7.0
1976	121.0	12.853	6.100	18.916	9.174	0.504	937.3	8.3	5.5
Total	1,529.7	54.712	89.401	–	135.418	59.393	28.869.3	66.4	43.9

[a] Both from central and state governments.
[b] Provided by the US under PL480, Title I. No provisions made in 1972, 1973 or 1974.

Source: Government of India, Ministry of Agriculture.

Figure 3.1 India: Foodgrain supplies, distribution and programme food aid: 1956–76

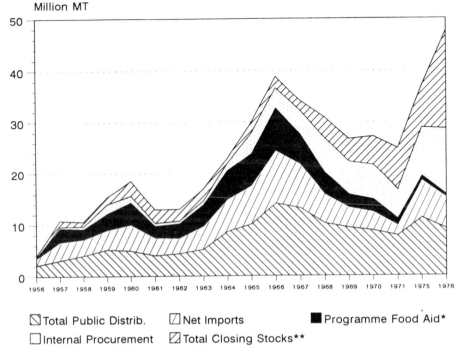

Million MT

Source: Government of India, Ministry of Agriculture

By the early 1970s, the accumulation of large rupee repayments from US programme food aid had become a source of embarrassment to both the Indian and the
US Governments. Owned by the US Government, these funds, were expected to grow
to more than Rs30 billion and, if spent, could have had an inflationary effect on the
Indian economy. Under the terms of a special agreement in 1974, therefore, the US
Government returned all rupees owed to it by the Government of India, amounting
to Rs16.8 billion, to be used for projects already budgeted for in India's fifth
five-year development plan. Some 60% was allocated to agricultural development,
including agricultural research and education, minor irrigation, animal husbandry
and dairy development, special programmes of rural development and employment,
soil conservation and land development. A further 18% was allocated to rural electrification projects, whilst the remaining 22% was invested in housing, health and
technical education programmes.

During the nine years 1968/69–1976/77, Canada provided more than US$361
million of programme food aid, about three-quarters of it in wheat, almost a quarter
in rape-seed and rape-seed oil, and the remainder in skimmed milk powder. Proceeds
from the sale of this food aid in India were invested mainly in agricultural development
projects.

Programme food aid had significant benefits. First, it filled a food gap during years
when many Indians faced hunger and famine. In the critical years 1964–7, between 5.6

and 8.2 million tons of food aid were supplied annually, accounting for between 67 and 89% of net imports. Secondly, part of the food aid provided saved foreign exchange that would otherwise have been spent on importing food commercially. Thirdly, the public distribution system was sustained during a period of acute food shortage when programme food aid represented between 40 and 89% of the food distributed. Fourthly, it helped to provide emergency food aid and to stabilize supplies and consumer prices. By issuing most of the supplies in deficit states where prices tended to be high, particularly in years of poor harvests, the system contributed to an equitable distribution of food throughout the country. Fifthly, funds generated from the sale of food aid commodities were also used for economic and social development projects, with priority given to investment in the infrastructure needed for the Green Revolution. The secret of India's success in food production has lain in raising crop yields through irrigation, technological progress and the use of new high-yielding varieties of seed. This required a policy commitment by the central government and considerable resources, which food aid helped to provide.

Project Food Aid

Programme food aid has not been supplied to India since the last agreement was signed with the United States in 1978. Instead, the focus has shifted to project food aid targeted on specific groups of poor, food-insecure people and on economic and social development activities designed to improve their well-being.

This transition should be seen against the background of a world-wide transformation in food aid. What began largely as a bilateral operation to dispose of unwanted and burdensome surplus stocks of agricultural commodities evolved into an international food aid system, accounting for about 10% of official development assistance, with a multilateral component. India served as an early testing ground for the development and expansion of project food aid. A pilot study commissioned by the FAO Council, and published in 1955, demonstrated convincingly how project food aid, if well-planned and executed within the framework of a recipient country's policy giving due priority to attacking the problems of poverty and hunger, could provide an additional resource to lift some of the constraints on economic and social progress, without significant adverse side-effects (Ezekiel, 1955).

Magnitude and dimensions: Much of the project food aid to India has been provided by the United States through the two largest international NGOs using food aid, CARE and Catholic Relief Services. Food aid has also been supplied by the European Community Commission (largely as assistance to dairy development), Canada and WFP. WFP is the largest source of multilateral grant assistance to India.

Over the three years 1987/88–1989/90, annual food aid to India in cereals (in grain equivalent) averaged about 268,000 tons through NGOs, 134,000 tons through multilateral channels (mostly WFP), and 121,000 tons from bilateral donors on a government-to-government basis.

The commodity composition of food aid to India has shown a marked shift over time as shown in Table 3.2.

Wheat and rice are no longer the principal commodities provided. They have been replaced by other commodities where there is a large gap between production and demand, including cereal-based blended and fortified foods, coarse grains and non-cereal products. Vegetable oil and dairy products have accounted for more than half of food aid transfers in value terms rather than physical quantities.

Table 3.2 *India: Commodity composition of cereal food aid: 1970/71–1988/89 ('000 MT)*

Year	Total cereals	Wheat[a]	Rice	Coarse grains[b]
1970/71	2,384.2	2,249.9	–	134.3
1971/72	1,776.6	1,444.8	185.3	146.5
1972/73	461.0	277.2	89.0	94.8
1973/74	252.1	197.0	–	55.1
1974/75	1,582.2	1,513.7	–	68.5
1975/76	1,107.8	1,000.0	20.5	87.3
1976/77	1,176.3	1,074.1	73.7	28.5
1977/78	568.4	523.9	6.2	38.3
1978/79	386.2	338.9	6.7	40.6
1979/80	343.9	304.9	–	39.0
1980/81	435.4	373.5	–	61.9
1981/82	337.6	280.4	–	57.2
1982/83	281.6	225.3	0.1	56.2
1983/84	371.3	287.2	6.9	77.2
1984/85	303.9	211.7	9.1	82.8
1985/86	257.4	170.8	8.3	78.3
1986/87	208.1	101.4	0.6	106.1
1987/88	222.7	103.8	30.3	88.6
1988/89	308.2	83.8	25.3	199.1

[a] Includes the wheat equivalent of wheat products.
[b] Includes the cereal component of blended foods.

Source: FAO, AGROSTAT.

Table 3.3 *India: Commodity composition of non-cereal food aid: 1977–88 ('000 MT)*

Year	Dried skim milk	Other dairy products[a]	Vegetable oil	Butter oil
1977	26.6	4.2	70.2	14.0
1978	43.2	5.6	96.1	11.1
1979	41.7	5.2	77.6	16.8
1980	28.1	4.8	57.5	2.5
1981	72.7	6.8	54.7	23.6
1982	36.4	2.9	37.7	8.2
1983	13.1	9.0	52.0	1.4
1984	69.8	12.7	69.6	27.5
1985	10.2	10.3	44.3	4.2
1986	4.1	11.0	100.0	3.8
1987	27.2	15.9	57.8	6.4
1988	20.2	15.3	111.4	13.9

[a] Includes the dairy component of blended foods.

Source: ibid.

Another significant shift is that food aid in wheat and rice no longer makes up a substantial proportion of imports of these commodities. Conversely, food aid in coarse grains has increased as a proportion of imports. Taking all foodgrains together, the proportion of food aid has declined from 33% to 20% of a much reduced level of total imports.

Table 3.4 *India: Average annual production, imports, exports and food aid in cereals: 1970/71–1988–89 ('000 MT)*

	1970/71–1974/75	1975/76–1979/80	1980/81–1984/85	1985/86–1988/89
Rice				
Production	41,632	47,886	54,488	62,980
Imports	298	112	171	322
Exports	22	203	449	313
Net imports	276	−91	−278	9
Total supplies a/	41,908	47,795	54,210	62,989
Food aid	55	21	3	16
Food aid as % of imports	18	19	2	5
Wheat				
Production	24,172	31,389	41,220	47,883
Imports	3,231	1,637	1,387	802
Exports	136	306	55	137
Net imports	3,095	1,331	1,332	665
Total supplies a/	27,267	32,720	42,552	48,548
Food aid	1,137	648	276	115
Food aid as % of imports	35	40	20	14
Coarse grains				
Production	26,639	29,243	30,586	27,820
Imports	419	97	16	136
Exports	1	19	20	4
Net imports	418	78	−4	132
Total supplies a/	27,057	29,321	30,582	27,952
Food aid	100	47	67	118
Food aid as % of imports	24	48	419	87
Total cereals				
Production	92,443	108,518	126,294	138,683
Imports	3,948	1,846	1,574	1,260
Exports	159	528	524	454
Net imports	3,789	1,318	1,050	806
Total supplies a/	96,232	109,836	127,344	139,489
Food aid	1,292	716	346	249
Food aid as / of imports	33	39	22	20

a/ Total supplies are based on production and net imports, taking no account of stock changes.

Source: FAO and WFP INTERFAIS Database

India's national food policy attaches prime importance to the establishment and maintenance of food stocks to cope with emergency situations and to stabilize prices. A stocking level of 21 million tons of wheat and rice has been fixed, which should be achieved by the end of June each year. In 1988 and 1989, official stocks were barely 55–60% of that level because of the large-scale public distribution of food following the serious drought of 1987. Stock levels subsequently built up again, and reached the stipulated level after the record harvest of 1989–90. The average annual level of food aid in wheat and rice over the years 1985/86–1988/89 was less than 1% of the annual average level of stocks of those grains for that period.

Closed monetization system: A distinctive feature of project food aid to India has been the evolution of WFP's assistance for FFW from the direct provision of food commodities as a component of wages in early projects to the present closed monetized system. Under this system, workers receive their full wages in cash. They can then choose whether or not to purchase all or part of the WFP family rations (for five or six people), consisting of cereals, vegetable oil and pulses, to which they are entitled from fair-price shops or from distribution centres established within project areas by the government department implementing the project in question.

WFP rations are priced at no more than 50% of total wages, and between 40 and 50% of prevailing local market prices. The savings on food costs provide a transfer of income to the poor food-insecure workers and their households, a high proportion of whose income is spent on food, thus increasing the amount of cash available for other basic needs.

The money generated from the sale of WFP commodities in each project is usually placed in a separate interest-bearing account. The funds are managed by a project steering committee consisting of state and central government officials and WFP country officers, and their intended use is set out in the plan of operations governing WFP assistance to the project. Investment of these funds has resulted in the purchase of local materials, thereby creating additional employment and income, a significant part of which has led to additional demand for locally produced food.

The central and state governments, in co-ordination with the WFP country office in India, have taken a number of steps to strengthen the programming, management and use of the funds generated. The impact of WFP assistance is being evaluated through studies carried out by Indian consultants. A monitoring and evaluation unit has been established in the WFP office, which has computerized a project-specific field reporting system to track project implementation and achievements. USAID, UNICEF and the Canadian International Development and Research Centre have provided support to strengthen this monitoring and evaluation capacity. An information and training unit has also been set up to organize training for national counterpart staff and nationals employed in the country office.

Types of Food-Aided Projects

The types of projects supported by food aid in India fall into two main categories: (i) agricultural and rural development, and (ii) human resource development.

Agricultural and rural development
Forestry projects: WFP assisted 13 forestry projects and expansions in 8 states between 1972 and 1990, totalling some US$258 million of assistance, comprising about 690,000 tons of food. These projects have generally aimed at improving forest management and use, while raising the socio-economic conditions of the poorest people living in the forest villages, who are dependent on the forest for their livelihood, by creating additional employment opportunities for them.

WFP food aid for such projects is reported to have supplemented the income of poor forestry workers, improved their nutritional status and helped to improve the living conditions of target groups through the development of socio-economic infrastructure. The additional plantations and forest management practices supported by food aid have contributed to the creation of sustainable, long-term employment opportunities, particularly for women who now form about half the work force employed in forestry activities. Funds raised from the sale of subsidized WFP family rations have been used for improving drinking water supplies, medical assistance, repair of dwellings and schools, and long-term income-generating activities.

However, the implementation of projects has encountered some difficulties; and procedural and inter-departmental problems have restricted the use of the funds generated. The full involvement of local people in project design, including the selection of species and areas to be planted as well as the sharing of produce, is necessary if such projects are to succeed.

Irrigation, rural infrastructure and settlement: Expansion of irrigation, feeder roads and other rural infrastructure has been a major factor in bringing about the large increase in India's food production. WFP has provided assistance to 26 irrigation, rural infrastructure and settlement projects and expansions in 11 states at a total cost to WFP of US$141.9 million. The major items supported with funds generated under the closed-circuit monetization system include social infrastructure (drinking water, primary school classrooms, primary health care centres and dispensaries, veterinary dispensaries and community facilities); transportation and marketing (feeder roads and agricultural stores); and facilities, such as shelter and mobile medical units, for the benefit of migrant labourers working on irrigation schemes. Problems that have arisen include a slow rate of expenditure of generated funds, a lack of clarity concerning priorities for investment, and delays in bringing newly constructed facilities into operation.

Livestock and dairy development: WFP assistance to livestock and dairy development projects has helped to increase poultry, pork and milk supply, to raise farmers' incomes, and to provide basic infrastructure.

Experience gained through the implementation of projects in the 1960s led to the formulation of a comprehensive dairy development and milk marketing project known as 'Operation Flood', which was launched in July 1970. This became the largest dairy development project in the world, to which WFP made its biggest single project commitment of 126,000 tons of dried skim milk and 42,000 tons of butter oil, valued at about US$166 million, over an 11-year period from 1970 to 1981. WFP-supplied dried skim milk and butter oil were provided to the National Dairy Development Board (NDDB), the project authorities, and mixed with locally produced milk to increase milk supplies at reasonable prices to New Delhi, Bombay, Madras, and Calcutta. The Rs1.2 billion funds generated were invested in a wide range of activities required for the development of the dairy industry on a sustainable basis. These activities raised the incomes of small farm households, the major milk suppliers.

The programme of aid to Operation Flood started by WFP continued with dairy commodities directly supplied by the EC Community Action programme and financial assistance from the World Bank. The aim has been to create a national milk grid connecting the milk producers' co-operative federations to the main cities of India. More than 6 million dairy farmers have joined 60,000 milk producer co-operatives throughout India during the past two decades. They earn more than US$1 billion a year, and now own some of the most successful businesses in the country.

The most immediate current concerns are: the need for more productivity enhancement measures through a well-functioning extension service; whether demand in the urban areas for milk and milk products will be sustained; the need for more diversified, high value-added products; a policy for the decentralization of organization and management; enhanced capacity in the co-operative unions and federations to handle price stabilization measures between the flush and lean seasons; and a reorientation of outlook as the enterprise moves from an economic environment driven by shortages to one of self-reliance, when demand will be satisfied without food-aided imports.

Whatever the concerns, the foundations of a modern dairy industry have been established, to which food aid and its generated funds have made a significant contribution.

Oilseed production and processing: Stimulated by the achievements of Operation Flood, the NDDB has used a similar strategy in its use of food aid and funds generated from its sale for oilseed production, processing and marketing through the co-operative movement. The objectives are to increase the productive capacity and economic strength of oilseed farmers to supply high-quality products in adequate quantity and at reasonable cost.

Although India is a major importer of vegetable oil, nutritionists consider that per capita the population consumes about half the level required for adequate nutrition, taking into account the predominantly vegetarian nature of the diet. Most of the edible oil processing is inefficient, yielding poor quality oil with limited choice for the customer. Distribution and marketing of oil are often not cost-effective.

The Canadian International Development Agency (CIDA) supplied crude rape-seed oil as food aid from 1981 to 1990. The Co-operative League of the US (CLUSA) provided vegetable oil from 1978 to 1988. The food aid and the funds it generated have been used to increase edible oil production, construct processing plants and establish a revolving fund to provide loans to stimulate oil production, processing and marketing activities. There are signs that producers encouraged by incentive prices and other supporting measures are beginning to achieve more rapid growth in oilseed production, which could reduce real prices and lead to more consumption by lower income groups in future.

Fisheries development: A WFP-assisted integrated rural development project begun in 1985 in the state of Haryana contained a fisheries development component which generated some 200,000 workdays of employment for enlarging fish ponds and excavating water supply channels. A second project was started in 1988 with WFP assistance in Assam centred on development of 16 naturally occurring inland lakes. WFP family rations are provided as part-payment of wages. A recent evaluation study has demonstrated that there has been a substantial increase in fishermen's earnings, and has confirmed the economic and social viability of the project.

Human resource development

Programmes for mothers and pre-school children: A series of nutrition and health programmes for vulnerable and disadvantaged mothers and pre-school children was launched by the government in the early 1960s. Early experience clearly indicated that child care programmes with inadequate coverage and very limited inputs cannot make much impact on the nutrition and health status of children. Moreover, sectoral and fragmentary approaches to the needs of children prevented the development of a co-ordinated strategy.

The Government of India took a series of significant measures in 1974–5, including the declaration of a National Policy for Children, the constitution of a National Children's Board and the establishment of a National Children's Fund. Inter-departmental teams were set up to study the situation in depth at the village level, and this led to a proposal for a scheme for Integrated Child Development Services (ICDS).

The ICDS was launched in 1975. It is one of the largest programmes of its kind in the world, and certainly one of the most comprehensive and imaginative. It focuses attention on economically and nutritionally vulnerable people, specifically expectant and nursing mothers and children below the age of six. It is designed to deliver a package of services, and adopts a holistic approach to improving child development.

This nation-wide programme now covers about 14.5 million beneficiaries. CARE provides assistance to about 7 million, and WFP to 1.8 million. The remaining 5.7 million receive supplementary meals from state and central governments. From the beginning of the programme, the central government has allocated about Rs8 billion and state governments have provided an additional Rs12 billion for the food component. These resources have been supplemented by other donors, the major ones being USAID, UNICEF, the World Bank and NORAD.

The ICDS is having positive results. For example, the infant mortality rate has been reduced from 129 per 1000 live births in 1976 to 98 for the country as a whole in 1988, and to 86 in ICDS areas. The incidence of severe malnourishment was reduced from 19% in 1976 to 6% in ICDS areas in 1985. The food component in the ICDS has acted as an incentive for mothers and children to participate in pre-natal and post-natal services. Pre-school children have particularly benefited from the nutrition supplement provided and from pre-school activities. Immunization of mothers and children has increased many-fold. The Government of India plans to expand assistance under the ICDS to cover the entire country. External assistance, including food aid, will continue to be required.

The CRS is also providing an imaginative programme of food aid support to mother and child health (MCH) centres. It focuses on mothers and infants up to three years old. Small enterprises have been started up under the scheme. The innovative aspect of this 'MCH and more' programme is that it serves as a starting point for development projects that address basic problems of rural women and children, in addition to providing nutrition and health services.

Women are encouraged to make small savings through credit co-operatives. These savings are matched with technical expertise and training provided by local NGOs. With low-interest loans, the members have started small enterprises, such as food processing, weaving and tailoring, for which market-potential surveys have been carried out. Other positive developments reported to have occurred in this programme are that family welfare schemes have resulted in a reduction in the number of children born to each participating mother and that the literacy level of children has risen as their mothers' appreciation of education has increased.

The need to incorporate MCH programmes into community development schemes that support income generation has led CRS to develop a women's economic and nutrition enhancement project, which began in 1990. Through the growth of self-confidence, mothers participating in the MCH programme are expected to become catalysts for positive change in their villages.

Primary school education: CARE has been supporting a midday meals programme for primary schoolchildren since 1962, with food aid commodities provided by the United States. The programme was gradually expanded to enable all the major states to cover a large part of their primary schoolchildren. All states attempt to cover children from poor households, and scheduled castes and tribes. However, CARE assistance has now been phased down from a peak of over 11 million recipients in 1970 to 2.7 million in 1990.

The midday meals programme was launched because it was seen as influencing the decision of economically disadvantaged households to enrol their children in school, to keep them there until they completed primary education and to act as an incentive for children to attend school regularly. The programme was thus considered an important support for the Government of India's aim of achieving universal primary education.

An assessment of this programme in 1984 concluded that it could have a stronger impact on enrolment in areas populated by poor people. Its impact on the retention of girls and of children from scheduled castes and tribes was lower than for others and was more strongly related to socio-economic than to education variables.

National and State Rural Employment Programmes

The central and state governments have instituted their own food aid programmes based on food produced in India, in addition to programmes supported by food aid from abroad.

Some poverty alleviation programmes have involved FFW. They have been based mainly on experience of the Employment Guarantee Scheme in the state of Maharashtra (MEGS), which began in 1972 after a seven-year pilot period. The purpose of this scheme is to provide economic security in general, and food security in particular, to the rural population by offering fall-back employment whenever other employment is not available and incomes are low.

MEGS is therefore basically a scheme for the residual labour force, and is so devised that only the really needy are reached. Employment is needed even in normal years during the slack agricultural season, and is particularly needed when crop failures have adverse effects on agricultural and rural employment, which sharply reduce income. The scheme provides a legal guarantee of employment in all the rural areas of the state at a cash wage somewhat below the prevailing agricultural wage. This ensures that only the really needy are reached. Any adult (male or female) seeking employment under the scheme must, under the law, be provided with work within a specified number of days (usually 15 days) after registration. The work provided is mainly of an unskilled, labour-intensive nature, usually involving the creation or strengthening of infrastructure needed for agricultural and rural development. District authorities maintain a shelf of planned and formulated projects on which construction work can commence as registrations increase. The scheme therefore not only provides a guaranteed income and work for poor unemployed workers but results in the creation of assets and infrastructure that reduce the risk of emergency situations in future.

The Government of India launched an FFW programme in 1977 to generate additional employment for the rural poor, to raise their income and nutritional levels, to create durable community assets and to strengthen the rural infrastructure. Most of the beneficiaries were from the scheduled castes and tribes. The central government provided state governments with foodgrains, while financial resources for the cash component, storage and non-food inputs were supplied by the state governments. This programme encountered some major difficulties, including shortage of food at distribution points, illegal sale of food aid commodities and infringement of workers' entitlements. It was reported, however, that, although employment generation was seasonal and short-term, it still had a positive impact on village communities.

In 1980, a National Rural Employment Programme was implemented as part of the national development programme. One of its main objectives was the alleviation of rural poverty. The strategy aimed at redistribution of income and consumption in favour of the poor by significantly increasing employment opportunities in the rural areas. It had a foodgrains component and also provided cash for the purchase of materials. In 1983 a Rural Landless Employment Guarantee Programme was launched to expand employment opportunities, particularly for rural landless labourers. The highest items of expenditure under both programmes were on rural road construction and social forestry. Other items included minor irrigation works, soil conservation measures, school buildings, housing, drinking water supplies and sanitation facilities. Meanwhile, in 1989 the Government of India announced another new programme, Jawahar Rozgar Yojna (the 'Jawahar employment plan', named after India's first Prime Minister), for 120 backward districts covering about a quarter of the country. This is specifically targeted at people below the poverty line, especially those in scheduled castes and tribes; 30% of the employment opportunities are reserved for women. All three plans were merged in April 1989, with a central government outlay of Rs21 billion for 1989–90, in order to increase the effectiveness of the rural employment schemes.

Experience gained through MEGS and FFW programmes shows the value of providing guaranteed employment with legal status. Such programmes have the advantage of incorporating a self-selection mechanism, which ensures that their benefits accrue to those most in need. They also have the merit of enhancing food security.

Emergency and Drought Management

One of India's most impressive achievements during the past 40 years has been the way in which its capacity to deal with large-scale emergencies has been developed. All developing countries, and especially those prone to recurring natural disasters caused by drought, have much to learn from the Indian experience.

The famines that racked India in the past have not recurred because agricultural and irrigation facilities and communications have improved and also because the government accepts responsibility for alleviating the distress of disaster victims. The success of relief measures is now determined not by the amount of assistance provided, but by the extent to which distress is mitigated.

The evolution of India's drought management policy has a long history. The approach which is now adopted leans toward drought mitigation, and is preventive in nature. Relief measures are not conceived in isolation, but are dovetailed into the development programme of each state. The primary responsibility for relief rests with each state government; and each state has its own relief code. A Calamity Relief Fund has been constituted for each state, with contributions from central and state governments in the ratio 75:25. State-level committees have been empowered to decide on all matters relating to relief operations. If an emergency is particularly severe, the central government provides additional assistance as the situation demands.

India's management of the drought of 1987, one of the worst this century, highlighted not only the resilience Indian agriculture had acquired during the previous four decades, but also the capacity and responsiveness of the people, and of both central and state governments, to deal with the consequences of drought without recourse to massive external assistance. About 285 million people were affected – more than a third of the total population – 93 million of whom were from vulnerable social and economic groups.

The immediate impact was on rural incomes. Priority was therefore given to providing employment opportunities, which absorbed over half of central government expenditure for drought relief. The Prime Minister set up a Cabinet Committee on Drought under his leadership to ensure timely and prompt measures for mitigating the impact of the drought. Priorities were established for the selection of work programmes so that employment generation resulted in 'drought proofing' and in the creation of durable and productive assets. Emphasis was laid on the proper use of available water resources to insulate agriculture from the vagaries of the monsoon.

More than a million tons each of rice and wheat were allocated to the states to increase the availability of foodgrains in the public distribution system. A special allocation of 440,000 tons of foodgrains was made to the drought-affected areas for relief measures. In addition, 200,000 tons of pulses, 30,000 tons of vegetable oil and 30,000 tons of dried skim milk were imported. The public distribution system was strengthened, and more than 7,700 additional fair-price shops were opened in drought-affected areas.

As there was a serious shortage of livestock fodder, a scheme was formulated for increasing fodder production in the drought-affected areas by extending subsidies to small and marginal farmers; free irrigation was also provided. The central government subsidized up to three-quarters of the cost of inter-state transportation of fodder and up to half the cost for within-state transport. As part of its response to the drought, the US Government donated 400,000 tons of maize, which was sold as poultry feed at subsidized prices. State governments established a system of regular monitoring of relief operations.

The Indian experience has demonstrated that emergency relief should be as much an economic as a nutrition intervention, providing employment as well as food, and should be planned as such. It requires a policy commitment and a high degree of government involvement at the national and local levels, with work programmes and financial allocations planned in advance. The efficiency of relief operations depends not only on the formulation of sound policies and programmes, but on their proper and timely implementation.

Food Aid Administration and Logistics

The Ministry of Welfare co-ordinates food aid provided by CARE and CRS. The Ministry of Finance deals with bilateral food aid from the US, the European Community and Canada. The Ministry of Agriculture is the nodal ministry for WFP's food aid programmes, and the Joint Secretary (International Co-operation) of that ministry serves as the central government's focal point on policy issues. Each state government concerned deals with operational matters.

The Ministry of Finance co-ordinates all types of development assistance to India. The Planning Commission formulates the country's five-year and annual plans. Project food aid is not included as part of development resources in the planning process; it is therefore not directed into the mainstream of development activities along with cash and technical resources for allocation to line technical ministries. However, most WFP FFW projects generate funds through the closed monetization system. The investment of such funds is implemented through the government department responsible for project management and operation.

India established a public distribution system for food in 1942 within the framework of a national food policy. The Food Corporation of India (FCI), established in 1965, mainly undertakes internal procurement of foodgrains and provides supplies to state governments according to allocations made by the central government. Grains are further distributed through a large number of fair-price and ration shops located throughout the country.

Food aid commodities are discharged at India's major ports. Rice and wheat are merged into the FCI stock as part of the food distribution system. The FCI can issue rice and wheat at any of its warehouses near food aid distribution sites at the request of the project authorities. These logistical arrangements are often referred to as 'foodgrain banking operations'. This mechanism makes it possible to transfer commitments to a number of projects dispersed throughout the country in accordance with actual project needs without additional transport and storage costs. Rice and wheat can also be issued to projects on loan from FCI stock. Flexibility has also been achieved in providing food aid through local purchase and exchange agreements. These arrangements have led to significant savings in cost and time in food aid operations.

India as a Food Aid Source

India is also a donor and source of food aid commodities. It has been a constant supporter of WFP, contributing to its regular resources for every pledging period since the start of operations in 1963. The Indian pledge has been in the form of tea and dried fish. From 1963 to the end of the 1991–2 biennium, India has pledged commodities valued at US$17.13 million to WFP. In addition, it has made contributions to the IEFR and made bilateral donations during the 1970s and 1980s to countries in Asia and sub-Saharan Africa, providing over 600,000 tons of wheat and rice.

India has also allowed WFP to borrow from its wheat stocks on a replenishment basis to provide food aid supplies to neighbouring countries, and has agreed to the diversion of ships carrying food aid to India to other countries where the need was acute.

Future Directions

Development strategy and areas of priority For many years India has given high priority to the alleviation of hunger and poverty. Considerable advances have been made, but the problems remain large and the resources required to overcome them will be considerable.

Several factors are causing shifts in the incidence and geographical concentration of poverty. One is the perception that agriculture alone will not be able to provide employment and income for all the rural poor. Productive employment must therefore increase rapidly in non-agricultural rural activities, in industry and in services. Another factor is the increasing concentration of the poor in specific regions and occupational groups. A third factor is the growing proportion of landless, wage-dependent households among the poor. These households account for 37% of the rural population, 46% of the rural poor and well over half of the poor in some states.

The Green Revolution has exacerbated regional and individual inequalities. There remains a large geographical concentration of poverty in the rainfed and dry farming areas that have not benefited from irrigation and high-yielding varieties of crops. The rate of decline in the incidence of poverty among the scheduled castes and tribes, many of whom live in the agriculturally poor regions, is about half that of the rest of the population.

The areas of priority for future action are closely related to the structural imbalances that have built up. Two central tasks have been defined. The first is to expand opportunities for productive employment at rising levels of real wages and incomes and at a sufficiently rapid rate to absorb the increase in the labour force caused by population growth, thereby progressively reducing the present level of unemployment and under-employment. The second is to improve the quality of life of the poor through improved health and nutrition, education, training and family welfare services.

The call for a national strategy for conservation and sustainable development implies a pattern of production that does not exploit natural resources at a rate faster than the rate of regeneration. Within that strategy, the priority now given to social forestry will continue in order to solve the serious fuel/energy problem.

The need will continue for integrated programmes, such as the ICDS, that protect and improve India's human resources. The crucial role that women play in this context, as well as in increased agricultural production and conservation of the environment, is now more fully appreciated. Under the National Commission for Women Act of 1990, statutory powers have been created to check the deteriorating condition of

Indian women; and the central government has formulated a national perspective plan for the years 1988-2000 to integrate women into the mainstream of economic development and to ensure equity and social justice for them.

Finally, there is concern about the growing number of urban poor. Programmes are required in urban areas to provide income-earning employment and safety nets for vulnerable groups.

Implementing effective poverty alleviation programmes on the scale required will demand considerable resources as well as a substantial reallocation of public expenditure. Problems in restoring and maintaining a sustainable macroeconomic balance must be addressed. At the same time, there will be a continuing need for external assistance, at even higher levels, and for a speedy and efficient disbursement of that assistance in programmes and projects specifically designed to benefit the poor.

Food aid uses and mechanisms India is approaching self-sufficiency in terms of market demand for the basic foodgrains, rice and wheat. But under-nutrition is still widespread; and the government's objectives of accelerating economic growth and the elimination of poverty will result in a significant increase in the demand for, and consumption of, foodgrains. This will call for unrelenting efforts to increase foodgrain production and productivity, at or even above current growth rates, if full self-sufficiency is to be attained. The large gaps between production and demand in other basic foodstuffs, such as vegetable oil and pulses, are likely to remain for some years.

These trends suggest a continuing role for food aid, especially in the context of India's extremely low human development index and the limited access of poor and vulnerable groups to adequate nutrition. Two main possibilities emerge for future food aid supplies: local purchase of wheat and rice for use as food aid in support of poverty alleviation programmes; and exchange of food aid commodities for domestically produced wheat or rice. In conducting these purchases and exchanges, particular attention should be given to the factors of price and quality. At the same time, monetization of food aid should be continued, in accordance with a coherent policy and clear operational guidelines.

Attention should also be given to strengthening the integration of food aid and its generated funds into the national development planning process, and to their co-ordination with financial and technical assistance provided to India. Many bilateral and multilateral donors and aid agencies have similar priorities in the allocation of their assistance. It would strengthen the impact of all types of external assistance if there was closer co-ordination within a coherent framework of support to India's economic and social development priorities. In that context, the closer involvement of the poor themselves, through their own institutions and through greater decentralization of decision-making, as well as through the large number of national NGOs with outreach to the poor, would help to ensure that all efforts, supported by both national and external resources, will reach those in need, thereby alleviating hunger and poverty and leading to equitable and sustained economic and social growth and development.

References

Ezekiel, Mordecai (1955) *Uses of Agricultural Surpluses to Finance Economic Development in Under-Developed Countries: A Pilot Study in India.* Reproduced in FAO (1985) *Food Aid for Development*, FAO Economic and Social Development Paper No. 34, Rome.

Appendix Table 3.1 *India: Cereal food aid receipts ('000 tons – in grain equivalent)*

	1987	1988	1989	1990	1991	1987–91 Average
Total:	177.9	560.9	497.2	333.5	176.3	349.2
By food aid channel:						
– Bilateral	141.0	348.5	434.8	240.3	108.2	254.6
– Gvt-to-Gvt	–	–	200.0	–	–	40.0
– through NGOs	141.0	348.5	234.8	240.3	108.2	214.6
– Multilateral	35.2	212.1	62.4	93.2	68.1	94.2
By food aid category:						
– Emergency Relief	0.5	25.5	0.1	–	–	5.2
– Project	177.4	535.4	297.2	333.5	176.3	304.0
– Agr./Rural Development	16.0	276.0	69.8	68.5	32.0	92.5
– Nutrition Intervention	161.4	250.8	68.3	41.0	39.0	112.1
– Other Development Project	–	8.6	159.1	224.0	105.4	99.4
– Non-project (Programme)	–	–	200.0	–	–	40.0
By donor [a]:						
– USA	141.0	347.4	434.6	240.2	108.2	254.3
– WFP	35.2	212.1	62.4	93.2	68.1	94.2
– Germany	–	0.6	–	–	–	0.1
– EC Community Action	–	–	0.2	–	–	–
– Switzerland	–	–	–	0.2	–	–
– NGOs	1.7	0.3	–	–	–	0.4
– Others	–	0.5	–	–	–	0.1

[a] Multilateral food aid provided through WFP appears under WFP as donor.

Source: WFP/INTERFAIS Database

Appendix Table 3.2 *India: Non-cereal food aid receipts ('000 tons)*

	1987	1988	1989	1990	1991	1987–91 Average
Total:	99.3	181.3	66.4	42.6	53.0	88.5
By food aid channel:						
– Bilateral	78.2	166.4	42.9	23.1	24.6	67.0
– Gvt-to-Gvt	48.2	136.5	15.1	–	–	40.0
– through NGOs	30.0	29.9	27.8	23.1	24.6	27.1
– Multilateral	18.7	14.9	23.5	19.4	28.4	21.0
– NGOs	2.1	–	–	–	–	0.4
By food aid category:						
– Emergency Relief	3.1	19.4	0.1	–	–	4.5
– Project	73.3	122.3	66.2	42.6	53.1	71.5
– Agr./Rural Development	54.6	83.5	37.3	16.8	24.4	43.3
– Nutrition Intervention	18.7	32.8	12.3	4.2	10.4	15.7
– Other Development Project	–	6.0	16.6	21.6	18.3	12.5
– Non-project (Programme)	23.0	39.6	–	–	–	12.5
By donor[a]:						
– USA	27.4	51.5	21.9	20.4	20.0	28.3
– WFP	18.9	14.9	23.5	19.4	28.4	21.0
– Canada	38.6	47.8	–	–	–	17.3
– EC Community Action	11.5	46.3	21.0	2.5	4.5	17.2
– Germany	–	10.3	–	–	–	2.1
– Netherlands	–	10.0	–	–	–	2.0
– Switzerland	0.7	0.4	–	0.2	0.1	0.3
– NGOs	2.1	–	–	–	–	0.4

[a] Multilateral food aid provided through WFP appears under WFP as donor.

Source: ibid.

Under a WFP-assisted road construction project new roads have been built, providing employment for 5,000 people paid partly with wages provided by the government and partly with WFP food rations. WFP/G. Di Majo

At a tree nursery in the Kaghan Valley boys put chir pine seedlings into plastic bags in readiness for transplanting. Under this food-aided project, access roads have been built and reforestation carried out. WFP/Banoun-Caracciolo

4 Pakistan

In the Wake of the Green Revolution & the Shadow of Afghanistan's War

Pakistan has been a major recipient of food aid. At the same time, the country has made considerable progress in increasing agricultural production. This experience, which goes against the grain of some conventional criticism that food aid has a negative impact on food and agricultural production, is of particular interest as a case study of food aid's evolution following the Green Revolution. Over time, the role of food aid has been transformed to cover a small part of the economy's deficit in non-cereals and to support specific development projects. Pakistan has also witnessed a massive relief operation for Afghan refugees in which the effective logistics of the country's food system have played a crucial role.

This review of Pakistan's experience focuses on four distinct features. First, Pakistan's success in combining substantial receipts of food aid over many years with progressive development in agricultural production. Secondly, as the country moves towards self-sufficiency and the regular export of certain food staples, there are some key socio-economic factors that the evolving roles of food aid will need to take into consideration including: differences in resource endowment, population and development potential among the country's provinces; imbalances in food production and distribution; inequitable distribution of income; and unemployment and under-employment. Thirdly, there is Pakistan's gradual emergence as a potential food aid supplier through triangular transactions, local purchases and commodity exchange arrangements. And, finally, there is its role as the host country in assisting the largest single refugee population in the world over a number of years, and the part that food aid has played in this.

Background

Pakistan had an estimated population of 126 million in 1991. Average GNP per caput was US$380 in 1990. If the population growth rate of over 3% per annum during the 1980s continues, the population will double in the next 20 years. Almost half the population is under 15 years of age. The adult literacy rate of 35% in 1990 is low compared with an average of 60% for low-income countries.

In general, development of the social sectors has not kept pace with the growth of the economy. As a result, a large part of the population continues to face poverty and to live in unsatisfactory conditions. Half the population has no access to clean water and three-quarters are without access to sanitation facilities. The situation is even more pronounced in the rural areas, where 68% of the population live. For example, only about one-third of the rural population have access to health services. Pakistan's seventh five-year national development plan (1988–93) emphasizes that the country's human capital should no longer be neglected.

The government's economic strategy has centred on the creation of a stable and growth-oriented environment. Real GDP increased during the 1980s at an average rate of over 6% per annum, with agriculture increasing by 4% and manufacturing by 8%. Other indicators of economic performance have shown steady improvement despite a number of adverse factors, notably a marked worsening in the country's external terms of trade, a declining trend between the mid-1970s and mid-1980s in real net ODA, and severe pressures for increased public expenditure on defence and refugee assistance associated with the large influx of Afghans into Pakistan.

Agriculture is the largest single sector of the economy, accounting for 26% of GDP, some 70% of export earnings, and employing half of the labour force. Much of the industrial sector, especially manufacturing, which accounts for a quarter of GDP, is agriculture-based.

Workers' remittances, mainly from the Middle East, have contributed significantly to the increase in economic prosperity. The large difference between GDP and GNP is accounted for by net factor income from abroad. Remittances have declined since the late 1980s, however, particularly as a result of the Gulf crisis.

Although the growth potential shows promise, the economy will continue to face serious imbalances, with a large current account deficit, increased deficit financing, low investment and savings rates and deteriorating terms of trade. In 1989, the debt-service ratio was 47% of GNP and 23% of export earnings. The government and aid agencies have expressed particular concern at the chronically low savings and investment rates. Steps are being taken to build confidence in the economy, especially in the private sector.

The federal character of the government provides a good basis for the delegation of administrative and developmental responsibilities to the provinces; but this has its limitations. Locally inspired and developmentally sound initiatives in food-aided projects, for example, often suffer from inadequacy of counterpart funding as a result of the central government's practice of withdrawing funds earmarked for such activities. There are also marked differences between the natural and human resources that individual provinces can call upon when formulating and implementing development programmes, with or without external assistance.

Overall Food and Agricultural Situation

Agriculture is the mainstay of the economy and occupies a high position in the government's scale of priorities. Wheat is the staple food. The area on which this crop is grown is higher than the combined area of all other cereals. Significant increases in production followed the introduction of a new strain of wheat in the late 1960s and an expansion in the area under irrigation. Rice production also increased owing to expanded cultivation and higher yielding varieties. Production of the main export crop, cotton, has also grown. Pakistan is a sizeable producer of vegetable oils, animal fats and oil cakes. It is also a substantial importer of vegetable oils, mainly of palm and soybean oils. However, dependence on imports should be less in the future as the government's promotion of oil seed production and the removal of controls take effect.

On the whole, Pakistan's agricultural economy is moving gradually towards self-sufficiency in the main staples and, ultimately, towards a not insignificant export capacity. Agricultural production has enjoyed a period of high growth over the past 30 years. However, despite the impressive gains made, there is a consensus within the government and among aid agencies that it is premature to declare that self-sufficiency in food production has been achieved and wheat imports of between 1 and 1.5 million tons a year have been recorded recently. The sector continues to face certain critical problems, particularly in the important irrigated areas, for which urgent solutions must be found. These include:

- the need to develop a balance in production strategies that gives adequate emphasis to increasing yields of the traditional crops, while promoting diversification in minor crops;
- formulation of a pricing policy package in view of the government's policy of phasing out subsidies for fertilizer and irrigation supplies;
- resolution of planning and institutional issues in irrigation and improvement in the operation and maintenance of the irrigation system;
- increased domestic resource mobilization, especially through effective measures for implementing capital cost recovery for irrigation projects;
- initiation of a salinity control and rehabilitation programme, with the aim of preparing for effective participation by the private sector.

Food Aid

Whereas Pakistan was a major recipient of food aid in the 1960s and 1970s, the successes of its agricultural growth strategy have resulted in a considerable decline in the volume of both cereal imports and aid. Food aid from all sources averaged 530,000 tons a year between 1989 and 1991, 77% of which was wheat. Relatively large amounts of non-cereal (edible oils, butter oil and dried skim milk) food aid receipts in the early 1980s, about 130,000 tons on average annually, were also received as programme food aid, principally from the United States. In the recent past, there has been a significant decline in non-cereal food aid receipts.

In recent years, the main donors of food aid to Pakistan have included the United States, Australia, the Netherlands, the European Community Commission, the Islamic Development Bank and WFP. Of the food aid received during the first half of the 1980s, 90% was supplied in the form of programme food aid. About 10% was provided as project food aid, mainly for use in support of forestry and watershed management, infrastructure development, and nutrition improvement for mothers and children. WFP has been the only project food aid donor. There have been no emergency relief operations specifically for Pakistan since 1976, but massive relief food has been supplied for Afghan refugees in Pakistan since 1979/80.

Despite relatively large receipts of programme food aid, Pakistan has sustained commercial imports of commodities that it has received as food aid. Programme food aid has replaced additional commercial imports, however, thereby helping the country's foreign exchange balance. Funds from the sale of commodities supplied have been used to support the annual development plan, although details of the precise use of the funds are not readily available.

Pakistan's ability to generate and, in good years, to export a substantial surplus of food, mostly rice, has raised questions regarding the continuing role of food aid. However, closer analysis of the agricultural sector, and of the economy as a whole, justifies its continued use and appropriateness. Within the food sector, rice, the main export crop, is an important foreign-exchange earner. But the country faces substantial shortfalls in the supply of edible oil, which will have to be met through imports for some years. Also, although important advances have been achieved in the production of wheat, annual fluctuations still occur as a result of changes in the weather and other factors. Furthermore, Pakistan's socio-economic profile has many characteristics which reflect structural underdevelopment, exacerbated by disparities in resource endowment among the provinces. These include severe unemployment and underemployment, particularly in the rural areas, uneven income distribution, malnutrition and a high rate of illiteracy. Food aid can play a significant and constructive role in alleviating socio-economic imbalances under targeted schemes designed to create employment, address problems of income distribution and combat malnutrition and illiteracy.

Food aid in support of Afghan refugee relief operations   Since 1979/80 food aid for Afghan refugees has been channelled to Pakistan, as the host country, by a consortium of 16 donors. This aid is based on assessments of the requirements of the refugee population; most of it has been in the form of wheat. Total relief food averaged 420,000 tons a year between 1989 and 1991, of which 86% was wheat. Although this assistance is quite distinct from the food aid supplied to Pakistan itself, it has been channelled through the national food distribution system. Wheat enters the port of Karachi and is drawn, whether from local or imported sources, from public stocks.

Food Aid Administration and Logistics

Development activities   The Ministry of Food and Agriculture co-ordinates project food aid activities for development. There is a close working relationship between the WFP country office in Islamabad and government officers concerned with food-aided development projects. However, there is no formal working relationship between WFP and the two ministries responsible for overall co-ordination of the economy – the Ministry of Finance and the Ministry of Economic Affairs and Planning. Thus, project food aid is not directly integrated into the country's planning framework. Reference is made to programme food aid in requests to donors made at Consultative Group meetings for aid to Pakistan organized by the World Bank, but not to project food aid.

WFP project food aid in wheat, once landed, is handed over to the Food Department to be merged with government stocks. Wheat is then released on a ton-for-ton basis from government depots closest to the distribution sites. This commodity exchange system reduces costs and contributes toward timely and regular distribution, promotes flexibility, and reduces the amount of storage required for individual distribution outlets, since releases are measured in close relation to specific periodic requirements. Food is usually readily available from the Food Department. When delays in food aid shipments occur, advances can be issued from government stocks thus avoiding disruption in project activities and food distribution.

The Food Department is also responsible for port clearance and handling of other WFP commodities. Charges are levied on the respective project authorities for associated costs. Commodities are stored in Karachi until the project authorities complete arrangements to transport them to project sites.

Afghan refugee relief operations Special administrative arrangements have been established for the Afghan relief operations. The Ministry of States and Frontier Regions has overall responsibility for these operations. WFP has been entrusted with co-ordinating all food aid matters with this Ministry and works with the UN High Commissioner for Refugees on detailed matters of food distribution. Regular meetings are held in Islamabad and at the provincial level to facilitate consultation among the agencies and bodies concerned, including the Ministry of States and Frontier Regions, WFP, UNHCR and representatives of the relevant technical departments in the provinces on all aspects of Afghan refugee operations. Items discussed include food, health, education and water issues.

Handling, logistics and transport arrangements and procedures are the same as those for WFP-assisted development projects. Some problems have arisen with regard to irregularity of supplies and the perennial issue of leakages. But most observers agree that the institutional and administrative structures established by the government, in partnership with the aid organizations, have been adequate to resolve any difficulties that may arise and to initiate remedial action.

Project Food Aid

Pakistan has used project food aid since 1969 in support of rural development projects, including forestry and watershed management, construction of infrastructure and dairy development. In addition, there has been support for health and nutritional improvements among vulnerable groups of mothers and pre-school children.

Forestry and watershed management Forestry programmes involving watershed management, soil conservation and fuelwood production can improve productivity and living conditions in rural areas. Such projects can benefit particularly from project food aid. They are labour-intensive and provide employment opportunities for unskilled workers. As forestry programmes often take place in poor, marginal and food-deficit areas, they provide an important additional source of income, and the food supplied serves as an additional source of consumption. Additional employment opportunities are made possible as a result of paying workers partly in food through funds released in the wage budget. As it is usually a long time before such activities show a return, project food aid may often constitute the only form of external financing. Such aid can therefore enable governments to embark upon these essential but long-term activities, while they continue to invest in other, shorter-term, production projects.

Large areas of the Hindu Kush foothills have been deforested and are subjected to severe soil erosion owing to population pressure and the need to exploit timber for income as well as for firewood and fodder. Besides destroying large areas of hillside which could produce fodder, firewood and timber and generate employment, erosi also results in the deposition of tens of thousands of tons of valuable silt in the voirs each year.

WFP has been assisting watershed management projects in the North We Province and elsewhere since 1972. In the period 1977–86 alone, WFP ass tributed directly to tree planting and soil conservation works on close t of bare hillsides. Nurseries supported through WFP assistance have produced over 300 million trees. Almost 9 million workdays have been devoted to soil conservation measures, providing substantial job opportunities for the rural unskilled and under-employed work-force.

The full benefits and costs of WFP-assisted forestry and watershed management projects are largely unassessed. However, as the country's watershed management network is vital, the projects that have been undertaken are of national importance. Workers benefit directly from the food aid itself. In addition, there are important, although not always quantifiable, downstream benefits to local communities in terms of trees planted, soil conserved, employment created and strengthened socio-economic stability. The projects have also played a crucial role in contributing towards the safeguarding of substantial national investments in hydroelectric and irrigation schemes.

Projects have sometimes suffered from a lack of adequate technical staff. This problem has been compounded by the fact that Forestry Department staff themselves do not always have all the multi-disciplinary skills needed to handle the broad range of tasks involved in sound watershed management. In view of the national importance of these activities, WFP project evaluations have concluded that the Federal Government needs to assume financial responsibility for organization and management activities. Similarly, the financial investment required for afforestation programmes in the catchment areas is beyond the means of the province and, therefore, requires budgetary allocations from the Federal government.

These problems are well recognized and have been the subject of considerable discussion between the government and WFP. Meanwhile, efforts are being made to secure the financial viability of these essential activities either through government guarantees or donor cash assistance.

Development of infrastructure WFP is assisting infrastructural development in the North West Frontier Province through local councils that are assuming development responsibilities at the grass-roots level. The activities that are being assisted aim to promote rural development through numerous small-scale projects as well as to create employment and help raise food consumption levels. Although the quality has varied, a large number of villages have benefited from infrastructure works. Villagers and their leaders have been encouraged to participate. WFP evaluations have observed a positive socio-economic impact of activities such as roads and irrigation schemes. However, in a number of cases, it was noted that the larger farmers had greater access to the benefits of these works. The lack of proper attention to appropriate sewage disposal also reduced the value of the water supply systems. Previous joint efforts by the government, WFP and the International Labour Organization to integrate women's participation in the projects have met with little success, although women have benefited indirectly from schemes that reduce the time needed to fetch water.

A number of proposals for improvement have been made. They involve provision for periodic technical reviews, improved selection of works and of beneficiaries to provide an equitable distribution of benefits, and inclusion of more social development work. The aim is to achieve a better balance in the development of social and economic infrastructure in rural areas.

Dairy and livestock development Between 1969 and 1981, the government received assistance from WFP for various projects in the livestock sector. These involved the supply of commodities to support production at milk plants and poultry farms until they became economically viable. It was intended to sell milk reconstituted from WFP-supplied commodities with the purpose of generating funds for investment in development schemes.

The overall aims of the projects were well-conceived in terms of the supply of food aid inputs to generate investment funds. However, the lack of clearly defined policy and operational guidelines on the generation, programming, use and control of funds generated from the projects created many problems, to the dissatisfaction of both the government and WFP. After careful joint assessment of the suitability of this form of assistance, it was mutually agreed that, although there had been some modest achievements, the overall lessons learned did not justify continuation. This is an example of how, if there are adequate mechanisms for consultation between the government and WFP, food-aided projects that fail to achieve their intended objectives can be either modified or discontinued.

Health and nutrition   Lack of purchasing power, coupled with some traditional food habits, have resulted in severe nutritional deficiencies, especially among the low-income and vulnerable groups of the population. WFP assistance was requested in 1975 for a nationwide nutrition improvement programme involving supplementary feeding, integrated with basic health services, for mothers and pre-school children. The basic objectives of this programme were to reduce the high incidence of malnutrition among children and expectant and nursing mothers, to promote knowledge and adoption of better child and family feeding practices, and to increase attendance at health centres at which health and sanitation education, immunization and mother and child health care services were provided.

The programme had a slow and difficult beginning, but later showed considerable improvement. It has evolved from being primarily a relief food distribution undertaking into an integrated health and nutrition programme, as originally intended. Much of the improvement is attributable to the government's increased commitment, as well as to technical assistance provided by FAO and financial support from UNDP, UNICEF and WHO. Steps have also been taken to improve the monitoring and evaluation of the project.

However, some problems remain. There is concern, for example, about slow progress in training adequate numbers of women health visitors and other project staff, who are indispensable for the proper running of the programme. And there have been gaps in the supply of WFP commodities to health centres because project support funding has been irregular.

Afghan Relief Operations

The large influx of refugees from Afghanistan since 1979 resulted in the mounting of a large-scale international relief operation. The number of refugees is estimated to have reached over 3 million. The Government of Pakistan appealed to the international community for assistance in the form of food, shelter and other basic requirements. A number of donor countries and international agencies responded in a common humanitarian effort to provide relief assistance.

The majority of refugees are organized into about 350 village units. Each unit was originally planned for 5,000, and later 10,000, refugees but the government has reported a population per unit ranging from 4,000 to over 23,000.

Initially, the refugees were supplied with emergency relief items: blankets, quilts, clothes, shelter materials, water and health facilities. WFP supplies basic food items. Other United Nations agencies, as well as governmental and non-governmental organizations, provide such basic needs as health care and drinking water. The infrastructure of the village units has been gradually improved and services have been extended. WFP has been asked to co-ordinate the supply of food commodities. About two-thirds of the food donations have been channelled through WFP, 15% through UNHCR (including purchases of sugar and tea) and 20% bilaterally. Even where food commodities are channelled bilaterally or through another agency, WFP assumes full operational responsibility, including purchases, logistics and transport handling and monitoring. UNHCR handles the larger part of external assistance in non-food items. For its part, the government provides 50 rupees, as a monthly cash maintenance grant, to each registered refugee. This contributes towards the purchase in local markets of basic necessities, including food items which may not be supplied under the refugee operation.

The emergency feeding operation satisfactorily fulfilled its principal objective of providing sustenance for the refugee population. Much of this success has been attributable to the commitment of the government as well as to the co-operation of the local population in the provinces concerned. Almost all refugee families have at least one member working mainly as a casual labourer and earning a regular income; the cash incomes earned supplement the government's cash maintenance grant and the relief supplies. Despite the establishment of a new government in Kabul in 1992, fighting has continued and as a result the large-scale repatriation of the Afghan refugees has been delayed.

Any relief operation of such magnitude is bound to encounter formidable difficulties, and this one has gone through a catalogue of problems. But it is a great testimony to the value of the overall approach that the relief operation has managed to withstand many technical and operational obstacles and has succeeded in its basic objective of delivering food and other basic needs to the refugees.

A number of significant features relating to the government's approach to coping with this relief operation are worthy of note and commendation. First, the level of commitment and material support has contributed greatly to generating confidence among donors in the determination of the government to assume responsibility for the welfare of the refugees. From the beginning, the government has assigned priority to the operation in terms of both resources and manpower. Secondly, and relatedly, strong administrative and institutional arrangements have been set up between the refugee community and the donor countries and aid agencies. Thirdly, the government has delegated technical and operational responsibilities to the agencies, while using the existing administrative and political structures to retain overall control of the operation. Fourthly, and particularly significantly, the open consultative and co-ordinated approach fostered by the government and supported by all concerned has been invaluable not only for resolving conflicts, but also for some constructive trial-and-error approaches.

Future Plans and Directions of Food Aid

Pakistan has the capacity to maintain and gradually increase its current level of agricultural production. Food aid could help in many ways to support a programme of adjustment in the agricultural sector. A major problem, however, will be the ability of a significant proportion of the population to purchase the food they need. Food aid could play a role, by supporting compensatory or entitlement schemes under carefully designed programmes that lead to additional consumption rather than substitution.

An associated use of food aid might be to support programmes to increase literacy rates significantly and to transmit and enhance skills. Such programmes could make a major contribution to the development of Pakistan's human resources and to the development of the economy. Furthermore, in order to stimulate the demand side of the agricultural economy necessary for supporting increased production, food-aided activities can support employment- and income-creating activities, especially given the high rates of unemployment and underemployment.

WFP assistance has recently been approved for a project designed to create awareness among the rural population of the need to undertake, through their own nominated local councils, various activities related to community development. Another project supported by WFP will promote female primary education in Baluchistan and North West Frontier Province by providing an incentive to parents to send their daughters to school as well as supporting female primary school teachers and teacher training.

Significant breakthroughs in the development and use of high-yielding crop varieties, coupled with more efficient input management practices, are commonly considered to be necessary if there are to be further increases in agricultural production. This will require the transmission of research results into farm-level practice. In this context, consideration might be given to the use of food-aid-generated funds (project or programme as appropriate) in support of research and extension services and training.

Increased attention might also be given to the design of projects under which a donor may provide some of the funds generated from programme food aid to support food-assisted activities. Such interventions could be targeted to strategic areas such as the operation and maintenance of the vital irrigation systems and the further development of education and health infrastructure, especially in rural areas.

As Pakistan gradually begins to generate structural surpluses, food-aid and technical agencies can play important roles in providing the required expertise in strengthening food management in areas such as marketing, quality control, pricing policy, storage, transport and logistics. Skills in these areas are indispensable if the country is to participate effectively in highly competitive international agricultural markets.

Increasing use might be made of the possibilities of obtaining supplies of food aid from Pakistan through triangular transactions, local purchases and exchange arrangements. Food aid supplies obtained in these ways might be used in other developing countries, as is currently being done by Japan, which purchases Pakistani rice for use as food aid in Africa and Asia, or in support of development projects within Pakistan itself, as has been done in the supply of Pakistani wheat for the Afghan refugee operations. Such food aid transactions could also contribute to the adjustment of Pakistan's agricultural sector.

Appendix Table 4.1 *Pakistan: Cereal food aid receipts ('000 tons – in grain equivalent)*

	1987	1988	1989	1990	1991	1987–91 Average
Total:	457.6	644.5	433.0	395.4	392.4	464.6
By food aid channel:						
– Bilateral	172.4	391.3	287.8	192.1	37.6	216.2
– Gvt-to-Gvt	172.4	391.3	285.9	188.1	36.0	214.7
– through NGOs	–	–	1.9	4.0	1.6	1.5
– Multilateral	285.2	253.2	145.3	203.4	354.8	248.4
By food aid category:						
– Emergency Relief	457.6	595.3	408.4	389.1	380.0	446.1
– Project	–	49.3	24.5	6.3	12.5	18.5
– Agr./Rural Development	–	34.3	24.5	6.3	11.8	15.4
– Nutrition Intervention	–	15.0	–	–	0.7	3.1
By donor[a]:						
– WFP	189.5	233.2	117.3	193.4	354.8	217.6
– Japan	115.5	113.0	130.0	60.6	–	83.8
– Canada	50.9	77.9	50.2	64.4	–	48.7
– EC Community Action	64.5	63.1	48.7	4.0	1.6	36.4
– USA	–	125.8	41.2	–	–	33.4
– Germany	31.1	20.0	26.6	50.0	30.0	31.5
– Netherlands	–	–	–	23.0	–	4.6
– France	6.0	–	13.0	–	–	3.8
– Austria	–	1.5	3.0	–	6.0	2.1
– Greece	–	10.0	–	–	–	2.0
– Belgium	–	–	3.0	–	–	0.6

[a] Multilateral food aid provided through WFP appears under WFP as donor.

Source: WFP/INTERFAIS Database

Appendix Table 4.2 *Pakistan: Non-cereal food aid receipts ('000 tons)*

	1987	1988	1989	1990	1991	1987–91 Average
Total:	206.7	401.4	207.9	156.0	13.1	197.1
By food aid channel:						
– Bilateral	168.2	376.3	195.0	147.0	1.7	177.6
– Gvt-to-Gvt	168.2	375.6	194.5	146.5	0.3	177.0
– through NGOs	–	0.7	0.5	0.5	1.4	0.6
– Multilateral	38.5	25.2	12.9	9.1	11.5	19.4
By food aid category:						
– Emergency Relief	37.7	30.5	12.9	17.3	6.5	21.0
– Project	6.1	11.5	3.4	3.7	6.6	6.3
– Agr./Rural Development	3.3	6.8	3.3	1.5	3.1	3.6
– Nutrition Intervention	2.8	4.2	0.1	2.2	3.5	2.6
– Other Development Project	–	0.5	–	–	–	0.1
– Non-project (Programme)	162.9	359.4	191.6	135.0	–	169.8
By Donor[a]:						
– USA	136.9	359.4	191.6	135.0	–	164.6
– WFP	25.8	24.6	12.2	6.7	11.4	16.1
– Canada	26.0	11.8	–	8.1	–	9.2
– EC Community Action	5.7	5.1	2.6	3.8	1.6	3.8
– Germany	12.3	0.5	0.4	2.0	–	3.0
– France	–	–	0.5	–	–	0.1
– Norway	–	–	0.7	–	–	0.1
– Switzerland	–	–	–	0.3	–	0.1

[a] Multilateral food aid provided through WFP appears under WFP as donor.

Source: ibid.

Women are encouraged to form groups to undertake productive or income-earning activities; in this case baking. Under this project women receive food coupons which can be exchanged in government-sponsored outlets which guarantee adequacy of supplies at fair prices. This is considered a quick and efficient way of transferring income to a large number of families living in extreme poverty. WFP/Mercedes Sayagues

5 Honduras

Responding to Economic Recession in an Environment of Instability

Honduras, one of the poorest countries in the western hemisphere, has experienced severe economic difficulties since the second oil price hike of 1979, exacerbated by regional political instability. In these circumstances, increased levels of food aid have met part of the urban demand for food, providing substantial balance of payments and budgetary support. Project aid has been used to combat poverty and malnutrition through supporting FFW programmes and food distribution to vulnerable groups, schools and training centres.

Efforts have been made to improve the planning of project aid. However, so long as such efforts remain partial, the integration of food aid with other development co-operation, which is essential to effective utilization, remains incomplete. As regional and political instability, which had previously resulted in food relief to refugees in Honduras, diminishes, the challenge in food aid planning and programming will be to foster effectively the process of economic recovery.

Background

About 60% of Honduras' population of more than 5 million live in rural areas with limited access to health and education and in generally poor conditions. More than half of them live below the absolute poverty level.

Honduras has not escaped the effects of the recession in the world economy. Gains in real economic growth achieved during the 1970s were erased as a result of the sharp economic downturn suffered from 1979 and they have not been recouped. At the same time, the population has continued to grow rapidly – in the 1980s by 3% per annum. As a result, there was a decline in per capita income equivalent to 1.9% per annum throughout the 1980s. The economic slowdown was particularly felt during the second half of the decade when industrial output was 9% below the level in 1980. During the 1980s the agricultural sector grew at an annual rate of 1.8%, well below population growth of 3.4% a year over the same period. Macroeconomic imbalances and a high level of external debt made it necessary to implement drastic adjustment measures, such as the introduction of new currency exchange regulations, adjustment in taxes and tariffs, removal of subsidies, liberalization of prices, and actions designed to streamline public sector expenditures. These measures, which are aimed at reducing inflation, promoting investment, and reversing unfavourable trends in exports and employment in the medium term, have adversely affected vulnerable groups and the unemployed in the short run. It was estimated that, in 1991, three-quarters of the population lived in poverty, with over half living in extreme poverty, without access to a minimum diet.

Although the contribution of the agricultural sector to GDP decreased from a third in the 1970s to a quarter in 1990, it still accounted for more than half of total export earnings (mainly from bananas and coffee) and provided employment for about 60% of the labour force. Agricultural production largely satisfied internal market demand in the 1980s, but there is evidence that the basic nutritional needs of large sectors of the population are still not being met, especially in remote areas where there are seasonal food shortages. The average nutritional intake of the poorest 50% of the population covers less than 80% of their minimum requirements. The diet consists mainly of maize, beans and small amounts of rice and potatoes. Data from surveys conducted in 1987 revealed that 57% of children below the age of five showed signs of calorie-protein malnutrition, with 45 % suffering from chronic malnutrition. It was estimated that there were over 500,000 malnourished children in the country, of whom about 200,000 suffered from second- and third-degree malnutrition and required urgent treatment.

Food Aid

Food aid to Honduras has generally been incorporated into development plans as an additional investment resource. However, its treatment has been neither systematic nor co-ordinated. Rather, the aid has been used as a resource which could support, and in some cases make possible, specific developmental objectives. One reason for this rather random treatment is that the Honduran planning entity, the Secretariat for Planning, Co-ordination and Budget (SECPLAN), does not directly co-ordinate all food aid provided from all sources.

Food aid has been supplied to Honduras regularly since 1959. The main donors and organizations involved are the United States, which provides programme aid directly to the government and project food aid through agencies such as CARE, CRS and CARITAS under PL480 Title II, WFP, the Honduran-German Co-operation for Food Security (COHASA) and the EC Commission.

Food assistance supplied includes wheat, skimmed milk powder, vegetable oil, rice, maize, pulses and blended commodities. There have also been sporadic donations of barley, lentils, and other food items, such as soups. Commodities are shipped from abroad, with the exception of those supplied by COHASA, which buys locally most of the commodities used in its food-aided projects.

Food aid increased considerably between 1979 and the mid-1980s, along with the growth in overall development assistance. However, volumes of food aid have declined slightly in more recent years. Since 1979, there have been changes in the types of foodstuffs supplied, mainly as a result of an increase in programme food aid in wheat supplied by the US. There have also been changes in the type of aid provided. In 1979, programme food aid represented 25% of the total food aid received, project food aid 68% and food aid for emergency purposes 7%. In 1991, programme food aid accounted for 74%, project food aid 24%, and food aid for emergency purposes 2% of the total food aid.

Food Aid Management and Administration

Arrangements for the management and administration of food aid in Honduras vary according to the source of the assistance. In some cases, food aid is channelled through the relevant government ministries or through autonomous agencies. In other cases, food aid programmes are carried out directly by non-governmental agencies, such as CARITAS,and several private groups that execute welfare programmes.

At the national level, SECPLAN programmes, co-ordinates and monitors food aid received from WFP, the EC Commission and COHASA, but not that supplied by NGOs. The internal costs of food aid vary according to the type of commodity and its source. These costs have increased significantly with time, and sometimes constitute the major obstacle to the use of food aid for development. About half of these costs are attributable to transport from port to project sites; more than a third are port charges, handling costs and other charges. The remainder arise in storage, fumigation and in loading and unloading. Total internal handling costs in 1991 were estimated to be US$70 a ton.

Impact of Food Aid

Food assistance, particularly programme food aid, has had a significant impact on the country's economy. The expansion of food aid to Honduras since 1979 coincided with a national financial and economic crisis. At a time when production of basic food crops was declining significantly, the increase in food aid served partially to offset the shortfall in supply. In addition, funds released or created through food aid sales allowed the government to meet some of the costs of the country's urgently needed economic and social development programmes. Food aid helped rural development, increased production of basic foods, strengthened farmers' organizations, improved the nutritional status of poor people and generally raised rural incomes.

Programme food aid   Honduras has received programme food aid mainly from the United States but also from the EC Commission. The commodities received have been sold through commercial channels on the understanding that the government uses the proceeds generated for broad developmental objectives.

US programme food aid constitutes long-term loans with grace periods of from 2 to 10 years at 2% interest, and with a commitment to repay within 20 to 40 years at an annual interest rate of 3%. If proceeds generated from their sale are used for mutually agreed development activities, the loan is changed to a grant. The funds generated have been used mainly to finance a credit programme for rural co-operatives through the National Agricultural Development Bank as well as to support various national agencies implementing development projects backed by US financial and technical assistance. Sales proceeds have been used to support an agricultural development project, which seeks to establish efficient and cost-effective public institutional structures and delivery systems to serve the needs of small farmers. This project comprises 11 activities carried out, among others, by the Ministry of Natural Resources, the Agricultural Development Bank and the National University.

US programme food aid has constituted the major share of total food aid to Honduras. It has helped the government fund development programmes at a time of serious financial difficulties and has substituted for some commercial imports of wheat. It has also resulted in some substitution in the consumption of maize by wheat flour, especially in urban areas. There have been no detailed evaluations of the impact of programme food aid in Honduras, but direct benefits in terms of budgetary support, import substitution and release of funds are evident. Programme food aid has supported the government's efforts to stabilize food prices. In addition to the creation of credit facilities for small farmers, funds generated from the sale of food aid commodities in local markets have supported the construction of storage facilities in food producing areas, price support measures for farmers and the establishment of fair-price food shops in rural areas.

Project food aid   Project food aid has supported development projects through FFW and feeding programmes for vulnerable groups, primary schools and training centres. FFW has been assisted particularly by COHASA, WFP and CRS. It has mainly involved the construction of basic rural infrastructure, the production of basic foods and the promotion of income-generating activities. A special feature of WFP assistance has been voluntary contributions by project participants equivalent to 5% of the market value of the food rations provided. These contributions have been pooled to finance production activities by project participants.

Food assistance to vulnerable groups has been channelled mainly through CARE, CRS and, since 1982, WFP. Projects have been designed to improve school feeding, to promote mother and child health care and nutrition, and to support supplementary feeding in areas where people have less than adequate diets and where seasonal food shortages occur. The Ministry of Health has established guidelines for nutritional rehabilitation and criteria for the selection of beneficiaries. Activities are carried out through rural health centres with the help of voluntary health personnel.

In some of the agreements signed between the government and the donor agencies, it is stipulated that evaluations of the assisted projects should be carried out on a continuing basis as well as through special studies conducted by SECPLAN. Evaluations of the impact of project food aid have not, however, been carried out systematically. *Food-for-work programmes:* One of the most significant FFW programmes in Honduras is one that has been executed by COHASA since 1975 in the southern part of the country. COHASA plans its activities in co-ordination with the Honduran Planning Council. Over the years an efficient and integrated approach to rural development has evolved which provides support to marginal farmers' groups. The general aim of the project has been to support the government's objective of incorporating these poor farmers into the mainstream of the economy by increasing food production, constructing rural infrastructure and creating employment opportunities, thereby improving living conditions. Food aid has been used in such a way as to stimulate community participation, while diminishing the risk of dependence on food assistance and avoiding disincentive effects on food production and local prices.

In 1982, SECPLAN evaluated a rural development FFW programme assisted by WFP. The evaluation noted that project activities had faced a number of constraints; operational deficiencies such as irregularity in food supplies, lack of co-ordination among the agencies in charge of implementation, inaccurate programming of activities and difficulties in achieving acceptability of some commodities were detected. Nevertheless, the evaluation observed definite accomplishments in terms of the construction of rural infrastructure and the quality of the work done, particularly on access roads, the level of community participation, and the amount of employment generated. In general, the evaluation emphasized the beneficial aspects of the project on communities that had not previously received development assistance.

SECPLAN evaluation in 1980 of a WFP-assisted FFW project for promoting basic grain production concluded that food aid, together with credit and technical inputs, had played an important role in increasing agricultural production and in settling farmers on new land made available through the agrarian reform process. A WFP evaluation the following year noted that the project had helped to support viable and highly motivated co-operatives and to promote full-time work on farmers' own land, relieving them of the need to seek work elsewhere for additional income and thereby increasing production. The Ministry of Natural Resources and the National Agrarian Institute considered the project to be an important element in support of land reform measures and of efforts towards increasing food production and farmers' productivity. A WFP/FAO technical review mission visited the project in 1985 and found that it had resulted in a real increase in annual food crop production of more than 10,000 tons, equal to the amount of commodities committed by WFP for the entire three-year duration of the project, and benefiting household incomes that were found to have increased 2.5 times.

Food assistance to vulnerable groups: Since 1957 CARE has supported a primary-school feeding programme, covering half the children attending primary school, followed by a programme to improve mother and child nutrition. There have been some criticisms of the first programme. It is open-ended, involves high operational costs for food distribution and management, and the food supplement provided does not amount to a significant percentage of the total energy requirements of the target group. School attendance and educational performance have improved, however, in the schools participating in the programme.

In the second programme, the food supplement provided covers a minimum of 30% of nutritional requirements. It operates nationwide through a variety of institutions. In the early years most of the beneficiaries were reached through community centres with no relation either to the Ministry of Health or to the National Board of Social Welfare (INBS). These organizations therefore had only limited opportunity to make an adequate selection of malnourished children, to offer pre-natal advice to pregnant women, or to provide services normally carried out in health centres. The programme has now been re-oriented so that the main emphasis will be on addressing the needs of vulnerable groups through health centres or community centres operated by the Ministry of Health or INBS.

Since 1982, WFP has assisted the Ministry of Health in its implementation of a nutritional rehabilitation programme. The main objectives of the programme are to improve the nutritional status of pre-school children and of nursing and pregnant women, to increase the attendance of mothers at health centres, and to promote community activities in food production and environmental sanitation. Although designed to achieve national coverage, the programme was initially conducted in only one area (Santa Barbara), with the participation of nearly 300 health volunteers serving more than 3,500 families. By 1992, the programme covered seven departments of the country and served over 8,600 families.

A joint Ministry of Health and WFP evaluation of this programme in 1984 found that food assistance had had a significant beneficial effect on malnourished children; the children had also received basic immunization and treatment of infectious diseases that facilitated nutritional recuperation. The main factors leading to nutritional deterioration among child participants were identified as the prevalence of infectious diseases or parasitical infections and unfavourable home environments. The evaluation emphasized that the nutrition education component of the project should be strengthened.

Food entitlement and compensatory programmes   The implementation of stringent economic adjustment measures in Honduras initially had an adverse effect on the incomes, employment and food intake of vulnerable groups. In order to protect these groups from this temporary hardship, and to cushion the impact of the adjustment process, in 1990 the government established a family allowance programme (PRAF) and the Honduran Social Investment Fund (FHIS). Since 1991 WFP has committed nearly US$13 million of assistance to a food-coupon programme executed by PRAF which benefits over 186,000 poor families and is linked to attendance at health centres and primary schools. WFP commodities are monetized to generate funds to finance the distribution of food coupons. In preliminary evaluation visits by WFP, the World Bank and USAID, it has been found that in poverty-stricken areas linking the distribution of food coupons to beneficiaries' attendance at primary schools and health centres has resulted in decreased drop-out rates in schools and increased frequency of visits to health centres, thus diminishing health risk among vulnerable groups.

Similarly, WFP has been co-operating with FHIS since 1992 in generating short-term employment for families suffering from extreme poverty. About US$1.6 million of WFP resources have been committed to assist FHIS in implementing this programme. Commodities supplied by WFP are monetized to pay wages to about 11,000 workers involved in building social infrastructure such as schools, health centres, latrines and wells.

In general, it has been found that food aid provided through these programmes is an effective way to provide compensation and transfer income to poor families suffering from the effects of structural adjustment.

Emergency food assistance   Food assistance for emergency purposes has been required for the victims of natural disasters, such as floods and hurricanes and, since 1979, for refugees as a result of political instability in the central American region. Relief food has been supplied by CARE, the EC Commission and WFP in co-ordination with the UN High Commission for Refugees.

During the 1980s food distribution for refugees was carried out by CARITAS and NGOs, such as World Relief, and was co-ordinated by the UNHCR through the National Commission for Refugees. This arrangement became a semi-permanent feature, since possibilities for the repatriation of refugees were limited, and continuing assistance was necessary as on the whole the refugees did not have the means to produce their own food.

The Honduran Government initiated a resettlement programme for about 15,000 refugees from Nicaragua with the help of World Relief in the mid-1980s, which resulted in a degree of food self-sufficiency, mainly in rice. Health and nutrition services were made available with the co-operation of another NGO, *Médecins sans Frontières*. Continuing food assistance was still required, however, for new arrivals and to consolidate the gains in food self-sufficiency. With the onset of the peace process in Central America, refugees from El Salvador, Guatemala and Nicaragua were able to return to their home countries. By 1992, only about 1,500 refugees remained.

Major Constraints and Difficulties

SECPLAN and donor agencies have studied the constraints and difficulties that face food assistance to Honduras. These arise from a variety of causes, including: the different modalities of the donor agencies; deficiencies in the design and formulation of food-aided projects; operational problems, including some in the management and administration of food distribution; inadequate monitoring arrangements during project implementation; and deficiencies in the assessment of the impact of food aid on the target population and development activities.

Procedures for assessing the feasibility of using food aid support for specific developmental objectives have often not been closely or systematically followed. At times, there has been little relationship between the specific priorities outlined in the national sectoral development plans and the food-aided activities undertaken. In other cases, food-assisted activities have been planned without reference to other development efforts already in operation in the same area or sector. The process of formulating some projects was also carried out without the knowledge of SECPLAN. As a result, the selection of project areas and beneficiaries has sometimes been inadequate; and there has been insufficient adjustment of food-aided efforts to take account of seasonal unemployment and underemployment and shortages of food supplies.

Operational difficulties have been caused by both internal and external constraints, a number of which have affected all forms of aid. Internal difficulties have included lack of counterpart funds and of adequate infrastructure for food management, inadequate staff, problems in commodity acceptability, inadequate systems for project control, monitoring and evaluation, concentration of activities in easily accessible areas, and lack of systematic involvement on the part of communities and participants.

External difficulties have included inadequate co-ordination among donor agencies in the planning and programming of activities, sometimes resulting in the overlapping and duplication of efforts; lack of continuity in food aid supplies when donor agencies have faced resource limitations; and delays in deliveries or substitution of commodities that are not easily handled. Donor agencies have frequently insisted on the direct distribution of externally provided commodities, not allowing the monetization of food aid, commodity exchange, or the local purchase of commodities. Donor requirements have sometimes included cumbersome or time-consuming administrative procedures that have resulted in irregularity of supplies.

The country has faced serious difficulties in absorbing larger amounts of needed food aid, mainly because of the reduced financial and personnel resources of the institutions handling food aid. This is unfortunate, given the proven beneficial effects of this type of assistance and the high degree of enthusiasm of the rural population in the support of food-aided projects.

The costs of distribution of food aid from warehouses to distribution centres have been absorbed with considerable difficulty by each government agency involved in the implementation of projects. Voluntary contributions to help cover these costs have been sought from project beneficiaries. However, COHASA-assisted activities have not been affected by these budgetary restrictions. COHASA does not depend on counterpart contributions from the government in order to effect food distribution; it has its own resources to operate its own distribution network.

Future directions

Large segments of the Honduran population still suffer from severe nutritional deficiencies as a result of food shortages, poor dietary habits, inadequate health and sanitary facilities and a lack of nutritional education. In the short to medium term, this situation will not be resolved: the problem is complex, and there are insufficient

resources to support appropriate intervention measures. Food assistance will, therefore, remain a useful and valid tool ·for development.

Some elements of a strategy for the use of food assistance have been developed by
SECPLAN based on food aid experience. Broadly, the strategy seeks to reorient food
aid, and the way in which it is programmed and used, so as to make it more effective
in contributing to the achievement of national development objectives and to integrate
it more fully into development planning. Linking food aid to programmes that
mitigate the adverse effects of economic adjustment on the poor is an example of how
this reorientation might be brought about.

Appendix Table 5.1 *Honduras: Cereal food aid receipts ('000 tons – in grain equivalent)*

	1987	1988	1989	1990	1991	1987–91 Average
Total:	131.0	180.4	135.7	140.0	122.1	141.8
By food aid channel:						
– Bilateral	118.9	150.9	133.8	125.0	107.1	127.3
– Gvt-to-Gvt	110.3	145.5	127.4	120.1	94.5	119.6
– through NGOs	8.6	5.4	6.4	4.9	13.2	7.7
– Multilateral	12.1	29.5	1.9	14.9	14.4	14.6
By food aid category:						
– Emergency Relief	5.1	11.2	0.4	5.5	1.9	4.8
– Project	18.2	52.4	19.8	18.3	25.7	26.9
– Agr./Rural Development	5.6	36.8	4.0	9.4	–	11.2
– Nutrition Intervention	2.7	4.4	2.2	–	7.2	3.3
– Food Reserve	2.5	–	–	–	–	0.5
– Other Development Project	7.4	11.2	13.6	8.9	18.5	11.9
– Non-project (Programme)	107.8	116.8	115.4	116.2	94.5	110.1
By donor[a]:						
– USA	111.6	136.8	125.6	125.0	106.2	121.0
– WFP	11.4	29.5	1.7	14.8	14.4	14.4
– EC Community Action	4.5	8.0	0.1	0.1	–	2.6
– France	–	5.2	–	–	1.5	1.3
– Germany	–	–	5.9	–	–	1.2
– Argentina	2.5	–	–	–	–	0.5
– Canada	–	–	2.2	–	–	0.4
– Spain	0.8	–	–	–	–	0.2
– Switzerland	0.2	0.9	–	–	–	0.2

[a] Multilateral food aid provided through WFP appears under WFP as donor.

Source: WFP/INTERFAIS Database

Appendix Table 5.2 *Honduras: Non-cereal food aid receipts ('000 tons)*

	1987	1988	1989	1990	1991	1987–91 Average
Total:	12.8	13.2	16.4	5.5	6.1	10.8
By food aid channel:						
– Bilateral	7.1	2.5	15.4	2.8	3.3	6.2
– Gvt-to-Gvt	2.2	0.3	14.2	–	–	3.3
– through NGOs	4.9	2.2	1.2	2.8	3.3	2.9
– Multilateral	5.7	10.6	1.1	2.7	2.8	4.6
By food aid category:						
– Emergency Relief	4.2	3.5	0.8	1.8	0.7	2.2
– Project	8.6	9.6	6.5	3.8	5.4	6.8
– Agr./Rural Development	1.6	3.7	1.4	1.0	1.7	1.9
– Nutrition Intervention	1.9	2.4	2.0	–	1.0	1.5
– Other Development Project	5.1	3.5	3.1	2.8	2.7	3.4
– Non-project (programme)	–	–	9.2	–	–	1.8
By donor[a]:						
– USA	4.8	2.0	7.5	2.8	2.7	4.0
– WFP	4.3	10.1	0.3	1.7	2.8	3.8
– EC Community Action	2.5	0.4	4.4	0.1	0.6	1.6
– Germany	0.8	0.5	3.2	–	–	0.9
– Canada	–	0.2	0.5	–	–	0.2
– France	–	–	0.1	0.9	–	0.2
– Switzerland	0.4	–	–	–	–	0.1
– Others	–	–	0.3	–	–	0.1

[a] Multilateral food aid provided through WFP appears under WFP as donor.

Source: ibid.

A type of spineless cactus is planted by project workers to provide fodder. This WFP-supported project for soil and water conservation works covers much of central and southern Tunisia. WFP/Banoun-Caracciolo

Small earthwork dams built in the Governorate of Medenine in southern Tunisia to prevent soil erosion and conserve water in semi-desert areas during the spring and autumn rains. WFP/Florita Botts

6 Tunisia

Food Deficits & Food Aid
in a Middle-income Country

Background

Economic planning was launched in Tunisia in the early 1960s. Government planners sought to introduce a needed realignment of the national economy, stressing the development of human resources and giving priority to education, health and agriculture. Continuity and coherence have been sustained through a succession of development plans that have maintained these priorities. Since the early 1980s, efforts have also been made to set up plans that target specific regions. These plans have been designed to improve the balance between regions, promote industrial decentralization, improve the standard of living of people in rural areas, keep farmers on the land and make farming attractive to young people in the expectation that they will become supporters of agricultural development and not migrate to urban areas, and achieve self-reliance in food.

Tunisia has undoubtedly made progress in terms of social and economic development. Its social indicators are among the best in Africa, resulting from the government's long-term policy of investing in human resource development and paying special attention to family welfare, education and training. Between 1960 and 1990, infant mortality declined by almost 60%, from 145 to 45 per thousand, life expectancy at birth rose from 51 to 67 years and adult literacy increased from 15 to 62%. An active family planning policy led to a decline in the birth rate from 44 to 30 per thousand. Demographic projections based on a gradual decrease in fertility and mortality rates as well as on contraction of migration abroad estimate the population to grow at an annual rate of 1.8%, reaching 9 million people in 1995.

However, Tunisia has to cope with the inherent problems faced by many developing countries. In view of its weak natural resource base, it has not yet been able to achieve food self-sufficiency. Over half its food requirements are imported. By the year 2000, according to the International Food Policy Research Institute projections, Tunisia will have an annual cereal deficit of 1.3 million tons compared with the current deficit of 800,000 tons and a meat deficit of about 200,000 tons against 55,000 tons in 1990.

The land is predominantly arid or semi-arid. Only 3% of the cultivable area is under irrigation. It is estimated that at least 80% of the country is subject to erosion, half of which is severe. Rainfed agriculture has been adversely affected by year-to-year fluctuations in weather conditions and irregular distribution of rainfall. Limited water resources and high wind and water erosion have aggravated farm land degradation and curbed agricultural production. For more than 20 years, the government has invested in efforts to reduce land degradation but the magnitude of erosion and desertification remains considerable and much remains to be done to check further destruction.

Specific government strategies essentially aim at improving the management of forestry, restoring the natural vegetation of rangeland and undertaking large-scale soil conservation works. This has resulted in better irrigation practices and in bringing additional land under cultivation. However, watershed management and water and soil conservation programmes to halt desert encroachment will continue to have priority. The government is now focusing attention on soil conservation activities to be undertaken by farmers on their own land in order to increase their awareness of the problem and involve them in environment protection works.

Tunisia has also not been spared the recessionary effects of the 1980s, which had a negative effect on the country's development. From being a fast-growing economy which averaged an annual 7.4% growth rate from the early 1970s to the mid-1980s, Tunisia is now facing the prospect of much reduced growth owing to low levels of private and public investment and adverse terms of trade. These difficulties, aggravated by high rates of rural and urban unemployment, have been exacerbated by the 1991 Gulf crisis, which resulted in a sharp decline in foreign investments, revenue from tourism and remittances. However, timely intervention, a progressive economic policy and exploitation of petroleum resources, albeit on a small scale, have made it possible for Tunisia to continue development despite external constraints.

A World Bank/IMF structural adjustment programme was adopted in 1986. The implementation of the economic reform programme was based on giving an export orientation to the economy and on expanding the role of the private sector, thereby easing the country's financial problems and promoting growth. The economy registered a relatively rapid recovery and now has a respectable rate of growth. Substantial improvements and prospects for long-term viability have been noted, in particular in the balance of payments despite the setback caused by the Gulf crisis. With a tolerable external debt, prospects for further economic growth are also encouraging.

However, rigorous implementation of the adjustment programme has brought certain social costs. The government gradually removed certain items from the basket of subsidized goods and shifted subsidies to goods mostly consumed by the poor. The poverty alleviation programme is also being reinforced to ensure a better targeting on the poor directly.

Tunisia is classified as a lower middle-income country by the World Bank with a per capita GNP of US$1,488 in 1990. This classification resulted in a considerable reduction in its foreign aid receipts in the early 1980s, as OECD countries redirected their aid in favour of the least developed countries. However, since the mid-1980s, Tunisia has attracted an increased number of foreign donors and institutions which, in addition to the IMF and the World Bank, are committed to support its liberalization policies and the structural adjustment programme adopted by the government. External financing in the form of loans and grants, including food donations, has ranged from 25 to 35% of total investments in development programmes.

Food Aid

Tunisia received food aid from the United States in 1957, one year after independence under an annually renewable bilateral agreement. Part of the aid was delivered directly on a government-to-government basis, and a smaller proportion was entrusted as project aid to US voluntary agencies and UNICEF. Project food aid was focused on improving the nutritional status of pre-school and school children and combating unemployment. This aid continued, mainly in support of pre-school and primary school feeding, until 1987 and was distributed through CRS.

More than 90% of the food aid that Tunisia received during the late 1980s was in the form of cereals, mostly wheat. The remainder comprised various foodstuffs, such as skimmed milk powder, butter and vegetable oil, tinned fish, cheese, sugar and tea. Virtually all of these non-cereals were donated as project food aid.

About 80% of all food aid to Tunisia over the period 1987-91 has been programme aid. Most programme food aid provided by Tunisia's major bilateral donors (Italy, France, the United States) is earmarked for sale. Supplementing commercial imports, it is sold by the Office des Céréales Tunisien (OCT), the national agency responsible for all cereal trading operations. Under annual and renewable agreements made on a bilateral basis with the different donors, Tunisia is authorised to sell all foodstuffs received, the proceeds being used to support the national budget or to cover expenses fixed and agreed jointly beforehand by the parties concerned.

Only the United States has sold agricultural commodities, mainly wheat and soya oil, to Tunisia on non-grant, concessionary terms in the form of long-term loans with a grace period and low interest charges. The funds generated have been used to promote agricultural development, mainly by granting loans to small and medium-sized farmers. Such funds have enabled the government to pursue a development investment programme and permit some savings on foreign exchange that would otherwise have been spent on food imports.

About a third of all food aid received since independence has been project food aid; the proportion has declined to 17% over the period 1987-1991. Project food aid has been used in the most disadvantaged regions of the country for the development of human resources and for agricultural and rural development. It is integrated with other forms of external aid and with public and private resources mobilized by the government for priority development projects.

WFP first provided assistance to Tunisia in 1965 on a modest scale, mainly for small pilot projects (institutional feeding, rural infrastructure, livestock development, etc.), which complemented to some extent the substantive US food aid programme.

Tunisia has had to appeal to the international community for emergency aid on a number of occasions, especially to help Algerian refugees in the period from 1958 to 1962, and flood or drought victims. However, appeals have been made only after the government has fully mobilized its own resources. Assistance supplied to meet emergency needs amounts to about 11% of all food aid received as donations.

Co-ordination and Integration of Food Aid

In general, project planning and co-ordination of international co-operation is the responsibility of the Ministry of Foreign Affairs and the Ministry of the Plan. Proposals for programmes and projects, drawn up by individual departments, are reviewed by the Ministry of the Plan to ensure that they accord, and are integrated, with the priorities of national economic and social development. However, each department is responsible for the use of food aid in accordance with programmes that are drawn up by common agreement.

There is no formal mechanism for co-ordination among the various agencies or donors represented in Tunisia. Nevertheless, there has been no duplication of effort by the assisting agencies or by the services or institutions that use food aid. Locally represented agencies and donors consult with each other and exchange relevant information on their activities.

The government attaches importance to food aid as it still plays a prominent role in the national development process. It is basically requested to support projects in disadvantaged regions of the country, where the people suffer most from problems of underdevelopment, particularly unemployment and poverty. It is in such regions that food aid is most justified. Food aid is an integral part of the investment effort, as shown by several pilot actions in the central and northwestern parts of the country where WFP aid and financial and technical contributions from the government have been co-ordinated. Food aid has also made it possible to implement and achieve the objectives of several projects in the national development plan.

Design and implementation of food-aided projects   The ways in which food-aided projects are designed and implemented vary depending on the type of contract drawn up between the donor and the recipient and on the product being supplied. Food donations to support projects have fallen into four categories:

(i) direct contributions by the US Government as concessionary programme food aid that have been sold and the proceeds used to support development projects;

ii) project food aid provided by the US Government mainly through the voluntary agencies CRS and CARE and through UNICEF;

iii) from the EC Commission as direct grant donations to the Tunisian Government or indirectly through CRS and CARE as distributing agencies;

iv) from WFP channelling food aid donations from about 30 donor countries as grant project food aid.

When a technical department receives an offer of food aid, or identifies a project in which food aid could rationally be used, it must request agreement in principle from the Ministry of the Plan. Once agreement has been obtained, a proposal must be submitted to the Ministry of Foreign Affairs and the Ministry of the Plan for final approval. No agreement is made without an in-depth study of the project and a request for food aid.

Pre-investment studies are prepared by the government's technical services in collaboration with bilateral or multilateral technical co-operation agencies. Several food-aided projects owe their success in part to the kind of joint pre-investment studies that have been carried out, especially those in watershed management and erosion and desertification control.

There have been differences between the approach taken by WFP and that of other donors. WFP requires the submission of a request by the government that may be appraised by an inter-agency mission comprising technical specialists from the concerned UN agencies as well as from WFP. Most other donors get in touch with the government service concerned when preparing their annual budget to make a joint study of food aid needs for project support. WFP is the only donor agency that plans food aid to projects over periods of up to five years. Other donors grant aid on a year-to-year basis, making it difficult to forward-plan project activities.

The food aid provided for development projects normally accounts for only a small portion of the total project cost. With or without co-financing from donors or financial institutions, the government's contribution has amounted to between 60 and 80%. In some cases, the government has contributed locally supplied foods out of its own budget in addition to the food aid provided by donors.

Food aid logistics   The government has set up a central service within the OCT in the Ministry of Agriculture with the sole task of handling the logistics of all products supplied as food aid and intended for various projects. This unit is responsible for the products from their arrival at Tunisian ports until their delivery to warehouses throughout the country near distribution and project sites. The OCT receives payment from the project authorities for services rendered.

Centralization of the food aid distribution system has reduced costs and increased efficiency. Food aid management has been streamlined and tailored to project needs through the network of storage centres and nationwide transport systems to which the projects have access.

Food-aided Projects

Project food aid, compared with other types of food aid, is easier to supervise and evaluate. Objectives can be determined, beneficiaries identified and the results measured and evaluated. About a quarter of all food aid-assisted projects in 1987-1991 have been used for the development of human resources; about three-quarters have focused on agricultural and rural development.

The first category comprises food aid which has been used to supplement the diet of vulnerable groups. It has been distributed through MCH centres for pregnant and nursing mothers and for children under the age of three; through pre-school centres; through elementary schools; and through vocational and artisan training centres and children's villages. Apart from improving the nutritional status of recipients, the aim has been to provide an incentive for increased attendance at health centres, schools and vocational training institutions.

Food aid for agricultural and rural development projects has been used as partial payment for workers and to stimulate small farmers to undertake activities designed to increase productivity and make better use of their land. A wide variety of projects have been supported in this category.

Since independence, Tunisia has had to cope with a serious unemployment and underemployment problem. In 1957, with assistance from USAID, the government launched a large-scale programme called *La lutte contre le sous-développement* (To combat underdevelopment). This was centred mainly on agricultural projects set up to give work to the masses of unemployed who were paid partly in wheat (as semolina). On average, the programme employed more than 100,000 workers a year to undertake reforestation, water and soil conservation projects, development of water systems, tree planting and maintenance, road and farm-road construction and rangeland management. Although the workers involved received little or no training and their productivity was very low, this basically relief works programme provided income in kind and in cash to the most needy and constructed infrastructure essential for agricultural and rural development.

In 1962, the programme was spectacularly relaunched under the Ministry of Agriculture and funds were allocated in the national budget. The United States continued to assist the project at a gradually reduced level until 1972. In the meantime WFP, at first on a modest scale and then, from 1968 onwards, at a more intensified level of participation, had taken over the soil and water conservation and agricultural development works under projects to stimulate small farmers to innovate and expand production. WFP aid is now focused mainly on reforestation, planting and maintaining fruit trees, fodder and food crops, and small irrigation works.

All these short- or long-term projects have been undertaken in the most disadvantaged rural areas, providing work and income (partly in kind) to the neediest. They have also created employment, particularly in agriculture.

The EC Commission has also supported rural development and employment creation projects by investing proceeds from the sale of programme food aid in wheat to an integrated rural development programme. The proceeds of EC milk powder and butter oil food aid sales to dairy plants have been used to upgrade dairy production.

Impact

Bilateral and multilateral food aid has made it possible for Tunisia to implement a number of major priority economic and social development projects, especially in agricultural and human resource development.

Food rations have helped upgrade the nutritional status of the most vulnerable groups, particularly pre-school children. They have also been given to elementary and secondary school children, girls in rural areas and others, including trainees in agricultural training centres. These rations, and other nutritional supplements, have helped to improve recipients' diet. They have also increased school attendances and led to greater participation in vocational training centres.

In 1988, WFP resumed its assistance to the social and education sector, which had been phased out in 1973, by supporting a feeding programme to vulnerable groups and primary school children that was previously assisted by CRS. WFP assistance was provided for 225,000 primary and 105,000 pre-school children. It was also given to mothers in rural areas as an incentive for them to attend community health and education centres regularly. In addition, WFP aid constituted an income transfer to rural youths in training centres and to poor rural families engaged in income-generating activities. WFP food was distributed in the form of cooked meals or snacks in primary schools and as take-home rations to the other types of project beneficiaries.

Food aid has also been a factor in implementing major agricultural projects, under both bilateral and multilateral co-operation. It has been used mainly as wage supplements and as an incentive to small farmers to develop their land.

Projects receiving food aid have been concerned primarily with erosion control, crop production, infrastructural work such as farm roads, rural housing and storage building and complementary activities such as the strengthening of co-operatives and agricultural extension.

An *ex post* assessment in June 1990 of WFP assistance for agricultural and rural development in central and southern Tunisia concluded that food aid, together with government inputs, had contributed significantly to increasing fruit tree and fodder production and had thereby increased the income level of small farmers, (WFP, 1990).

In the second half of the 1960s, WFP also helped to install the first unit to manufacture concentrated livestock feed, mainly maize-based. By the mid-1980s, there were about 168 units of this sort throughout the country, producing concentrated feed for poultry-raising and livestock and helping to develop poultry-raising and livestock in general. These projects not only had a catalytic effect on the country's development: they have also helped to generate jobs in agriculture and rural development and to increase the income of the most disadvantaged groups in this sector.

Internal and external conditions have had favourable and not so favourable effects on the launching and implementation of projects receiving food aid. Favourable internal factors include Tunisia's geographical location, with good port and other logistical facilities, a stable social and political climate, continuity and coherence in government planning, the availability of trained personnel, good nutrition and health services, a good reputation among international aid agencies, and a willingness to make effective use of local and externally supplied resources. There has been good administration and management of all phases of project identification, implementation and review. Food aid has been integrated into priority projects as defined by the government and as components of projects executed or assisted by other bilateral and multilateral financial and technical co-operation agencies; and there has been good collaboration among national and international organizations.

On the other hand, the country also faces a number of difficulties. These include low and erratic rainfall, widespread wind and water erosion, limited natural resources and the backlash of the world economic crisis of the 1980s, which resulted in the return of a large number of migrant workers and in high unemployment, worsened by the flight from the countryside. A significant part of the population is semi-nomadic and scattered throughout the rural areas, making access and outreach difficult for projects which by their very nature often take place in the most remote, disadvantaged regions.

Future Directions

Food aid has helped Tunisia to close the national 'food gap' and to obtain additional funds for the national budget to finance economic and social development projects, which are now bearing fruit. Good administration has led to rational utilization of food and other aid in accordance with a policy aimed at reaching the neediest groups of people.

Aid in the form of grain, though sometimes sizeable in comparison with domestic production, has overall represented about 5% of total wheat consumption and has not impeded an increase in domestic cereal output. The government has given price support to grain producers and cereal production has gradually increased.

Aid in general, including food aid, can be justified for a middle-income country such as Tunisia as a way of attaining self-reliance. It is even more to be recommended in the light of the government's commitment to development policies designed to benefit the poor and to lead to equitable and sustainable economic growth.

WFP's assistance to Tunisia in the 1990s has been revised taking into account WFP's resource constraints and the country's encouraging economic performance. The new approach is based on targeting WFP assistance to low-income groups in the most disadvantaged regions and to supporting the government's poverty alleviation programme. It also envisages the gradual phasing out of WFP assistance before the end of the decade.

In this context, WFP is supporting a rural development project in the poorest north-western region. WFP food aid will be provided as a supplement to the cash incentives paid to locally recruited labour undertaking soil conservation works and road construction. It will also encourage small farmers to adopt new agricultural techniques and to undertake soil conservation and improved planting activities on their own farms. By focusing on small farmers, the project aims to foster greater community participation in planning and implementing project activities. WFP is also maintaining its support, albeit on a smaller scale, for the government's poverty alleviation programme by providing food assistance to a primary school feeding project targeted exclusively on schools in remote rural areas. WFP assistance, intended to provide budgetary support for the government and to strengthen the school programme, will also contribute to reinforcing parent/teacher associations so as to enable them to assume responsibility for running the school canteens following the phasing out of its assistance.

Reference

WFP (1990). *Report on the Retrospective Evaluation of Overall WFP Assistance to Co-operatives and Other Legally Constituted Farmers' Associations in Central and Southern Tunisia*, CFA: 30/SCP: 5, Rome, October.

Appendix Table 6.1 *Tunisia: Cereal food aid receipts ('000 tons – in grain equivalent)*

	1987	1988	1989	1990	1991	1987–91 Average
Total:	340.8	402.6	335.0	372.3	244.3	339.0
By food aid channel:						
– Bilateral	340.8	338.9	301.0	311.2	230.3	304.4
– Gvt-to-Gvt	283.0	335.0	300.7	310.7	229.8	291.8
– through NGOs	57.8	3.9	0.3	0.5	0.5	12.6
– Multilateral	–	63.7	34.1	61.2	14.0	34.6
By food aid category:						
– Emergency Relief	57.8	10.8	6.8	11.1	–	17.3
– Project	–	177.6	63.5	50.5	29.2	52.1
– Agr./Rural Development	–	113.7	25.3	37.9	14.0	38.2
– Nutrition Intervention	–	3.9	0.3	0.5	0.5	1.0
– Other Development Project	–	–	37.9	12.1	14.7	12.9
– Non-project (Programme)	283.0	274.1	264.8	310.7	215.1	269.5
By donor[a]:						
– USA	315.3	200.6	169.8	301.0	186.6	234.7
– WFP	–	63.7	34.1	61.2	14.0	34.6
– France	–	71.0	50.0	–	21.0	28.4
– Canada	25.4	41.4	28.7	–	14.7	22.1
– EC Community Action	–	25.0	45.3	0.5	0.5	14.3
– Italy	–	–	7.2	9.6	7.5	4.9
– Spain	–	0.8	–	–	–	0.2

[a] Multilateral food aid provided through WFP appears under WFP as donor.

Source: WFP/INTERFAIS Database

Appendix Table 6.2 *Tunisia: Non-cereal food aid receipts ('000 tons)*

	1987	1988	1989	1990	1991	1987–91 Average
Total:	6.6	31.2	11.2	10.3	9.2	13.7
By food aid channel:						
– Bilateral	3.4	26.6	6.7	8.8	7.3	10.6
– Gvt-to-Gvt	3.3	25.0	6.6	8.1	7.0	10.0
– through NGOs	0.1	1.6	0.1	0.7	0.3	0.5
– Multilateral	3.2	4.6	4.5	1.5	1.9	3.1
By food aid category:						
– Project	3.6	7.3	11.2	5.1	5.2	6.5
– Agr./Rural Development	3.2	5.6	6.3	4.1	4.3	4.7
– Nutrition Intervention	0.1	1.6	–	0.6	0.3	0.5
– Other Development Project	0.3	0.1	4.9	0.4	0.6	1.3
– Non-project (Programme)	3.0	23.9	–	5.1	4.0	7.2
By donor[a]:						
– USA	–	22.5	–	–	–	4.5
– EC Community Action	3.1	3.0	3.1	3.6	3.3	3.2
– WFP	3.2	4.6	4.5	1.5	2.0	3.1
– Italy	0.3	0.1	3.1	5.1	4.0	2.5
– Germany	–	1.0	0.5	–	–	0.3

[a] Multilateral food aid provided through WFP appears under WFP as donor.

Source: ibid.

Railways are essential to a country's development. Under a national food-for-work scheme to improve the rail system, workers receive food rations for themselves and their families. WFP/Andre Girod

7 Benin

The Multi-purpose Project Approach in Action

Benin has had long experience with the multi-purpose project approach supported by food aid for both development and to meet emergencies. A number of the positive features in this experience may have wider relevance, especially for relatively small developing countries.

Since the beginning of WFP operations in 1963, it has been recognized that it is uneconomic to support small development projects in isolation, in view of the high administrative and logistical costs. A narrow application of cost-effectiveness criteria could penalize small countries, however, or small projects in larger countries. The governing body of WFP therefore decided, in 1965, that, although it had generally encouraged the submission of projects for WFP support with a commodity value of at least US$200,000, small developing countries should not be prevented from submitting smaller-scale projects for consideration. It was felt that, wherever possible, countries should combine several small projects into one multi-purpose project. This approach would facilitate the synchronization of commodity shipments in order to keep transport costs at an economic level. It would also encourage the establishment of inter-departmental co-ordinating machinery for dealing with food aid for local or regional development programmes.

Benin was the first country in West Africa to adopt the multi-purpose project approach. Its experience has shown that this approach can yield real benefits if adequate technical guidance, equipment, materials and food are provided. Rural communities can engage in many activities outside the agricultural season and thereby improve their productive capacity and the environment. In food-deficit situations, the provision of food aid can be a critical input to support villagers in the heavy work involved and to attract the additional workers required. Many of the activities to be performed are short-term and require only limited quantities of food. The multi-purpose project approach is sufficiently flexible to accommodate such activities within an overall plan adapted to the felt needs of local rural communities.

The Benin experience also shows how a flexible, multi-purpose project approach supported with food aid may help a country tackle emergency situations. Emergency food aid deliveries take time to reach a country and may be distributed as free relief rations, which is not always the most appropriate response in a disaster situation. A programme of reconstruction following an emergency can be started immediately by adjusting and/or expanding food-aided multi-purpose projects to meet the needs of the affected population. Adapting such projects to immediate needs can ensure that productive work is available, can maintain human dignity by providing work in place of handouts, and can make savings in the delivery time and costs of food aid.

There are also significant administrative advantages from the multi-purpose project approach. WFP has supported one nation-wide, multi-purpose project in Benin. It is operated under a single legal agreement and budget. There is sufficient flexibility within the agreement to allow adjustment and amendment involving the least amount of administrative time for the government and WFP. Shipments to the project are automatically combined, with resulting savings in transport costs.

Administrative arrangements within Benin have been combined for the receipt, handling, storage and distribution of WFP food aid. The monitoring of the progress of project activities and food aid operations is also centralized. Single, combined reports are prepared and single evaluation missions are usually undertaken. A national committee and a national administrative and logistics directorate have been established, with similar units at the provincial and local levels in accordance with the government's policy of decentralization. UNDP has provided assistance for technical support, training, materials and transport for the national food aid directorate in Cotonou, and for the directorates in six provinces, in recognition of the important part they can play in improving the management of food in the country. The WFP country office has trained local staff, strengthening the management and administration of food aid and enabling local personnel gradually to assume full responsibility for food aid operations throughout the country.

Background

Benin is a small, poor nation on the coast of West Africa. It has a population of about 4.7 million. By UN criteria, it is one of the world's least developed and food-deficit countries. It is therefore given priority in the allocation of food aid and is eligible for concessional lending from the International Development Association (IDA) of the World Bank.

About 60% of the population live in rural areas. Population growth has increased from an annual average of 2.7% in the period 1961–80 to 3.2% per annum during the 1980s. Almost half the population is less than 15 years old. Life expectancy increased from 35 to 47 years at birth between 1960 and 1990, reflecting some improvement in living conditions in the country, but is lower than the average for sub-Saharan Africa. There is also a high rate of infant mortality. At 113 per 1000 births in 1990 it is above the average for low-income countries. The levels of medical services and health care are improving but are still inadequate. Malaria is the single main cause of death. Only about one-third of the population has access to a safe drinking water supply. Access to education has expanded rapidly in recent years, but schooling rates are still low and less than one-quarter of the adult population is estimated to be literate.

The real growth rate of GNP during the 1980s averaged 2.2%, substantially higher than in previous years, when it was less than 1%. Agriculture, supplemented by commercial activities revolving around Benin's traditional transit role with the landlocked countries of the Sahelian region of West Africa and trade with neighbouring countries, particularly Nigeria, is the primary basis of the economy. Much of the industrial sector is agriculture-based. Agriculture grew at under 2.5% per annum in 1980–87, lagging behind the population growth rate of 3.2%. To redress this situation, in the mid-1980s the government adopted a policy aimed at improving agricultural incentives. As a result, certain food crops that enjoy a strong demand in Benin and in neighbouring countries have performed well. Exploitation of local petroleum, cement and sugar resources has also begun. Earnings from the export of these commodities are expected to be considerably more than the revenue currently obtained from traditional export crops.

The agricultural sector employs about 70% of the active population, and accounted for about 37% of GNP in 1990. Food crop production is predominant, representing more than 90% of the total value of agricultural output and occupying over 80% of the cultivated area. The main food crops produced are yams, cassava, maize, sorghum, millet, beans, potatoes and small quantities of rice. The main export crops are cotton, oil-palm products and groundnuts. Farming patterns vary considerably throughout the country, influenced by soils, which are generally poor, and by rainfall. Annual precipitation is much lower than in other coastal West African countries.

Agriculture is dominated by small family farms, which account for the bulk of production, although the number of co-operatives has increased. Production of food crops is in the private sector. The marketing of export crops was liberalized by the new government in 1991.

Traditionally, Benin has been self-sufficient in food production, and has generated significant foreign exchange earnings from export crops. Some of its food production is unofficially exported to Nigeria. Although food production has increased, it continues to lag behind population growth. Accordingly, food imports have grown. It is estimated that only about 16.5% of Benin's agricultural land is under cultivation, mainly because small farmers lack adequate farm inputs and services. The growth in the urban population, at a rate of about 5% a year, during the 1980s, and trade with neighbouring countries have also led to rising pressure on food prices.

The government attached a high priority to promoting increased agricultural production and productivity in its outline plan drawn up for the 1981–90 period. Special attention was given to food production and to the export crops, cotton and oil palm, to help meet the costs of imports. Food production above subsistence needs has also been stimulated in order to raise incomes in the rural areas, to increase rural savings and improve living standards.

The current emphasis in agricultural development is on decentralization. Priority has been given to regional action centres for rural development that receive credits from the government and external assistance for farmer training and for research aimed at increasing production. The elimination of subsidies, the institution of charges for improved seed and the initiation of specific interest rates on seasonal credit were all expected to help in assuring inputs and services and in providing financial stability to the institutions supplying them.

Food Aid

During the period 1987–91, total food aid averaged 14,100 tons a year. Cereals accounted for about 86% of this, representing about 14% of total cereal imports. Data are not available, however, on the proportion of food imports that were re-exported unofficially to neighbouring countries. Relatively small quantities of non-cereal commodities amounting to 2,000 tons were received annually as food aid over the same period. The main suppliers of food aid have been the EC Commission, WFP, the non-governmental organization CRS, France and Japan.

During 1987–1991, about 23% of the food aid provided was in the form of pro-gramme (non-project) aid, mainly wheat for sale in urban areas. The funds that accrued from such sales were used for investment in development activities. Some 74% of total food aid provided was in the form of project food aid, 44% of which was used in support of agricultural and rural development activities, mainly in the context of the WFP-assisted, nationwide, multi-purpose project. The other 30% of project food aid was used to improve the nutritional status of mothers and pre-school children, largely through activities supported by CRS. Emergency relief assistance accounted for 3% of total food aid receipts during the 1980s.

For planning purposes, the government distinguishes between the use of food aid for (i) emergencies and (ii) for structural adjustment.

Emergency aid   The government operates in every district a centre, managed by the Ministry of Social Affairs, to provide for the needs of vulnerable groups (mothers and children, old people and invalids) and to establish an adequate infrastructure to come to the assistance of all citizens in times of disaster. Emergency aid is also necessary when disasters strike the entire population, or are so large that the district centres cannot cope. In such cases, a National Civil Defence Committee is responsible for co-ordinating activities. A state of emergency is officially declared and the inter-national community is asked to come to the country's assistance.

Structural adjustment   The government has also placed priority on providing food to those in need through a programme of structural adjustment, which has three basic elements: (i) improving the health and nutrition of vulnerable groups; (ii) attaining national food security; and (iii) using food as an investment resource for economic development.

Vulnerable groups: The district centres that provide emergency food relief are also designed to supply special assistance for the development of human resources. This includes improvement in the health and nutrition of mothers and pre-school children and a school feeding programme, both of which are seen as essential components of a long-term development strategy aimed at improving the productive capacity of the population and reducing social expenditure.

National food security: In 1983, the government established a special office, Office Nationale de Céréales (ONC), to deal with all matters pertaining to national food security, including stabilization of agricultural prices and stimulation of increased agricultural production through a policy of guaranteed producer prices. ONC's activi-ties have been limited by lack of funds for the construction of warehouses and silos, the provision of transport facilities, seed and fertilizer and support for training and research. The government has supported other initiatives, however, such as improve-ment in the traditional methods of household food storage and various measures for reducing post-harvest food losses. These initiatives have increased food security at the individual household level but their contribution to national food security has been less effective as uncontrolled trading in food with neighbouring countries continues to take place.

Food aid as an investment resource for development: The government has established three basic principles for the use of food aid within the national develop-ment strategy.

(i) First, to reduce the use of food aid as a means of emergency relief. It is considered that problems caused by natural disasters can largely be resolved by good planning and the establishment of a system capable of mobilizing the affected population in a joint effort aimed not only at combating the effects, but also the causes, of a disaster by, for example, constructing reservoirs, wells, and dams, by land rehabilitation, reforestation and seed improvement. Distribution of free emergency rations should be provided only in rare cases, such as when large-scale unforeseen disasters strike.

(ii) Second, giving emphasis to a labour-intensive, as opposed to capital-intensive, strategy for development, whereby the people are motivated and mobilized to participate actively in projects related directly to their own economic and social situation. This approach provides employment during the period outside the agricultural season and avoids competition for labour during the farming cycle.

(iii) Thirdly, and following on from the second, to use project food aid as part of the wage or as an incentive in FFW programmes, and to use the counterpart funds from the sale of programme food aid for the purchase of complementary inputs of tools, equipment and materials.

Integration of food aid in national development: The Ministry of Planning and Statistics makes estimates and prepares a plan for the internal costs and utilization of food aid in development programmes. This procedure is intended to ensure that food aid, along with other forms of development assistance, is fully integrated into the national planning process since the Ministry of Planning and Statistics is also responsible for drawing up the government's five-year plans.

Co-ordination among donors: A committee chaired by a senior official of the Ministry of Planning and Statistics, and including representatives of bilateral and multilateral donors, international financial institutions and the government, meets regularly, thus facilitating discussion on priorities and fields of intervention. Within the UN system, the UN Resident Co-ordinator convenes regular meetings of UN agency representatives to discuss their individual assistance programmes and to co-ordinate them to the maximum extent possible. The WFP country office also organizes regular meetings with the NGOs involved in rural development during which ideas are exchanged and collaboration established.

Food Aid Management and Administration

Different administrative structures have been established for handling food aid received from various donors for different purposes. Programme food aid, mainly in the form of wheat, is sold to national millers for use in urban areas. The funds generated are deposited in a government account and used, in consultation with the donors concerned, for investment in development projects.

Food aid provided by CRS is controlled and managed by that organization from the port to the beneficiary.

A special national committee (Comité National de Gestion du Projet PAM) has been established to provide overall co-ordination in the management and administration of food aid provided by WFP. The Ministry of Planning and Statistics has created a National Directorate to monitor day-to-day food aid operations. There are also individual committees in each province, which co-ordinate and control the use of WFP food aid at the provincial level and advise the National Directorate on the management and administration of assistance received from WFP.

The administrative arrangements for WFP food aid facilitate close monitoring of the assistance provided as well as the training of local personnel by the WFP country office staff. The administrative structure that has evolved reflects the government's policy of decentralizing decision-making and allowing more direct participation by local leaders. Responsibility for food aid administration is separated from the management of the technical aspects of WFP-assisted projects. As a result, technical staff do not have to spend time on the handling and distribution of food aid, and the aid itself is managed efficiently. This separation has, however, sometimes resulted in insufficient technical assistance in community development activities, for which food aid has been provided.

Project Food Aid: Uses and Impact

The government has given priority to rural development, with the double aim of satis-fying the basic needs of the population and of attaining self-reliance in food produc-tion. Improving rural living conditions is considered to be a prerequisite for preventing the drift of the population to urban centres. Project food aid has been generally used to support Benin's rural development strategy.

Multi-purpose rural development project WFP has been providing food aid to Benin since 1964. Special emphasis was given to rural development in the WFP pro-gramme of assistance in 1968. WFP aid was first approved for a nation-wide multi-purpose project for rural development in 1974. The project comprises 8 sub-projects in two categories: (i) production and infrastructure activities; and (ii) human resource development. WFP assistance has been provided as part-payment of wages or as an incentive for beneficiaries to take part in various activities. Financial, technical and material assistance for the sub-projects has been provided from many multilateral, bilateral and non-governmental organizations.

Production and infrastructure: The major sub-project of production and infrastructure activities has been community development works for rural develop-ment. The availability of food aid provided under this sub-project during the non-agricultural season has been an important factor in mobilizing the rural population to carry out works that they consider essential for improving their living conditions, pro-duction and incomes. WFP assistance has been provided for small-scale rural develop-ment projects financed by other aid organizations or donor countries including Canada, the European Community, France, Germany, the Netherlands and the United States. WFP assistance has acted as a catalyst in attracting assistance from bilateral sources.

This community development works sub-project has been the most successful of the eight sub-projects. Work undertaken can be grouped into three categories: (i) economic infrastructure, including small dams, wells, water tanks, bridges and community stores; (ii) health infrastructure, including health centres, village health units and latrines; and (iii) education facilities, including primary schools. As a result of the sub-project, a growing number of villages now have basic facilities for the rural population, reducing the inclination to migrate to the urban centres. A more stable labour force is thus being created to support increased agricultural production. Women have benefited especially from the infrastructural works, especially those relating to improvement in water supplies and health centres.

Another important sub-project supports afforestation to increase the supply of fuelwood and other wood for local use and timber and road works in the national parks. Financial assistance was obtained from the EC, the African Development Bank and Germany. WFP assistance has been used to attract workers, to maintain the labour force at remote work sites and to create new employment opportunities in rural areas. Workers are given WFP rations in addition to the minimum daily cash wage.

A further sub-project supports the government's programme to develop a comprehensive framework of feeder roads throughout the country as a basic requirement for rural development. Financial and technical assistance has been received from the World Bank and the UN Capital Development Fund (UNCDF). WFP rations have been provided to workers engaged in road construction, in addition to a minimum daily cash wage. This assistance has attracted workers and maintained the labour force at the worksites as well as improving productivity.

A well-digging programme was launched to improve the availability of drinking water, particularly in the north of the country where there is a long dry season. WFP food has been given to workers as an incentive and a supplement to their wages. Financial and technical aid was obtained from a number of sources including UNICEF, IDA, USAID and UNCDF.

The government is undertaking mineral prospecting programmes in isolated areas. The provision of WFP rations in addition to the minimum cash wage has helped to attract and retain seasonal workers. Financial and technical assistance was received from UNDP, the EC and the former Soviet Union.

Human resource development: Three sub-projects of the WFP-assisted multi-purpose project relate to the development of human resources. They include a school feeding programme, various types of training, and assistance to rural youth clubs.

Over 50,000 children in both primary and post-primary education have been fed under the school feeding programme, which has attracted more children of poor families to attend school; average rates of attendance at schools with canteen facilities have increased by 20%. Health authorities, teachers and parents have reported that the children's health and nutritional status has improved noticeably. Each school has a co-operative production unit, comprising a vegetable garden, a poultry yard and a communal production field. These units aim to achieve a better integration of education into the rural environment and to contribute to school running costs. Some produce from the gardens is eaten by the children themselves, and some is sold in the local market. The proceeds are used to buy school equipment or additional locally produced foodstuffs.

Similarly, the use of food aid to provide meals at training centres has been an important factor in enabling poor people to attend a wide range of training courses. Training in the management of co-operatives has been provided. The provincial health authorities have organized training and refresher courses for voluntary village health agents, first aid workers and midwives. The Benin Red Cross has also arranged training sessions for first-aid volunteers as well as helping handicapped people become better integrated into society. Ministries concerned with education and training have given teachers refresher courses in education and development and have organized training for extension agents and for officials who, in turn, disseminate improved agricultural technology to farmers in their own villages. The Ministry of Functional Literacy and Culture has launched a national literacy programme. Financial and technical aid has been provided from a number of UN organizations including FAO, UNCDF, UNESCO, UNFPA, UNICEF, UNIDO and WHO.

Rural youth clubs have been set up as a first step toward the establishment of village co-operatives with the aim of increasing food production. It is expected that these clubs will reduce the exodus of rural youths to the urban areas by providing them with training in improved farming techniques, thereby increasing their income and enabling them to form groups as young farmers who can improve the living conditions of their villages by increasing production and utilizing their resources more effectively. Each club has been given land for cultivation. Part of the harvest is divided among the members and the remainder marketed through the local agricultural credit banks, and this enables the clubs to buy agricultural tools and other small equipment. Seed is obtained from the government on a reimbursable basis. Food aid has played an important role in supporting the activities of these clubs. Financial and technical aid has been provided by UNICEF, UNCDF, UNDP, FAO, the World Bank and USAID. There have been some difficulties with the youth clubs, however, in terms of insufficient regular and effective guidance, lack of diversification of activities and insufficient resources and technical expertise.

Catholic Relief Services   CRS has provided project food aid from the US Government to Benin since 1959. Its main activity is a programme of food distribution and nutritional improvement for mothers and pre-school children throughout the country, reaching about 150,000 mothers and children. The programme also involves monitoring growth charts of pre-school children, giving mothers education in nutrition, encouraging community health activities and supplying supplementary food to participating households. Surveys have shown that the programme has improved the nutritional status of beneficiaries and has encouraged attendance at training sessions. Drought assistance and support for children in institutions has also been given by CRS in some years. In addition, CRS has given financial support to village-level, rural development activities. Financial and material support has also been given for village schools and classrooms.

Future Directions of Food Aid

Food aid will continue to be requested as an appropriate form of assistance to support development activities in Benin. The government is of the opinion that food aid will lose its *raison d'être* when the poor become self-reliant, rather than self-sufficient, i.e., when they have enough money to buy the food they need. The potential for increasing food aid to the country, in particular project food aid of the type provided by WFP, is closely related to its absorptive capacity in terms not only of transport, handling and storage facilities, but of the capacity to prepare and implement sound development projects.

Appendix Table 7.1 Benin: Cereal food aid receipts ('000 tons – in grain equivalent)

	1987	1988	1989	1990	1991	1987–91 Average
Total:	14.9	14.1	12.5	13.3	5.8	12.1
By food aid channel:						
– Bilateral	12.0	9.1	10.9	8.8	4.2	8.9
– Gvt. to Gvt	11.6	8.0	10.9	1.5	1.8	6.7
– through NGOs	0.4	1.1	–	7.3	2.4	2.2
– Multilateral	3.0	4.9	1.5	4.5	1.7	3.1
By food aid category:						
– Emergency Relief	–	2.3	–	–	–	0.4
– Project	10.5	8.3	7.9	11.8	4.1	8.5
– Nutrition Intervention	5.9	1.6	0.7	5.8	2.4	3.3
– Other Development Project	4.6	6.7	7.2	6.0	1.7	5.2
– Non-project	4.5	3.6	4.6	1.5	1.8	3.2
By donor[a]:						
– USA	3.5	5.2	6.4	6.9	2.4	4.9
– WFP	3.0	4.9	1.5	4.5	1.7	3.1
– Japan	4.5	–	4.6	1.5	1.8	2.4
– Germany	4.0	–	–	–	–	0.8
– Italy	–	4.0	–	–	–	0.8
EC Community Action	–	–	–	0.4	–	0.1

[a] Multilateral food aid provided through WFP appears under WFP as donor.

Source: WFP/INTERFAIS Database

Appendix Table 7.2 Benin: Non-cereal food aid receipts ('000 tons)

	1987	1988	1989	1990	1991	1987–91 Average
Total:	2.6	2.0	1.5	1.5	2.4	2.0
By food aid channel:						
– Bilateral	1.8	0.4	0.8	0.6	1.0	0.9
– Gvt-to-Gvt	1.7	0.4	0.6	–	–	0.5
– through NGOs	0.1	–	0.2	0.6	1.0	0.4
– Multilateral	0.8	1.6	0.7	0.9	1.4	1.1
By food aid category:						
– Project	2.6	2.0	1.5	1.5	2.4	2.0
– Nutrition Intervention	1.8	0.4	0.8	0.5	0.9	0.9
– Other Development Project	0.8	1.6	0.7	0.9	1.5	1.1
By donor[a]:						
– WFP	0.8	1.6	0.7	0.9	1.4	1.1
– USA	1.4	0.4	0.6	0.4	0.7	0.7
– EC Community Action	0.3	–	0.2	0.2	0.3	0.2

[a] Multilateral food aid provided through WFP appears under WFP as donor.

Source: ibid.

The provision of school meals encourages parents to send girls to school as they know their children will be fed, thereby augmenting family income. WFP/Peyton Johnson

8 Lesotho

Sustaining Development in a Small Landlocked Economy

Lesotho has one of the longest experiences of project food aid in Africa, extending over almost three decades. Within the constraints imposed by being not only landlocked but entirely surrounded by the Republic of South Africa (RSA), assistance in the form of food aid came to play a critical role in sustaining development and food security. The further constraints of an economy in which more than 40% of the adult labour force was employed in the RSA, necessitated a further social development role for food aid where effectively a large proportion of households are female-headed.

Lesotho's experience shows how project food aid can be organized to support the development and maintenance of rural infrastructure, and increases in sustainable agriculture and human resources. Lesotho's extended experience provides useful insights into the constraints on the effective use of food to support economic and social development, such as problems of the dependence of some groups on entitlements from projects, management problems in maximizing the effective use of resources, problems faced by different donors in seeking to work together in a complementary way; but all in a broadly constructive context. The rapid political changes now going on in RSA imply potentially different priorities and possibilities for development and external assistance, including food aid.

Background

Lesotho faces a unique set of circumstances and problems that derive primarily from its geographic position, as noted above. It is a small country with limited natural resources. Remittances from its migrant workers are essential in financing the heavy deficit in its balance of trade. Revenues resulting from its ties to the South African Customs Union and the Rand Monetary Area Commission account for a major portion of the funds available to finance the government budget. Its dependence on external activities and resources (including those from aid) has resulted in its GNP being nearly twice its GDP.

Another feature of Lesotho's geography that conditions its agricultural and economic potential is its altitude. The whole country is at or above 1500 metres, and most of it is mountainous. Only 9% of the land area – a narrow strip along the western side of the country, and the lower slopes of river valleys in the mountains – is suitable for

119

cultivation. Lesotho had a population of only 1.8 million in 1990, and even fewer if migrant workers are excluded. The population is largely concentrated in the limited cultivable areas, and so population density on the arable land is as high as in the heavily populated countries of Asia.

Land is held communally. Although adult males are heavily involved in wage employment in the RSA mines, farming continues to supplement incomes and to secure a place of residence in Lesotho, as there is no security of employment or right of permanent residence in the RSA. Two-thirds of farm production is for household consumption. Although the traditional land-use system operated until recently ensured that all households had access to land, in recent years intense pressure on land has resulted in a rapid increase in the number of landless households. The average size of holding is only two hectares or less. The task of achieving income and food self-sufficiency for the growing population is, therefore, becoming ever more difficult.

Agricultural problems have been exacerbated by an oscillating rainfall pattern of ten years of below-average rainfall followed by ten years of above-average rainfall. In addition, there are limited areas of readily irrigable land, a risk of hail damage to crops, and much of the cultivable soils are fragile and easily eroded.

The people of Lesotho share their limited land area with a large number of livestock. Their attachment to cattle stems from their pastoral background. Cattle have important social as well as economic roles; they serve as bride wealth as well as traction power for agriculture and as providers of milk. Sheep and goats are also kept in large numbers; they produce saleable wool and mohair, which have been important components of agricultural export earnings. As a result of the increased earnings from mining in the RSA, there has been a substantial increase in consumption of sheep and goat meat (and secondarily of beef) and a fall in wool and mohair production. There is considerable overstocking, a factor contributing to low returns from livestock and to soil erosion. Livestock have increased during the 1980s, but the number of farmers holding livestock has decreased. The major grazing herds have become more concentrated in the mountain areas among fewer owners.

Women have a heavy responsibility in Lesotho's economic and social life. Women (mostly widows) head 30% of rural households with another 30–40% managed by women whose husbands are working in the RSA. Women in Lesotho are also generally better educated than men, with higher female than male attendance at all levels of the school system except university, and higher female literacy rates. This situation has resulted from the livestock herding responsibilities of males that fell heavily on young boys as their fathers and older brothers became migrant labourers. Women also constitute 50–60% of workers on FFW programmes. Many chiefs are women, acting on behalf of absent male relatives. However, men retain authority over important production decisions, thus placing constraints on agriculture. Some agricultural activities are also gender-related, for example women almost never participate in ploughing and planting.

Lesotho faces a severe challenge in generating jobs for its growing labour force, particularly in view of the stagnation and current decline in employment in the mines in the RSA. The present unemployment rate is estimated to be about 35%. Agriculture will have to provide most new jobs as other sectors of the economy are very small. This will be a difficult task because many of those currently considered to be employed in agriculture are underemployed.

Food Aid

WFP assistance to Lesotho began just before independence in 1966 and has been included as an integral part of a succession of five-year plans beginning in 1970/71. In all four planning periods to date, emphasis has been placed on four areas that have accounted for approximately 75% of anticipated expenditure: (i) increasing agricultural productivity, primarily through large area-based projects; (ii) expanding and remodelling the country's education system; (iii) constructing an economic infrastructure, with special attention to roads; and (iv) developing the social infrastructure, including health and nutrition services, water, sewage and sanitation. Food assistance has been provided for implementing projects in all these areas. Despite the growing recognition of the contribution of food aid to development, however, it has tended to be viewed only as a resource to facilitate the implementation of specific projects. Its use has not been seen as a contribution to the achievement of the government's overall aims.

Lesotho has received a high proportion of its food aid from WFP. Other major donors have been the EC Commission and Japan. The United States has been the principal source, however, as it has not only supplied the food and resources to CRS but is also the major provider of food to WFP.

The first food aid request approved by WFP in 1965 related to a pre-school and school feeding project. WFP assistance to primary school feeding has continued up to the present, although the project has been reoriented towards self-sufficiency and a gradual phasing out of assistance. Similarly, WFP assistance for FFW for soil and water conservation and road improvement approved in 1966 is still in operation. WFP has supplied some wheat for sale under this project to generate funds to provide other inputs needed for road construction. WFP also supported an institutional feeding programme from 1970 until 1989 and has been involved in two projects to establish strategic reserves of maize and wheat. WFP has provided considerable emergency assistance in response to drought in 1968, 1970, 1983 and 1986. It also co-ordinated food relief from other donors for the widespread drought in 1992.

CRS also began project food aid operations in Lesotho at independence in 1966, distributing food commodities from the US Government. The CRS programme reached pre-school children and workers and their dependants in FFW programmes. It has also supplied other resources to improve food aid management, such as warehouses for the storage of commodities at district locations and at individual project sites.

WFP transferred implementation of its pre-school feeding activities to CRS in 1974 in order to avoid duplication and because CRS had the facilities for overseeing operations at MCH centres. WFP supported the CRS programme for several years thereafter with supplies of dried milk powder and blended foods. Other donors supplied limited amounts of food in the early years of the feeding programme but it was not until the late 1970s that they began to provide aid in significant quantities. CRS phased out its operations in Lesotho in 1990.

While WFP and CRS provided project food aid only for specific projects and groups of people, the EC Commission began providing programme food aid to Lesotho in 1978. This food aid has been sold and the funds generated used for projects agreed between the Lesotho Government and the EC Commission. Funds were used at first to pay for additional warehouses; more recently, they have been used to relieve drought conditions and for agricultural development projects. The EC Commission has also provided limited amounts of sugar for sale, and milk and butter oil that have been used mainly in the primary school feeding programme. Rice was supplied in 1983 for the drought emergency programme and distributed to hospital patients.

Japan also provides about 2,000 tons of cereals annually, which is sold and the funds generated used to support WFP-assisted development projects.

Quantitative overview of food assistance

Nutritional considerations: In 1976, 41% of food supplies were provided direct from farms, 23% from locally marketed farm surpluses, 29% from commercial imports and 7% from food aid. However, since then, food aid and commercial imports have increased significantly, while local production has declined, principally because of drought and the decrease in cultivable land. Food aid now accounts for 5% of the country's total cereal requirements. Calorific availabilities are now adequate, according to available nutritional information. Protein availabilities are only barely sufficient, however, and there are still deficiencies in niacin, calcium, riboflavin and vitamin A. Thus, the nutritional value of the food aid programme is important.

The contribution of food aid is especially significant in the diets of the poor. A food survey carried out in 1976 (Colorado University/National University of Lesotho, 1978) found that a third of households had insufficient income in cash or in kind to meet their basic energy requirements. As surveys indicate that a high proportion of the participants in FFW, in particular, are from landless households, or from households headed by elderly widows, food aid is important in their total food supply (Lawry, 1986).

Production and imports: Concern has been expressed at the possible disincentive effects of food aid on Lesotho's agricultural production and trade. Both food aid and commercial imports of major commodities have increased significantly as Lesotho's self-sufficiency with respect to these foods has declined. Cereal food aid has increased but also non-cereal commodities as the number of children in the primary school feeding programme has increased.

Food aid administration Several departments of the government are involved in different aspects of the administration and management of food aid. Donors and NGOs involved also participate more or less extensively in food management, depending on the nature of their aid programmes and the operating procedures they are required to follow.

Since 1978, a Food Management Unit (FMU) in the Office of the Prime Minister, from 1986 under the Military Council, has had general responsibility for the overall programming and management of food aid, including co-ordination with donors. Line ministries and NGOs are responsible for the day-to-day field operations of the various project activities. The NGOs most closely associated with the programmes have been, until recently, CRS, and now Save the Children Fund. At the field level, feeding activities or food distribution take place at nearly 1,000 sites. Donor organizations generally maintain only an overview of operations and have been most extensively involved in project evaluation. Some donors have also supplied technical personnel to serve in operating positions in the government related to food assistance activities.

FMU serves as a central co-ordinating point for all food-aided projects and programmes and is responsible for receiving and storing commodities and transporting them to district warehouses and substores. All ministries advise FMU of their food needs, the timing of supplies and the amounts required by feeding district. FMU liaises with donors to negotiate agreements with respect to programming of supplies and to assist in the resolution of problems. It also supplies the food management accounts required by donors. Ministries take responsibility for transportation and accounting for food aid commodities from the time they leave FMU warehouses.

The major administrative problem of the food aid programme is logistical. Organizing commodity movements within the country presents difficulties, given both the costs involved, particularly in transporting food to the mountain areas, and the state of the road network. All organizations now rely on the government transport company or on private contractors for food movements. The Save the Children Fund (UK) has had to use all modes of transport to reach some of the more remote schools included in the school feeding project, including, in some cases, donkeys and head-loading. Problems are compounded by limited storage space available at schools. Another major administrative problem is a general lack of management information on current stock levels and requirements.

Project Food Aid

Project food aid dominated the Lesotho food aid programme until 1978, and still accounts for most foods donated to the country.

FFW programmes: FFW in Lesotho has a multiplicity of purposes. Descriptions of FFW in the development plans and in donor documents clearly identify its developmental contribution. However, FFW was begun in Lesotho for volunteer workers and to alleviate drought conditions, and has continued to have significant welfare features that are a barrier to the achievement of development targets. Essentially, there has been a dichotomy between the achievement of specific development goals and targets (such as a completed road), that are time-limited in nature, and the open-ended welfare objective to support the poorest and most disadvantaged members of society.

At independence in 1966, the government faced the task of generating progress in a mountainous country with very poor infrastructure. Until the mid-1960s there was only one mile of tarred road in the whole country. Outside the western and southern border areas there were virtually no roads and only some tracks leading into the mountains. The newly independent government appealed for villages to undertake voluntary road building activities as well as dam construction and soil conservation works. There was a substantial response, particularly from women who were in the majority in the rural labour force. The mid-1960s was also a period of drought. The government wanted to provide food to relieve the situation in the villages, but was opposed to simply giving food away as a hand-out as it could create a disincentive for future production when the drought lifted. It was decided to give the food to people who volunteered to work on roads and dams.

A system evolved of village-level management with government overview of projects. Village development committees (VDC) submitted proposals for projects to district-level committees which, in turn, submitted their approved list to the central government for final selection of the projects to be supported. Upon notification that a project was approved, the VDC concerned organized a roster from which workers for each work session were chosen. The workers elected their supervisors and the VDC supervised payment of workers when food supplies arrived in the village.

The villages used this system partly to meet the welfare needs of the community and included on the rosters a high proportion of landless, aged and/or handicapped people. Other welfare features also became apparent over time, especially the tendency to organize numerous projects spread around the countryside, each involving a small number of workers, thus distributing the food resource as widely as possible. Very few resources were available to provide the other inputs needed for effective development activities (except where FFW was programmed as a component of development projects, as discussed below). Workers often provided their own tools. There was only very limited technical assistance, training, effective supervision and material resources to assure the quality of the structures being built. When the welfare features of FFW were coupled with these shortcomings, it is easy to appreciate why the rural participants in FFW considered that they were working mainly to obtain food. Less emphasis was placed on their expectations with respect to benefits to be derived from the development activity.

FFW has also been used to some extent in large area-based agricultural development and in a woodlots project, where significant levels of technical and material resources were made available, largely by donors, in addition to food aid. Village-level control of the selection and supervision of workers was maintained in most cases, although in some projects funds were provided for cash wages or supplements, in addition to food, for workgang supervisors. It has been used for such tasks as building roads, constructing terraces, grassing waterways, maintaining tree nurseries and planting and tending trees. Most of the projects have been highly ambitious, especially in view of the limited number of trained staff of the Ministry of Agriculture. In some cases, initial successes were registered in increasing crop yields but these tended to disappear when the material inputs and technical assistance provided by donors were phased out.

The accomplishments of FFW are difficult to isolate from the other elements of development projects. When projects have been unsuccessful, they have detracted from the value of the FFW contribution. Yet the FFW programme as a whole has had three important achievements: the construction of three-quarters of the country's road network (at least 3,000 km out of a total of 4,000 km); important soil conservation works; and the establishment of about 9,000 hectares of trees in the period up to 1992, which will make a major contribution to the fuelwood and timber needs of the country in future as well as helping soil conservation.

Considerable effort has been expended on improving the management of FFW programmes. The need to improve productivity and to strengthen the developmental approach of FFW activities has been recognized. Measures to achieve this include: tools and equipment acquired with funds generated from monetization, use of monetized funds to assist in harvesting and marketing of wood from forest plantations, increased cash incentives paid to workers in addition to the food ration, improved work norms and experiments in compensating workers according to a piece-work approach instead of the number of hours worked, and in establishing day-care centres to look after young children in order to enable their mothers to participate in FFW road construction. These new arrangements have several advantages for the workers. They can organize their FFW work more flexibly in relation to their domestic and other responsibilities. Workers can earn the same wages in less time. And increased responsibility for organizing their work is given directly to the villagers. Early results are positive. In some cases, road construction has progressed at twice the former rate.

Food assistance for vulnerable groups: The nutritional problems of Lesotho were starkly revealed by a nutrition survey conducted by WHO between 1956 and 1960, which provided the first comprehensive data on malnutrition in the country (see Colorado University/National University of Lesotho, 1978). The survey found widespread dietary deficiencies: 30% of the children were underweight, 15% of the population suffered from pellagra during the summer period, and 15% had goitre. As a result, a Permanent Bureau of Nutrition (PBN), which included representatives of various government ministries, donor organizations and NGOs, was set up in 1961 to co-ordinate activities in nutrition improvement.

The Save the Children Fund began a primary school feeding programme in 1961. An Applied Food and Nutrition Programme (AFNP) was started in 1962 as a joint project of the government and FAO, WHO and UNICEF. Its objective was to improve the nutritional status of the population through increased production and consumption of nutritious foods. It originally began in seven pilot areas and was eventually expanded to cover most of the country.

The PBN was intended to be the co-ordinating body for the AFNP and was responsible for organizing primary school feeding activities in AFNP areas. It was also expected to be the government agency responsible for overseeing other nutrition programmes supported by WFP and CRS that involved food supplements. It was not very effective, however, as it was an advisory committee without administrative personnel or executive powers. An Office of the Food Aid Programmes (FAP) was therefore created in 1967 within the Prime Minister's Office, with responsibility for all food aid activities. The SCF was made an agent responsible to the FAP. In the late 1970s, a Food and Nutrition Co-ordinating Office (FNCO) was created, originally in the Prime Minister's Office but it later moved to the Ministry of Agriculture. This was to serve as a focal point for nutrition concerns, the analysis of nutritional data and co-ordination of the programmes of the various ministries.

Primary school feeding: SCF (Lesotho) is almost entirely composed of volunteers and derives its funds from voluntary donations. Its outstanding achievements have included reaching schools throughout the country with food supplies and providing each school with the materials necessary to establish a school garden as well as building kitchens and storage areas at many of them. Other voluntary organizations, especially OXFAM, have assisted with kitchens and kitchen equipment, eating utensils and water supplies.

By the early 1970s, the school feeding programme had reached 87% of all primary schools in the country and almost two-thirds of the total enrolment. The programme continued to expand, reaching 70% of total enrolment by 1980. SCF (Lesotho) found it difficult to keep up the level of deliveries required to cover the higher percentage of enrolment, however, and WFP supply targets were also set lower than the enrolment increases. The programme also ran into some other difficulties. For example, it appeared that a much higher proportion of urban than rural children were being reached. In 1980 it was decided to strengthen the management of SCF activities, and SCF (UK) took over the project management and provided a field director and other staff. All schools recognized by the Ministry of Education are now covered by the programme, and almost all enrolled children receive school meals. With the delivery problem under better control, SCF has been able to turn its attention to other pressing problems, in particular the need to provide or improve adequate storage and cooking facilities and water supplies at schools.

The government has consistently committed 20% of its national budget to education, half of which goes to primary education. A high proportion of children now attend school. The government views the school lunch programme as part of the country's education programme, but the Ministry of Education has limited staff who already have to cope with other problems such as shortage of trained teachers and classrooms, and lack of educational materials and textbooks. The Ministry is therefore understandably reluctant to take over responsibility for the large school feeding programme. Nonetheless, it is important that this large-scale effort be institutionalized within the government. Steps are now being taken to promote self-reliance among schools for their own feeding programmes and to pass over responsibility to the government as WFP assistance is gradually phased out.

Mothers and pre-school children: In 1965, WFP began support to the government to help improve the health and nutritional status of expectant and nursing mothers, pre-school children, tuberculosis out-patients and persons suffering from severe malnutrition. The following year, CRS started a programme which initially concentrated on children but was later extended to include mothers. WFP judged that its recipient groups would be served more effectively if they were included in the CRS programme. Accordingly, in 1974 WFP decided to phase out its own programme and provided food to CRS for distribution, including milk and blended foods that CRS found difficult to procure. This arrangement continued until 1979, when CRS received adequate supplies for all activities from the US Government.

Significant improvements in nutrition have been achieved since the WHO survey in the 1950s. These improvements have resulted from food assistance programmes and nutrition interventions and from general improvements in the standard of living brought about especially by rising wages from mining in the RSA.

Emergency Operations and Strategic Food Reserves

Expansion of on-going food-assisted projects rather than the provision of emergency food relief helped to relieve the consequences of drought in 1968/9 and 1970/72. However, considerable emergency assistance was supplied by a number of donors to help 200,000 people severely affected by the famine after a particularly bad harvest in 1982/3.

At that time, the government again wanted to use FFW as a mechanism to distribute drought relief, since it was concerned about the disincentive effects of food relief hand-outs. However, donors felt that the efforts being made to improve the technical standard of FFW programmes would be undermined by over-burdening them with large numbers of additional workers to supervise. A decision was made, therefore, to make a free distribution of only three months' food supply to needy households. Criteria for determining whether households were in need of emergency food aid were established for the use of village development committees. Considerable difficulties were experienced at all levels of the operation and commodities were slow to reach the intended beneficiaries. However, by 1984 the government believed it had eased most of the bottlenecks in the system.

Income from mining in the RSA during the prolonged drought of the early to mid-1980s was much higher than during previous drought periods, and cushioned many households against the effects of loss of production. The households most affected were the poor without access to wage income who had too little to eat even in favourable years.

In addition to drought, Lesotho has also faced the problem of control of the movement of supplies into the country by the RSA. Concern with this problem became acute in the late 1970s after the closure of the border with the Transkei. A UN mission visited Lesotho in 1977 and recommended the establishment of a national reserve consisting of 20,000 tons of wheat. It was also recognized that there was need to hold stocks of maize in the mountain areas, as they were worst served by commercial marketing operations. Plans were developed to use food aid donations as a basis for establishing reserve stocks for both purposes.

Two types of reserve were therefore set up: (i) strategic reserves to be held at the wheat and maize milling plants, and (ii) stocks of maize that were to be held in FMU warehouses and Co-op Lesotho stores in the mountain areas. These stocks were to be continuously recycled; after the initial food donations, the government was to replace stocks using the funds realized from the sale of donated foods to finance purchases. However, this approach was not fully implemented. WFP has been the only donor to provide grain. Only a 2,000 ton reserve of maize held by the Lesotho Milling Company has been maintained; white maize consigned to Co-op Lesotho and fortified yellow maize meal managed by FMU have been used and not replaced. As a result, reserves of maize amount to only one month's supply.

Future Directions of Food Assistance

Food aid has played a positive role in Lesotho's development and the welfare of its population. Women have been the principal recipients. There is now concern that greater emphasis should be placed on activities that generate permanent employment in rural areas faced with an uncertain economic situation, which could include retrenchment of thousands of workers from the mines in the RSA. Ways of increasing the productivity and developmental impact of FFW also need to be explored. Even if donors are prepared to permit total monetization of food donations to pay wages in cash rather than in food, many government officials feel that problems of misappropriation and other negative effects, such as male monopolization of employment and the use of wages for purposes unrelated to family welfare, would cause considerable suffering in rural areas. The consensus appears to be that FFW should continue but with changes in the types of project supported, improvements in planning and management, increased technical and material inputs and increase in the cash supplementation of largely food wages. A clear separation of welfare needs and development requirements would help resolve the problem of the low productivity of FFW projects.

Although concerns about production disincentives can be excessive, Lesotho remains economically vulnerable because of its dependence for its food supply on mine wage remittances from the RSA and external donors. Lesotho has no control over restrictions that could be placed on mining employment or over donor decisions. Neither situation has been seen as desirable in terms of the country's long-term food security or its wider economic independence.

Higher returns from agriculture could be achieved if there was a shift to the production of high-value food crops and to intensive livestock production. Such a move could also improve the nutritional status of the population. It would represent substantial new risks for rural households, however, and would require new skills. The process of change would have to be supported by programmes to cushion the risks, especially those relating to family food supply, and to tide the poor farming communities over the period of adjustment. The creative use of food assistance could support the process, particularly if it formed part of programmes that included other resources (financial, technical and material) necessary to change farming systems and generate production increases.

The government's Central Planning and Development Office recognizes the need to develop a comprehensive plan for disaster mitigation and food security that incorporates food aid, but it lacks the planning resources for such an extensive effort. Political change in the RSA opens up the prospect of radical changes in the economic environment for Lesotho. But before these developments take effect, and despite the progress made with the help of food aid, there is a considerable body of opinion, both amongst the population and within the donor organizations, that holds that rethinking is required about future food-assisted projects. Women's leaders have pointed out that women have been working on the infrastructure for many years, but villages for which structures have been built are still food insecure and employment ends when FFW programmes are completed. Many villagers believe they are working only for the food aid they receive. If food assistance is to result in lasting benefits and the sustained and equitable economic growth needed to make real improvements in the standard of living of rural people, changes should be made in FFW programmes to remove their welfare image and to plan and execute effective development projects. Changes in donor attitudes, especially concerning multi-year programming of food aid and monetization to provide funds for other necessary inputs, also suggest that broader and longer-term planning of Lesotho's food assistance activities is both necessary and possible. There is now the added challenge of redefining priorities and possibilities in the potentially far more positive, but uncertain, environment of a post-apartheid South Africa.

References

Colorado University/National University of Lesotho (1978). *An Exploratory Study of the Food System of Lesotho*. Report to the Lesotho Food and Nutrition Co-ordinating Office. Boulder, CO and Roma, Lesotho.

Lawry, S. (1986). *The Selabathbe Household Survey 1986*. Government of Lesotho, Ministry of Agriculture.

Appendix Table 8.1 *Lesotho: Cereal food aid receipts ('000 tons – in grain equivalent)*

	1987	1988	1989	1990	1991	1987–91 Average
Total:	43.5	44.5	25.6	39.1	20.2	34.6
By food aid channel:						
– Bilateral	22.0	34.3	17.2	9.7	10.3	18.7
– Gvt-to-Gvt	17.0	31.0	8.8	9.7	10.3	15.4
– through NGOs	5.0	3.3	8.4	–	–	3.4
– Multilateral	21.4	10.1	8.4	29.4	9.9	15.9
By food aid category:						
– Emergency Relief	–	–	0.1	–	–	–
– Project	31.2	23.1	16.8	29.4	9.9	22.1
– Agr./Rural Development	14.1	9.2	5.7	14.9	5.5	9.9
– Nutrition Intervention	2.7	9.6	5.4	–	–	3.6
– Other Development Project	14.4	4.3	5.7	14.5	4.4	8.7
– Non-project (Programme)	12.2	21.4	8.8	9.7	10.3	12.5
By donor[a]:						
– WFP	21.4	10.1	8.4	29.4	9.9	15.9
– EC Community Action	10.0	15.7	7.0	7.0	7.9	9.5
– USA	9.9	13.0	8.4	–	–	6.3
– Japan	2.2	5.7	1.7	2.7	2.4	2.9

[a] Multilateral food aid provided through WFP appears under WFP as donor.

Source: WFP/INTERFAIS Database

Appendix Table 8.2 *Lesotho: Non-cereal food aid receipts ('000 tons)*

	1987	1988	1989	1990	1991	1987–91 Average
Total:	13.9	5.2	5.2	4.3	2.8	6.3
By food aid channel:						
– Bilateral	7.3	2.7	0.9	–	–	2.2
– Gvt-to-Gvt	5.2	2.7	–	–	–	1.6
– through NGOs	2.1	–	0.9	–	–	0.6
– Multilateral	6.6	2.4	4.3	4.3	2.7	4.1
By food aid category:						
– Project	13.9	5.2	5.2	4.3	2.8	6.3
– Agr./Rural Development	2.9	0.3	0.6	0.8	0.8	1.1
– Nutrition Intervention	5.6	2.7	0.7	–	–	1.8
– Other Development Project	5.4	2.1	3.8	3.4	1.9	3.3
By donor[a]:						
– WFP	7.3	2.7	0.9	–	–	2.2
– USA	6.6	2.5	4.3	4.3	2.8	4.1

[a] Multilateral food aid provided through WFP appears under WFP as donor.

Source: ibid.

Sisal was formerly known as 'green gold' in Tanzania. A WFP-assisted project, which provides housing and subsidized food, has made working in the sisal industry more attractive, increased productivity and reduced absenteeism. WFP/Michael Pickstock

Nurses receive WFP food aid while undergoing training. WFP/Francis Mwanza

9 Tanzania

Self-reliance, Economic Growth & Equity

Experience of Tanzania's development policies and strategies highlights a number of the dilemmas that face many countries in sub-Saharan Africa. Self-reliance, economic growth and equity issues are particularly relevant to the roles and effectiveness of food aid.

The Tanzanian experience brings out several issues of special concern for food aid policies and programmes. First, Tanzania has an evolving policy framework within which the government's long-held objective of self-reliance is being pursued alongside policy adjustments designed to attain a better balance between growth and equity. This has implications for food aid. Secondly, significant adjustments are taking place in the agriculture sector, which is the mainstay of the economy. Food aid has provided support to that sector through a range of different programmes and projects. The adoption of thoroughgoing reform measures is likely to influence the future roles of food aid.

Thirdly, Tanzania has regional disparities, which affect food production, marketing and distribution. Cyclical droughts further complicate national and regional food security. In view of shortages of foreign exchange to pay for commercial food imports, food aid is likely to be required in the years ahead to meet shortfalls in supplies. Fourthly, problems of suitable storage, transportation, marketing and distribution exist alongside the country's export potential. Food aid can assist in overcoming these problems and in fostering exports through FFW, monetization, triangular transactions, local purchases and exchange of commodities. Fifthly, structural adjustment measures need to incorporate programmes for the alleviation of poverty for the most vulnerable groups as an essential element, including programmes for the promotion of employment. The roles that food aid could play in supporting such programmes need to be examined.

Sixthly, the effectiveness and appropriateness of food aid will depend on careful planning, targeting and co-ordination with other development resources. Multi-year programming of food aid would facilitate decisions regarding commodity selection and forward planning. Funds generated from food aid sales provided by different donors require co-ordination, perhaps in a common fund that would also facilitate their better integration into overall government development planning.

Finally, the Tanzanian experience includes successful food-aided refugee settlements

131

involving a large number of people, and these have resulted in productive and self-sustaining village communities. This experience provides an example for other countries hosting refugee populations.

Background

Tanzania became independent in 1961. Following the adoption of the Arusha Declaration of 1967, the government pursued, consistently and determinedly, the objectives of 'socialism and self-reliance'. The international community gave strong support to these endeavours, providing Tanzania with development assistance which, in per capita terms, has been among the highest in Africa. Although Tanzania made impressive gains in the social sectors, however, it was recognized that economic growth was essential if its achievements were to be sustained. The Economic Recovery Programme (ERP), launched in June 1986 as part of the government's evolving development policy framework, reflected an assessment of two decades of experience following the Arusha Declaration, and represented a bold effort to put the country on a course of growth with equity after several years of serious economic decline.

The United Republic of Tanzania comprises mainland regions and the islands of Zanzibar. It is one of the largest countries in sub-Saharan Africa both in terms of size (about 945,000 sq km) and population (24.5 million in 1990). It is also one of the poorest, with per capita GNP of only $ 110 in 1990. The population growth rate was estimated at 3.1% per annum during the 1980s.

As already noted, the country has made notable progress in providing social services to its population. Since 1986, adult literacy has been 90%, compared with the sub-Saharan African average of 49%. Life expectancy, at 54 years in 1990, is also above the sub-Saharan African average. Child mortality has fallen in recent years largely because of an immunization rate of 80% in 1990. In rural areas, 46% of the population had access to safe water in 1987-90, compared with an average of 28% for rural sub-Saharan Africa as a whole. However, poor economic performance has resulted in a lack of adequate resources to maintain the high delivery of social services. Malnutrition, and regional imbalances in food supplies, have also become causes for concern.

The government's policy has been to extend the role of the state to all sectors of the economy. As in many other African countries, there is a large traditional rural sector and a small, capital-intensive, modern urbanized sector. Linkages between the two are not strong. The agricultural sector could produce the bulk of the raw materials needed for domestic industry and food for the urban population, as well as export earnings. Large foreign-owned sisal, tea and coffee estates have been nationalized, but food production is still predominantly dependent on private subsistence farming. In the late 1960s, the government began to group scattered settlements into what were called 'ujamaa' (communal) villages. This approach was not without merit, although the pace and manner of its implementation caused considerable controversy.

The economy has declined significantly since the late 1970s for a number of external and internal reasons. The country's international terms of trade have deteriorated. Several years of unfavourable weather have reduced domestic agricultural production and increased the need for food imports. Adverse developments in the economy have also been affected by domestic policies, such as the abolition of co-operatives in the early 1970s, inadequate producer prices (that have persisted over a long period), an over-valued exchange rate, and the lack of basic consumer goods.

Persisting balance of payments difficulties led the government to place renewed emphasis on agriculture, and the production of both food and cash crops. A National Economic Survival Programme (NESP), introduced in 1981, was succeeded in 1982 by a three-year Structural Adjustment Programme. The ambitious targets of these programmes were largely not met, but they constituted the beginning of a necessary adjustment process.

The ERP, launched in 1986, was a comprehensive programme designed to combat the country's economic problems. A meeting of the Consultative Group of donors for Tanzania, organized by the World Bank in July 1987, supported the ERP and indicated that the total financing requirements (including further debt relief) of US$955 million in 1988 would be met. As in the case of other developing countries, food aid was not included in the overall external resource requirements drawn up for the meeting, although such aid could help ease foreign-exchange constraints, since scarce foreign exchange is often spent on food. It could also assist reconstruction and development activities by helping to meet local and recurrent costs.

By the end of the 1980s, government policies were beginning to have an impact, although many problems remained and much of the country's infrastructure continued to degenerate. The reform measures have included progressive exchange-rate and interest-rate adjustment, tight fiscal policies and liberalization of the trade regime. The adoption and on-going implementation of some major economic and financial policy reforms, the inflow of external resources (bilateral and multilateral), and generally good weather conditions, have contributed to improvements in economic performance particularly in agriculture. In terms of overall performance as measured by GDP, the result has been relatively impressive. GDP grew by an average of 3.7% in real terms in 1987–90 compared with 0.9% a year over the period 1983–6.

Trade liberalization and related reform measures have helped to stimulate exports, in particular, non-traditional exports. A deterioration in the social sectors was experienced during implementation of the Structural Adjustment Programme. Those most seriously affected were health and education. In consequence the government initiated a Priority Social Action Programme (PSAP) as a medium-term programme designed to address pressing social needs and to provide a framework for long-term development of these sectors as an integral part of the socio-economic transformation process. Sectors being addressed through PSAP are health, education, water supply, food security, and income and employment generation.

Traditionally, Tanzania has received strong support from the international community through relatively large inflows of external assistance. Total official development assistance in 1989 was US$906 million, or over $30 per capita. Although food aid constitutes a relatively small part of total ODA, the funds generated from the sale of bilateral programme food aid, and some project food aid, are sizeable. Food aid therefore brings significant budgetary and economic benefits, but requires systematic co-ordination by the government and among donors.

Food and Agriculture

Agriculture accounted for 59% of GDP in 1990, 59% of export earnings, and employed 85% of the labour force. About 80% of the population live in the rural areas. Small-scale farming provides about 75% of agricultural export earnings and about 80% of the value of marketed cereal production.

Lack of water, poor soils and insects are major constraints on crop production in most of Tanzania. Except in the highlands, there is often either too much, or too little, rainfall. Agricultural production is therefore vulnerable to erratic rainfall, especially as only 3% of the area under cultivation is irrigated. Programmes to combat soil erosion and deforestation are urgently needed.

The main cereals grown and marketed are maize, rice and wheat. While maize and rice production has increased steadily, wheat production has fluctuated considerably. A high proportion of the food produced is consumed on-farm. There are wide differences in agricultural production and potential across the country. The predominance of eight regions (out of 20) in food production has major implications for planning, marketing and distribution, as well as for an import strategy. The main food producing areas are inland, generally far from the largest areas of consumption along the coast. The national food strategy has attempted to address this problem by encouraging regional specialization in the production of particular crops.

There is considerable unrealized potential in the livestock sector, which is dominated by traditional livestock husbandry. Similarly, there is scope for large increases in fish production, but this is threatened by destructive fishing practices along the coast.

Cash-crop farming, manufacturing, mining, transportation and construction activities rely heavily on imported inputs, while foreign-exchange earnings rely heavily on the export performance of a small group of primary commodities, mainly coffee, cotton, tea, tobacco, sisal, cashewnuts, and cloves. Tanzania is extremely sensitive to fluctuations in commodity prices and to deteriorations in its terms of trade. Intra-African trade accounts for a minor part of foreign trade. However, the prospects for growth in trade with neighbouring countries look promising with Tanzania's active role in the Southern African Development Community (SADC) and the Preferential Trade Area (PTA).

Coffee has been the most valuable export product since the mid-1970s. During the period 1980–85, it accounted for almost half of total agricultural earnings, and a third of all export earnings. Total coffee production increased steadily in the early 1980s, but since then has slowly declined. Tanzania is the third largest sisal producer in the world, contributing about 9% of world output. Sisal accounts for 2% of foreign-exchange earnings. Production fell during the 1970s and early 1980s, but a rehabilitation programme has since resulted in increased production.

The agricultural sector as a whole is severely hampered by problems related to the distribution of production inputs which are closely related to the inadequate provision of credit. In 1984-5, co-operative unions were revived and parastatal bodies reverted to their former status as essentially marketing boards. Co-operatives took over the collection of crops from farmers and transportation to a much reduced number of National Milling Corporation (NMC) depots. Meanwhile, an open market system has flourished resulting in a wide difference between official and unofficial prices. In addition, the government took steps in the second half of the 1980s to diversify marketing of food grains and to reform the institutional structure for the marketing and processing of export crops. It recognized that adequate price incentives were necessary to stimulate increased agricultural production and exports.

Food production has generally lagged behind the demands of a growing and increasingly urbanized population for most of the past two decades. Cash-crop production has not been able to produce the foreign exchange that is crucial to sustained growth and development. As a result of a combination of policy reforms and favourable weather, tentative steps have been made towards re-establishing self-sufficiency in maize production. However, deficient rainfall since mid-1991 has contributed to reduced crop yields and overall self-sufficiency in food is still far from being achieved. In addition, the country's considerable potential in the livestock sector and in fish production remains largely unrealized. Food aid could therefore continue to play an important part in promoting food security for some time to come.

Food Aid

Tanzania has received food aid since independence in 1961. At the height of critical domestic food shortages during the early to mid-1980s, it played a crucial role in averting crises, especially in the major urban centres at a time when most commercial imports were reduced as foreign-exchange earnings from exports declined. Cereal food aid declined significantly, however, during the latter half of the 1980s. Non-cereal food, comprising only 4% of the total quantity of food aid receipts, has been mainly in the form of dried skimmed milk, butter oil, vegetable oil, dried salted fish, canned fish and pulses. Over the period 1989–91, WFP has been the most important provider of cereal food aid to Tanzania. Over the same period, programme food aid accounted for about a fifth, project food aid over half, and emergency food aid about a quarter of the total quantity of food aid receipts.

Tanzania received significant quantities of maize from Zimbabwe and of wheat from India in 1983-4 under triangular food aid operations, a good example of the use of food aid to strengthen South-South co-operation and stimulate trade among developing countries.

Food aid does not appear as a separate component in the country's development plans. It is linked directly to annual plans, however, in the sense that development activities earmarked for funding from food aid sales are included in national budgetary exercises.

Administration and logistics   The Ministry of Finance and Economic Planning is responsible for the overall administration of programme food aid. Cereal food aid deliveries are received by the NMC, the parastatal body responsible for all grain milling and marketing in Tanzania. Funds generated from the sale of programme food aid are channelled to the government Treasury through the Ministry of Agriculture, Livestock Development and Co-operatives. Project food aid is normally co-ordinated by the sector Ministry concerned.

A National Disaster Preparedness Unit in the Office of the Prime Minister and First Vice-President co-ordinates emergency relief operations. A number of emergency operations have been mounted since 1978, mostly in aid of drought victims. Emergency food needs can be quickly communicated through well-defined lines of communication from village committees throughout the country. Experience from past emergencies has revealed a lack of adequate logistical support, however, that has been a major constraint to effective distribution of relief assistance. The WFP country office in Dar es-Salaam maintains close co-operation with the FAO-assisted Early Warning Unit in the Ministry of Agriculture, Livestock Development and Co-operatives. This unit monitors food production countrywide.

In response to the chronic drought situation and consequent food insecurity in the north-central region in 1987, the member agencies of the Joint Consultative Group on Policy (IFAD, UNDP, UNICEF, UNFPA and WFP) launched a number of joint projects aimed at addressing some of the root causes of the region's agricultural and economic vulnerability. They included dam construction, seed multiplication, forestry and community development activities. FAO and ILO joined in these collaborative efforts.

Food Aid for Agricultural and Rural Development

Monetized programme food aid: Substantial funds have been generated from the sale of food aid, and more are expected to accrue from future food aid supplies. These have provided substantial budgetary support for development activities in various sectors of the economy, especially in agriculture and livestock production, and constitute an important supplementary resource to implement priority activities in the ERP. Efforts need to be made, however, to find even more effective and better co-ordinated uses of sales proceeds in order to enhance their developmental impact and to speed up the utilization of funds. This could be achieved through the establishment of a common fund for all food aid donors, in the ERP.

Food aid has made a substantial contribution to the balance of payments. However, poor co-ordination between the government and donors on overall import planning has tended to reduce potential foreign-exchange savings from food aid.

Cash crops and agricultural diversification: The sisal industry has been in decline since the early 1970s, mainly because profits and investment have not been sufficient to sustain growth. The main reasons for this have been an unfavourable exchange rate, high production costs and competition with synthetic fibres. Problems faced by the industry have been aggravated by the deterioration of equipment and the loss of experienced management and labour, especially sisal cutters, worsening terms of trade and depressed prices caused by a glut of sisal on the world market.

WFP assistance was sought to assist the sisal industry by helping to stabilize the workforce through improving workers' housing on the sisal estates and by supplying commodities to the labour force at subsidized rates. Labour is critical to the industry. In turn, the availability of food and housing together provide a powerful incentive to attract and retain workers. Most of the workers' settlements are located far from food production and marketing centres, making the availability and price of food a critical factor influencing the retention of labour. The provision of WFP food rations to 17,000 sisal workers tempered what would almost certainly have been a collapse in labour supply for the estates, with far-reaching and perhaps irreversible effects for the industry. In preventing that collapse, WFP assistance also served as a catalyst for attracting additional resources from donors including the International Finance Corporation (IFC) and Germany. Proceeds from the sales of food aid to the workers at subsidized prices have been used for the construction of workers' houses.

Measures adopted under the ERP have set the stage for improvement in the sisal industry more generally. A modest recovery in production has already been achieved. Further progress will depend on the successful implementation of the government's overall plans for the reorganization and rehabilitation of the industry.

Agricultural diversification and production on Zanzibar: Though part of the United Republic of Tanzania, Zanzibar retains autonomy over its economic and social institutions and planning. The islands are inhabited by about 600,000 people, almost a quarter of whom live in Zanzibar town. Agriculture is the mainstay of the economy. Clove production is the major economic activity, accounting for more than 93% of total export earnings. Coconut oil, copra and a limited tourist trade make up the remainder.

Balance of payments problems have placed severe constraints on the government's capacity to finance badly needed imports for economic and social development programmes. The pattern of exports and imports gives rise to serious concern. Clove production has reduced markedly: the trees are old and disease-ridden. Food imports have varied over time, but have always been substantial, demanding outlays of scarce foreign exchange.

The government has taken steps to formulate policies and programmes to tackle Zanzibar's severe economic problems, giving priority to agriculture, with particular reference to achieving self-sufficiency in food production, and diversification of the economy. WFP food aid to Zanzibar has been directed towards supporting these priorities with project food aid in support of dairy production, rice cultivation and rubber plantations, as well as provision of emergency food aid to cushion the effects of drought and pest attacks on crops. In the rubber development scheme, food aid has played a substantial part in the establishment of several plantations covering over 1,000 hectares. The profitability of rubber could be enhanced if its development in Zanzibar was tied to rubber production, manufacturing and marketing activities on the mainland. WFP has also been providing dairy commodities that generate funds for investment in dairy development activities with the objective of increasing self-sufficiency in milk production.

In concert with a number of donors and aid agencies, WFP has also since 1981 provided food rations to an average of over 1,000 workers a year (40% of whom are women) in a FFW land development programme that seeks to increase irrigated rice production. The main activities completed by 1988 included over 630 hectares of land levelling, 560,000 cubic metres of excavation, the construction of 150,000 metres of bunds, 180,000 metres of drainage, 105 kilometres of irrigation canals, 45 kilometres of access roads, 20 small dams and the drilling of 34 productive boreholes. The project's labour-intensive approach had enabled 3,500 smallholders to obtain on-the-job training in canal, drainage and bund construction, in addition to crop establishment, water management and erosion, pest and weed control. Training and extension have been augmented by several demonstration plots and the establishment of an audio-visual department which produces instructional materials for extension through mobile radio and television units. The developed land has been distributed to small farmers for cultivation.

This programme has also yielded a number of associated developmental benefits. These include the supply of safe drinking water to rural areas; the provision of new roads that have facilitated the outreach of health extension and electrification activities into remote areas; the introduction of drainage systems in formerly swampy areas, thereby reducing water-borne diseases; increased nitrogen fixation and soil erosion control; and the introduction of intensive inter-cropping that has enabled more food to be grown. A rice development fund has been created from the savings generated by part-payment of wages in WFP food rations. Part of these funds have been used for the installation of emergency fuel reserve tanks, the purchase of reserve fuel, agricultural tools and building materials, and the establishment of an incentive bonus scheme for workers.

The government is obliged to import nearly three-quarters of Zanzibar's rice requirements, using scarce foreign exchange, at the expense of other vital imports. At a time when foreign-exchange earnings from cloves are falling, this situation has created severe problems. WFP assistance is a useful link in a chain of efforts to increase domestic production and reduce dependence on imports. It is a particularly good example of the appropriate use of food aid, in concert with other technical and capital assistance, to promote development in a sector accorded highest priority by the government.

Dairy development: Most milk in Tanzania comes from the traditional herd. Although there is potential for increasing production from this source, emphasis is being placed on expanding and increasing the productivity of an improved dairy herd.

WFP assistance in support of the government's dairy development plan began in 1976. Since then, a number of other donors, particularly EC member countries, have also provided substantial aid. WFP provided dried skimmed milk and butter oil for milk processing plants in the urban areas of Dar es-Salaam, Arusha and Tanga, that were recombined with local milk to increase supplies. Funds generated from recombined milk sales were used for investment in the development of the dairy industry.

The initial emphasis of the dairy development plan was on the establishment and expansion of large dairy farms. This encountered a number of difficulties, mostly because the government failed to deposit the funds from recombined milk sales in a special account and to use them for the purposes agreed upon. The government then took corrective measures and it was also subsequently agreed that the generated funds would be directed towards the support of smallholder dairy farming to the maximum extent possible. Where funds were invested in large-scale farming activities, it was recognized that there should be clearly demonstrated benefits between these activities and those of the smallholder sector.

Although difficult to quantify in precise terms, much of the investment since the mid-1980s will have an impact on milk production long after external assistance comes to an end. There is some evidence that total local milk supplies have been increasing, and there is no evidence that dairy food aid has acted as a disincentive to local production, largely because there remains a large unmet demand in the three main urban areas. Recombined milk sold at regulated prices accounted for only 5% of total supply in 1987. Free market prices of fresh milk have been consistently higher than regulated prices. There is, therefore, an attractive incentive margin. EC Commission and WFP pricing policies for food aid dairy products are co-ordinated, with the aim of preventing counter-productive effects. Effective collaboration of this kind is pivotal to efforts aimed at preventing excessively cheap imports from causing domestic prices and production to collapse.

The management of this project has improved progressively as a result of a painstaking process of negotiation and collaboration between the government and WFP, with technical assistance from FAO. Transport and financial problems have caused a steady decline in fresh milk intake at the dairy plants, however, and an increasing reliance on food aid commodities. Such developments could potentially break the link between the processing plants and the dairy sector and the continuation of dairy food aid could hamper the long-term development of the sector. The government's policies under the ERP of encouraging private sector participation and rationalizing the public sector have set the stage for reform, but additional corrective measures are imperative.

Settlement of refugees: Social strife and civil war in neighbouring countries in the 1960s and 1970s caused large numbers of people to flee into Tanzania. Under the 1951 Convention on Refugees, the government recognized these immigrants as refugees and marshalled manpower and resources to enable them to settle in the country. Appeals were also made to various United Nations organizations and NGOs, all of which responded generously with assistance.

WFP committed US$20 million of food aid over the decade from 1972 to help tide more than 100,000 refugees over the initial period of settlement while they prepared land received from the government for cultivation. UNHCR and the Tanzanian Christian Refugee Service (TCRS), together with the Lutheran World Federation, allocated funds for water supplies, roads, schools, dispensaries and communal and commercial centres. They also provided technical advice and extension services, and agricultural inputs such as machinery, tools, seeds, insecticides and fertilizers.

As the settlements developed, vocational training and adult education programmes were instituted. These contributed towards enhancing the skills necessary for income-generating activities, such as poultry and animal production, carpentry and tailoring. Once the settlements started to become self-reliant, in some cases producing surpluses in food as well as cash crops such as tobacco, the government became responsible for their services. In 1980, some 36,000 refugees assumed Tanzanian citizenship in one of the biggest mass naturalization ceremonies in history.

Surveys sponsored by UNHCR in 1980 indicated that 23,000 refugees had remained spontaneously settled in villages. The surveys noted differences between the refugees and the local population that affected the former's opportunities for self-improvement. UNHCR and TCRS, in collaboration with the government, drew up a programme of assistance to the spontaneously settled refugees that received WFP assistance from 1984 to 1987. The purpose of this project was to expand agricultural production and to further the development of social infrastructure in selected villages. Currently, about 15,000 refugees from Mozambique receive food assistance in a settlement in southern Tanzania.

There are some 175,000 refugees now living in Tanzania. The majority are in self-reliant rural settlements that no longer need food aid. Tanzania's record in helping refugees has been exemplary. Food aid and other assistance, combined with the government's policy of hospitality, has led to the promotion of durable, development-oriented settlements.

Strategic grain reserve: A strategic grain reserve project supported by a number of food aid donors and organizations was undertaken between 1978 and 1982. It was not successful, basically because of differences of opinion between the government and donors over its purpose. Since then, policies and circumstances have changed sufficiently to enable a workable strategic grain reserve to be put in place. During early 1992, stocks amounted to 90,000 tons of cereals, mainly maize.

Future Plans and Directions

Food aid to Tanzania has played a variety of positive roles. Programme food aid has contributed mainly to the generation of investment resources for development, while helping to meet periodic food shortfalls. Project aid has generally been applied effectively in support of activities aimed at increasing agricultural production, encouraging diversification and promoting the government's overall policy of self-reliance. In most cases, food aid has been used wisely and, where problems have been encountered, corrective managerial and institutional measures have been adopted that have led to substantial improvements in programming, administration and logistics.

Transport and storage Transport and storage together constitute one of the most serious constraints on Tanzania's rural and agricultural economy. Late evacuation of food and cash crops from the producing regions, coupled with inappropriate storage facilities and techniques, cause considerable post-harvest losses and damage. The government is giving attention to these problems and donors have shown a willingness to respond with help. However, piecemeal efforts which concentrate only on such inputs as the provision of vehicles and the construction of stores are unlikely to have a lasting benefit. It is of the utmost importance that any measures taken are preceded by a carefully elaborated government policy for the food and cash-crop sectors. FAO is initiating action, which needs to be supported by a comprehensive plan of action linking road and storage construction with community participation, and which clarifies further the respective roles of co-operatives, marketing boards and private traders in agricultural marketing. Food aid can play a positive role both in food-for-work activities and, through the use of funds from food aid sales, for financing such projects.

Strategic grain reserve   Tanzania can produce surpluses in its main staple crop, maize. In drought years, the relative scale of famine and malnutrition depends largely on the speed and efficiency of the government's action. This, in turn, requires a reliable response capability and a national early warning system with disaster-preparedness plans and relief measures supported by a properly functioning strategic grain reserve. Food aid can contribute to the establishment of such a reserve, but its role will be meaningful only if it is coupled with the technical and financial assistance required to establish an early warning system and disaster-preparedness strategies, as well as for stock and financial management of the reserve under a broad food security programme. Such a programme could include, *inter alia*, price stabilization arrangements, a multi-donor mechanism to operate jointly funds generated from food aid sales, and a special revolving fund for stock purchases and repurchases.

Growth with equity   Food and cash-crop production is concentrated in a few regions of the country. Some regions are faced with regular shortage of rainfall leading to increasing aridity. These problems are further exacerbated by over-grazing and uncontrolled tree-felling, which have caused excessive soil erosion and deforestation. The role of food aid in soil conservation and reforestation programmes in these areas should be fully explored. Such programmes might be linked to ILO's special public works programme for rural areas. In addition, resources from monetized food aid could be used in the areas where direct distribution of food is considered inappropriate. There is scope for collaboration with bilateral donors in this area.

Adjustment programmes must increasingly include specific provision for protecting the vulnerable groups and for supporting the incomes of the poor during the transitional period of adjustment. Public works or other schemes supported with food aid offer an approach which needs to be explored, especially in view of the government's desire to encourage urban to rural migration as part of its efforts to promote agriculture and rural development. These schemes should be combined with compensatory programmes to protect the health and nutrition of the most vulnerable groups, especially women and children.

Food aid in Tanzania faces a panoply of problems and opportunities. The size and terrain of the country give rise to high transport and logistical costs and constraints. Problems still remain regarding such issues as the adequacy of accounting and programming for the large amounts of funds generated by food aid sales, the effects of foreign-exchange shortages on project implementation, and the extent of transparency in the official assessment of shortfalls. The multiplicity of donors also calls for careful co-ordination of activities. However, these problems are not insurmountable and there are also opportunities, arising mainly from the country's growth potential and its generally good record in the overall application and management of food aid. There is increasing recognition that, given an appropriate policy framework and careful project design, food aid can assist significantly in promoting growth while safeguarding equity. Within this recognition lies the challenge for food aid in Tanzania for the years ahead.

Appendix Table 9.1 *Tanzania: Cereal food aid receipts ('000 tons – in grain equivalent)*

	1987	1988	1989	1990	1991	1987–91 Average
Total:	53.9	53.8	51.7	33.4	14.1	41.4
By food aid channel:						
– Bilateral	53.8	29.1	34.9	18.0	6.4	28.4
– Gvt-to-Gvt	53.8	28.2	31.9	18.0	6.4	27.6
– through NGOs	–	0.9	3.0	–	–	0.8
– Multilateral	0.1	24.7	16.7	15.3	7.7	12.9
By food aid category:						
– Emergency Relief	0.1	24.7	11.2	14.5	2.0	10.5
– Project	27.9	1.2	5.7	6.9	5.7	9.5
– Agr./Rural Development	3.6	0.5	5.6	6.9	5.7	4.5
– Nutrition Intervention	14.0	0.2	–	–	–	2.8
– Other Development Project	10.3	0.5	0.1	–	–	2.2
– Non-project (Programme)	25.9	27.9	34.8	12.0	6.4	21.4
By donor[a]:						
– WFP	0.1	24.7	16.7	15.3	7.7	12.9
– Japan	13.6	12.4	8.4	4.9	5.4	8.9
– USA	10.3	5.6	13.4	–	–	5.9
– Australia	4.7	7.0	–	6.8	–	3.7
– EC Community Action	7.7	0.6	6.3	–	–	2.9
– Canada	12.4	–	–	–	–	2.5
– France	3.5	3.5	–	–	1.0	1.6
– Italy	–	–	3.9	3.7	–	1.5
– Switzerland	–	–	2.9	0.5	–	0.7
– Uganda	–	–	–	2.0	–	0.4
– Spain	1.5	–	–	–	–	0.3
– NGOs	–	–	0.1	0.1	–	–

[a] Multilateral food aid provided through WFP appears under WFP as donor.

Source: WFP/INTERFAIS Database

Appendix Table 9.2 *Tanzania: Non-cereal food aid receipts ('000 tons)*

	1987	1988	1989	1990	1991	1987–91 Average
Total:	4.0	5.4	1.5	5.0	2.1	3.6
By food aid channel:						
– Bilateral	1.0	3.2	0.1	1.6	0.1	1.2
– Gvt-to-Gvt	0.6	1.6	–	1.4	–	0.7
– through NGOs	0.4	1.6	0.1	0.2	0.1	0.5
– Multilateral	2.9	2.2	1.4	3.4	2.0	2.4
– NGOs	–	–	–	0.1	–	–
By food aid category:						
– Emergency Relief	0.9	0.4	0.9	2.7	0.4	1.1
– Project	3.1	3.4	0.5	2.3	1.8	2.2
– Agr./Rural Development	2.3	1.8	0.5	2.2	1.7	1.7
– Nutrition Intervention	0.2	0.3	–	–	–	0.1
– Other Development Project	0.6	1.3	–	0.1	0.1	0.4
– Non-project (Programme)	–	1.5	–	–	–	0.3
By donor [a]:						
– WFP	2.9	2.2	1.4	3.3	2.0	2.3
– EC Community Action	0.3	1.6	0.1	0.1	0.1	0.4
– USA	0.6	1.3	–	–	–	0.4
– Italy	–	–	–	1.3	–	0.3
– Canada	–	0.3	–	–	–	0.1
– Switzerland	0.1	–	–	0.2	0.1	0.1
– Luxemburg	0.1	–	–	–	–	–
– NGOs	–	–	–	0.1	–	–

[a] Multilateral food aid provided through WFP appears under WFP as donor.

Source: ibid.

10 Australia

Focus on Poverty Alleviation

Food aid has been a significant but decreasing component of Australia's overseas aid programme since the inception of the Colombo Plan in 1950. Australia has a strong commitment to assist developing countries, particularly the poorest, and especially those in its own geographical region. Historically, it has been the fourth largest donor of cereal food aid, and the fourth largest contributor to the Food Aid Convention (FAC). It is a strong supporter of WFP and a regular contributor to the IEFR.

The agricultural sector contributes only about 4% to Australia's GDP and only about 5% of the labour force are in agricultural employment. However, agricultural production accounts for about a third of the total value of Australian exports.

Although Australia is a major food exporter, food aid represents a much smaller proportion (about 8%) of its annual official development assistance than is common among the large food aid donors of Europe and North America. Food aid also represents only a very small part of domestic food production and exports. This seems paradoxical given Australia's comparative advantage as a cost-efficient food producer and a major food trading country. Unlike other major food-producing developed countries, the Australian government provides only very low levels of assistance to domestic producers and does not maintain food stocks. For Australia, therefore, food aid does not represent an alternative use for costly stored surpluses. Nor would Australia's ODA be less if it did not give food aid. The food commodities provided are normally purchased out of the aid budget from domestic production (with the exception of some emergency food aid) and are paid for at the full prevailing market price.

Policy Framework

A committee carried out the most comprehensive review ever undertaken of Australia's overseas aid programme and submitted a report (known as the Jackson Report) to the government in 1984. The recommendations made in that report underlie later developments in Australian food aid policy.

Government policy on the provision of overseas aid seeks to balance humanitarian

143

concerns and economic and political interests. The aid programme is designed to promote sustainable and equitable development in the assisted countries. It is reasoned that Australia will benefit from the economic activity that will flow from such development. Australia has recently developed a new strategy for its aid programme that represents a commitment to focus more deliberately on the alleviation of poverty in the developing countries it helps.

Australia has acceded to successive Food Aid Conventions because of its desire to achieve international rationality and agreement in world cereal trade. From 1967, when it became a signatory to the first FAC of the International Grains Agreement, FACs have provided a constant international stimulus for the provision of its food aid. It reduced its minimum FAC commitment from 400,000 tons to 300,000 tons of grain (in wheat equivalent), however, in the 1986 FAC; this was because of economic difficulties and a desire to avoid the possibility that food aid might either unduly displace other forms of Australian overseas assistance or require a substantial increase in the aid budget if food commodity prices rose significantly. Australia sees its FAC annual commitment level as a guaranteed minimum obligation, irrespective of production and price fluctuations, which it has regularly exceeded, sometimes significantly. There is, therefore, no diminution in its resolve to do all it can to assist in providing the food aid that continues to be needed in many developing countries. This was clearly demonstrated in 1982/83 when, as a result of a serious drought and the sharp reduction in domestic food production that followed, Australia met its food aid obligations by purchasing food from other countries.

Food Aid Administration

A separate office to administer Australia's overseas aid programme was first established in 1973. It was substantially reorganized in accordance with the recommendations of the Jackson Report, with a view to improving effectiveness through a concentration on country programmes rather than on different forms of aid. Management resources have not increased commensurate with the expanding size of the aid programme, however, and the administrative overhead is one of the lowest among donor countries.

The new aid administration, renamed the Australian International Development Assistance Bureau (AIDAB), is an autonomous Bureau within the Department of Foreign Affairs and Trade. AIDAB has three divisions: Country Programmes; Policy, Planning and Management; and Community, Commercial and International. The last division includes a Food Aid Section which is responsible for providing policy advice on food aid issues, operations and evaluation; analysing food needs in developing countries and, in conjunction with AIDAB's Country Programme Sections, proposing allocations; proposing, in co-ordination with the International Organizations and Programmes Branch, the level of Australia's pledges to WFP and the IEFR, and the commodity composition of these commitments; managing, until 1990 in conjunction with AIDAB's Procurement Management Section, the delivery of Australia's food aid programme; liaising with Australian producers, suppliers and other agencies concerning food procurement and distribution; and establishing and maintaining information systems for reporting on Australia's food aid programmes and practices.

In December 1990, AIDAB's Procurement Management Section, which managed the procurement of food commodities and goods for the various country and global aid programmes, was disbanded and its various components were absorbed by relevant sections. The food procurement component was absorbed by the Food Aid Section. As a result, the Food Aid Section is now more easily able to monitor food procurements, payments and shipping, and is involved with commodity suppliers directly, thereby improving its efficiency and effectiveness and expanding its corporate knowledge.

A more significant modification occurred in January 1992 following a comprehensive review of AIDAB's organizational structure. While retaining the three-divisional structure, two divisions now comprise a mix of bilateral and multilateral programme delivery activities: the Pacific and International Programmes Division (PIP), and the Asia, Africa and Community Programmes Division (AAC). The Food Aid Section is now placed in the Asia, Africa and Food Branch of the AAC division. This provides both the necessary degree of strengthening and continuity of resources. It also enhances opportunities to integrate food aid more closely with country programme activities.

AIDAB operates the aid programme through three main components: country programmes, community and international programmes and corporate services.

Country programmes: These programmes aim to promote development in designated countries by assisting government and regional organizations in the planning and implementation of activities designed to improve economic and social conditions. Strategies are designed in consultation with recipient governments, the overriding consideration being to deliver the various types of aid in ways that best match recipient countries' needs. There are two critical steps in the country programme management process: first the preparation of a country paper setting out the objectives and strategies, and second the holding of an annual, high-level consultation with the recipient government to review progress to programme for future activities.

Community and international programmes: These programmes operate through voluntary agencies and commercial and international organizations, to promote co-ordinated Australian and international efforts to assist development in Third World countries, including the provision of humanitarian relief, assistance for disaster preparedness and prevention measures. The United Nations and International Programmes Section in AIDAB has responsibility, in consultation with the Food Aid Section, for determining Australia's pledges to WFP. The latter section is then responsible for determining, with WFP, the types of commodities to be supplied. In close co-ordination with the Food Aid Section, a Refugee and Disaster Co-ordination Section determines funding of food aid allocations for refugees and the victims of natural disasters.

Budgetary process: The government establishes overall levels of aid for each financial year. Allocations for each programme are set by the Minister for Foreign Affairs and Trade, in consultation with the Federal Treasurer and the Minister for Finance and on the advice of senior AIDAB officials. A public budget paper on the aid programme is produced each year.

Aid expenditure has been reduced in recent years in line with overall budgetary restraint owing to acute economic difficulties. For the financial year 1987-8 official development assistance as a proportion of government budget outlays fell to its lowest level of 1.3%. The ratio of ODA to GNP fell to 0.36, the lowest ever, well down from the average of 0.45 to 0.53 during the 1970s and early 1980s, but close to the average of 0.35 for the major donor member countries of the OECD Development Assistance Committee. The government has, however, accepted the UN recommended level of 0.7 as a desirable target, consistent with the need to determine aid levels within broader economic considerations. The reduction in the overall aid budget has particularly affected programmes, including food aid, for which there was no forward commitment at the time the cuts were made. Food aid in 1988 accounted for the lowest proportion of Australia's ODA in the recent past – of 8.4% compared with over 16% in 1982.

The Australian Government has adopted a system of programme budgeting. Departments set their own priorities within overall budget allocations, describe strategies to achieve stated objectives and give details of performance indicators. The new AIDAB administrative structure facilitates this new approach, which focuses more attention on the achievement of objectives, including those involving food aid. Approved allocations must be disbursed during the financial year (July-June) or funds will lapse. All aid appropriations are subject to the same scrutiny and accountability as other expenditures.

There is no separate food aid budget under AIDAB's new structure; instead, annual budgets covering all aid (including food aid) are approved for each country programme, for emergency aid and for multilateral organizations. The only legally binding commitment concerning food aid disbursements is the minimum obligation entered into under the FAC, which serves to protect the continuation of some food-aided programmes despite overall budget cuts. Within the annual budget, overall country and global allocations, grain and other food prices, transportation costs, multi-year commitments and FAC contributions all have to be taken into account in establishing each year's programme of food assistance.

Food procurement and transportation   Two main methods of obtaining food from domestic production are used for the food aid programme. For Australian suppliers with sole responsibility for exports of the food commodity concerned (wheat, rice, skim milk powder and dried fruit), AIDAB negotiates price, quality and shipping arrangements with them prior to placing orders. Wheat prices are based on the monthly average of the Australian Wheat Board's daily spot prices. Rice prices are negotiated at the beginning of the financial year. Where there is no single supplier, as in the case of vegetable oil, wheat flour, sorghum and pulses, an open tender arrangement is used, in which all specifications to be met (quantity, quality, timing and shipping arrangements) are detailed.

AIDAB uses a shipping agent to manage bilateral food aid shipments. As a consequence, it tries where possible to charter vessels for development food aid shipments rather than, as in the past, relying on suppliers and using liners. This has resulted in considerable savings. Charters, which normally involve consolidated shipments for a number of recipients, are easier because most recipients of Australia's bilateral food aid have Indian Ocean ports of access. It is customary for freight on shipments for Bangladesh, Egypt and Sri Lanka to be paid for and arranged by the recipient governments; for all other bilateral food aid shipments, Australia pays cost and freight to the ports of recipient countries. AIDAB liaises with the Programme's Australian shipping agent in arranging WFP food aid consignments; prior to the appointment of its own shipping agent, it frequently made use of WFP's services to arrange bilateral shipments. Australia usually pays a varying but significant proportion of the internal transport, storage and handling costs in recipient countries of the development and emergency food aid it provides. In the case of Mozambique, it made a cash grant, and for Ethiopia, it donated an additional amount of food aid to be sold there to cover these costs.

Monitoring, evaluation and co-ordination   AIDAB undertakes an annual monitoring programme, subject to available staffing and funds; the Evaluation Section has been strengthened to assess the impact of the aid programme, including food aid. Designated officers in Australian missions in recipient countries are also expected to monitor the aid programme. NGOs distributing Australian emergency food aid are required to produce a monitoring report six months after receipt of the food. AIDAB has also used WFP's services to monitor Australian bilateral food aid programmes, especially in sub-Saharan Africa and Bangladesh.

Australia has been a member of the Committee on Food Aid Policies and Programmes since its inception and has played an active part in its deliberations concerning WFP activities and food aid from all sources. AIDAB is expanding its regular bilateral contacts with officials of other donor countries. Formal annual aid consultations are held with Japan, New Zealand and the United Kingdom, and AIDAB also meets regularly with aid officials from Canada, the United States, Germany and the EC Commission. There is scope for discussion of food aid at such meetings.

Flow, Direction and Uses of Australian Food Aid

During the 1980s, Australia's food aid shipments ranged between 246,000 tons and 486,000 tons annually; supplies increased steadily to reach a peak in 1981/82 but have subsequently decreased. Australia's cereal food aid as a proportion of the global volume increased progressively to reach 5% in 1981/82, but declined to about 3% in 1990/91. In the past, the bulk of Australia's food aid was channelled bilaterally but the proportion provided multilaterally through WFP increased to 28% in volume and 40% in value in 1986-7. A small but growing proportion was also provided through NGOs, reaching 7% in volume and 8% in value in 1986-7, mainly as emergency food aid to sub-Saharan Africa.

Australia has been a strong supporter of WFP from the Programme's beginning, and has made substantial increases in its pledges in recent years. For the biennium 1989-90, it pledged US$69 million to WFP's regular resources, US$14 million for WFP's protracted refugee operations and US$0.9 million for the IEFR. The main commodities provided are wheat, rice, wheat flour, sorghum and maize, and non-cereal foods such as pulses, sugar, vegetable oil, dairy commodities, high protein biscuits and dried fruit.

Between 1981 and 1987, Australia also supplied the equivalent of US$1.3 million in non-food items for WFP-supported development projects. For the biennium 1989-90, US$1.1 million was provided for this purpose. WFP has provided purchasing, transportation and monitoring services for Australian bilateral food aid, mainly for countries in sub-Saharan Africa but also for some countries in South-East Asia and the Middle East.

Commodity composition   Wheat typically accounts for about two-thirds of the total volume of Australia's food aid. The other main commodities are rice, maize, and wheat flour. Almost the entire sorghum production, a relatively new grain crop for Australian farmers, has been provided for food aid. Australia also provides high protein biscuits through WFP as part of its emergency food aid, and sugar as part of its WFP commodity pledge. The provision of dairy products as food aid has steadily declined. Meat products, provided in earlier years, are not currently given as food aid. Dried and canned fruits are sometimes included when requested by WFP, and pulses have also been supplied.

Regional distribution of bilateral food aid   Bilateral ODA has been provided to more than 90 countries; food aid, including emergency assistance, has been supplied bilaterally to around 20 of these countries. Countries in the Asian and Pacific regions typically receive some 60% of Australia's bilateral ODA and about 43% of its total ODA.

By contrast, about two-thirds of the value of Australian bilateral food aid has gone to Africa. This shift in regional distribution is relatively recent, although Egypt has historically been a major recipient. The Australian Government has a special programme of assistance to countries in southern Africa, in which development food aid figures prominently.

Two countries alone, Egypt and Bangladesh, have received a large part – up to 50,000 tons a year each – of Australia's bilateral development food aid. Ethiopia and Mozambique are also significant recipients. There has been a steady decline in bilateral food aid to South-East Asia. Previously, both the Philippines and Indonesia were major recipients. Other regions receive only small and intermittent amounts of Australian bilateral food aid.

Australia's emergency food aid is provided through the IEFR, bilaterally on a government-to-government basis, with small amounts supplied through NGOs or multilaterally through WFP. Australia has regularly exceeded, often substantially, its minimum pledge of 50,000 tons annually to the IEFR. In the mid-1980s sub-Saharan Africa received two-thirds of Australian bilateral emergency food aid, with Ethiopia and Mozambique accounting for more than three-quarters of these deliveries. Somalia and Sudan are also major recipients. South Asia also benefited, receiving about a quarter of Australian bilateral emergency food aid, most of it for the Afghan refugees in Pakistan. Although Oceania receives only a small proportion of the total bilateral emergency food aid, Australia is the major donor when calamities strike the small islands in the region.

Impact of Australian Food Aid

Various aspects of Australia's food aid programme have been studied and reviewed in order to increase its effectiveness and efficiency.

Monetization policy and procedures   As nearly all AIDAB's bilateral food aid is monetized, a review of problems encountered has presented policy guidelines on how best to carry the process out in different circumstances. It does not, however, advocate monetization above other ways of using food aid.

As noted above, Australia's bilateral food aid for development has been concentrated on a small number of countries in Africa, South Asia and the Indian Ocean. In most of these countries, the food aid commodities were monetized, that is, sold in the recipient country. AIDAB's general policy objective is to use the funds generated from food aid sales to support food security-related development activities. Funds have been used to help meet the local costs of AIDAB development projects and to support programmes and projects financed by other aid organizations.

Where bilateral food aid is sold by the recipient government, the net funds generated are deposited in an Australian food aid counterpart fund account, which is jointly managed by representatives of the Australian and recipient governments. Normally, joint signature is required to authorize the use of these funds. Problems with monetization have included establishing the price at which food aid sales should take place, unauthorized deductions from sales proceeds to meet administrative and local costs, lack of clarity concerning the use of funds generated, and delays in their use.

Bilateral development food aid programmes A series of papers have been produced in AIDAB giving policy and operational guidelines on its bilateral food aid programme. One provides a comprehensive set of criteria and discussion of issues that need to be considered in country programmes when weighing the effectiveness of food aid against other forms of assistance. Another provides general guidelines and comments on the ways food aid can be used in structural adjustment programmes. A third aims to improve the effectiveness of bilateral food aid through the provision of a set of monitoring guidelines to be used by officials in Australian missions in developing countries.

Concern has been expressed in AIDAB about the effectiveness of its bilateral programme in helping to meet the food needs of the poorer segments of the population in the recipient countries. It was agreed that evaluations should be undertaken in a number of countries to assess the impact of food aid and to recommend ways of enhancing its role in promoting social and economic development.

The first desk review of a country food aid programme was undertaken in 1979 in relation to Sri Lanka (AIDAB, 1979). Since then, a number of country studies have been carried out including Bangladesh, Ethiopia and Tanzania (AIDAB, 1982, 1983,1984), plus another desk review, this time of Egypt (AIDAB, 1983), and a review of a land rehabilitation project in Ethiopia.

Sri Lanka: The 1979 review concluded that in general Australian food aid was not dependent upon the existence of domestic surpluses and that the regularity of supply of food aid played a temporary indirect food security role. While the Sri Lankan Government subsidized wheat flour prices, returns from monetization were poor and the use of the foreign exchange saved through the provision of food aid could not be determined. The review recommended that food aid to Sri Lanka should be continued, and that non-food forms of aid should be provided to assist with improvements in food security. While the review recommended that part of the food aid allocations should be directed to maintaining stock levels, Australian policy has been to monetize its food aid to provide support for projects related to improving food security.

Bangladesh: The bulk of the food aid provided to Bangladesh was originally distributed at subsidized prices through the public food distribution system. A country study conducted in 1982 observed that food distributed through that system only marginally benefited the poorest people. Australia also directed some of its food aid allocation for food-for-work in a rural public works programme and for a vulnerable group feeding programme, which were also supported by other donor countries and WFP. This reflected the Australian Government's concern that food aid should benefit the poor and that it should be related directly to social and economic development programmes.

The study concluded that multi-year food aid allocations, with a fixed forward commitment, would allow for more effective planning and implementation of the FFW and VGF programmes by the Government of Bangladesh. It noted that the long-term developmental impact of these programmes could be enhanced by the provision of associated training and assistance for improved planning capability and technical design. There was also a need for more attention to be given to the development of a maintenance programme for rural infrastructure works. The study found that food distributed through the FFW and VGF programmes had significantly less adverse effect on domestic producer food prices than rations provided through the public distribution system. It recommended that data collection and analysis should be regularly undertaken to assess the impact of Australia's aid in the light of Bangladesh's changing food situation, which should provide guidance for determining future food aid. As a result of the study, Australian bilateral food aid for the public distribution system was terminated and transferred to the FFW and VGF programmes.

Egypt: A desk review of Australian bilateral food aid undertaken in 1983 concluded that a significant factor influencing Australia's aid programme to Egypt was the latter's importance as a commercial purchaser of Australian grain. The food aid provided had supported the Egyptian Government's objectives of controlling consumer and producer prices and of making cheap food readily available as well as of obtaining foreign exchange through export crops. During the late 1980s, Australia also provided local cost financing from the proceeds of food aid sales for the construction of wheat silos and for projects designed to increase agricultural productivity and food security in Egypt.

Ethiopia: Australia has provided emergency food aid to Ethiopia since the late 1970s. In more recent years, a development approach has been introduced through the provision of food-for-work in a land reclamation and afforestation project in the southern province of Gamu Gofa under the management of the Ministry of Agriculture. A country study in 1983 endorsed that a greater developmental emphasis should be given to the use of Australian bilateral food aid by targeting it on specific groups through food-for-work programmes or by channelling it through agencies and NGOs implementing developmental programmes in areas of need. The Ministry of Agriculture project was considered to have had a significant developmental impact; food-for-work assisted in improving the livelihood of farmers in the area. The study considered that technical advice, assistance for training and other inputs from Australia were required, and that forward provision of food aid should be made for three years.

A review of Australian assistance to Ethiopia for land rehabilitation and reforestation conducted in 1985 noted that the use of food aid for food-for-work had two objectives. First, it provided an incentive to smallholders to participate in these activities. Second, it contributed to the food needs of peasant communities in areas where drought and famine were endemic and where food was accepted as, or even preferred, to, cash wages. The review noted that the food aid provided as food-for-work tended to be self-targeting as those who were better-off were not willing to work for payment in food commodities. Women participated significantly in FFW activities, and did the same type of work as men, for which they were paid at the same rate. The findings of the review suggested that the economic status and security of farmers in Ethiopia would be increased in the longer term. At the same time, they indicated that the impact of severe drought and famine could be reduced in an economically efficient way by using food aid for long-term development purposes. Australia's assistance was recommended for a further three years from 1986/87 to 1988/89, and this was approved.

Tanzania: Tanzania has been one of the largest African recipients of Australian bilateral food aid, provided essentially to meet the country's growing food deficit and for budget support. The bulk of the food aid was provided to urban areas at subsidizd prices through government retail outlets. A country study undertaken in 1984 concluded that the developmental impact was difficult to determine. There had been little direct contribution to long-term development and no targeting of food aid beyond the provision of cheap grain to urban residents. Access of the poorer sections of the community to the food aid was limited; many of those whom the government wished to assist through subsidized sales were unable to purchase sufficient food grains to meet their daily requirements.

Little information was available on the use of proceeds generated from the sale of food aid and no assessment could be made of the developmental impact of these funds on the agricultural sector. The study recommended a number of changes, most significantly the linking of sales proceeds to development projects. As a result, an agreement was signed governing the use of sales proceeds, including support for a women's credit programme and a co-operative development credit programme. The study also proposed that greater emphasis should be placed on co-ordination among food aid donors to Tanzania and recommended a fixed forward programme of Australian food aid with a three-year commitment. This was subsequently implemented, although the amount of food aid has been reduced.

A further review of Australia's bilateral food aid programmes is to be undertaken. This will look at AIDAB's management procedures concerning food aid and the experience of other major food aid donors. The review will consist of in-depth country studies complemented by a comprehensive desk study of AIDAB's experience and an international assessment of food aid, leading to conclusions that suggest improved use of food aid for development.

Emergency food aid   Steps have been taken to increase the speed and efficiency of Australia's emergency food aid. For quick-strike action within the South-west Pacific region, where tropical cyclones and other sudden natural disasters regularly occur, AIDAB uses the services of the Australian Natural Disasters Organization. This agency also co-ordinates the provision of disaster-related assistance within Australia and has close working relationships with a range of government departments, including the Defence Forces. Arrangements have been made to bring such resources as aircraft and ships from these departments to a state of readiness when a disaster occurs or is expected. As a further aid to rapid response, stocks of high protein biscuits, water containers and other non-food items are held in store. Guidelines have been formulated for AIDAB country programme managers for quick action when natural disasters strike.

A Plan for the Australian Response to Disasters in Other Nations (PLAN AUSAID) has been used since 1988 governing the organization of the response to disasters overseas. Cash grants can be obtained from a special provision in the aid budget for unforeseen disasters, which can be used to provide grants to governments or organizations for the purchase of disaster relief supplies, including locally available food or food from neighbouring countries. In 1987-8, for example, cash grants were given to WFP and to the NGO, World Vision, for procurement of rice in Thailand to be delivered to drought victims in Laos and Kampuchea. AIDAB also made a cash grant to a consortium of Australian NGOs, the Working Group on Food Aid to Africa, for the purchase and shipment of emergency food aid to Ethiopia. In addition, funds were approved in 1987-8 for the purchase of 62,000 tons of grain (wheat equivalent) for refugees in Pakistan, Ethiopia, Mozambique, Somalia, Laos and Kampuchea. If funds have been fully utilized, revised and additional budget estimates can be sought for emergencies.

An Australian Overseas Disaster Relief Organization (AODRO) has been established to co-ordinate the response of Australian NGOs to disasters. This organization is almost entirely funded by AIDAB. AODRO does not engage in fund-raising but disseminates information and organizes food procurement and shipping.

Exchanges, triangular transactions and local purchases   AIDAB has undertaken exchange of food commodities, triangular transactions and local purchases in times of emergency. Australian wheat has been exchanged for maize in Zimbabwe, for example, which was then transported by Australian NGOs to use as emergency food aid in Mozambique at AIDAB's expense.

Examples of triangular transactions and local purchases have included the purchase of wheat in Pakistan for the Afghan refugees in that country at a time when drought in Australia made it impossible to provide wheat from domestic production; of sorghum in Sudan for refugees in Ethiopia; of wheat from Saudi Arabia for emergency feeding in Ethiopia; of Thai sorghum for people affected by drought in Tanzania; and of Burmese and Thai rice for Kampuchean refugees. Local purchasing arrangements of this sort have been made only in emergency situations when there has been good reason for doing so, such as, for example, to provide food more quickly, or when Australian-produced foodstuffs were not available.

Such transactions have been undertaken at commercial prices with no concessionality and have had a number of mutual benefits. The country in which the exchange has taken place has saved foreign exchange on imported wheat and storage costs on locally produced maize. The donor has saved sea freight costs, which have been borne by the country in which the exchange of commodities has taken place. The country receiving the maize has benefited from receiving a food commodity acceptable to the victims of the emergency situation in a shorter period of time. And regional food security measures have been fostered by stimulating food trade among neighbouring countries.

Future Directions

Historically, all Australian aid, including food aid, has been conditioned by a mix of humanitarian, political and economic considerations. In the past, political considerations have predominated in relation to the more significant bilateral concerns of the aid programme; economic advantage for Australia has, for the most part, been of secondary importance. The influence exercised by the general public and NGOs has been relatively small.

However, the situation is changing. An important concern is future developments in world food trade for Australia's products. The policies of other major food exporters which have led to high producer subsidies, protectionism and market intrusion through aid-supported practices are likely, if unchecked, to have a considerable adverse effect on Australia's agricultural trade. Unlike other major food exporters, Australia provides only very low levels of assistance to some of its farmers. Australia has strongly supported the Uruguay Round in the GATT negotiations aimed at liberalizing agricultural trade and strengthening GATT rules and disciplines. Pressures on the government to safeguard Australia's agricultural interests have increased, however, and the relationship of aid to trade has assumed added significance. Thus, the government is under a continued injunction to use Australian commodities in its food aid programme.

Food aid is seen as being administratively economical compared with other forms of aid, a favourable factor in AIDAB, which has to cope with continuing constraints on staffing. Food aid also benefits from an association in the public mind of the urgent need to provide food to alleviate the consequences of famine and disasters, and the desire to see Australia's food bounty shared with poor people in less fortunate countries. The recent policy decision to enhance the poverty alleviation focus of Australia's aid programme has also increased attention to the food assistance component. Food aid has been integrated into the country programme budgeting system and is being brought more fully into the mainstream of AIDAB's country programme planning activities and integrated with the other development resources and instruments. While the larger part of Australia's non-food bilateral assistance continues to be allocated to countries in its immediate geographical region, however, the food aid component has been focused increasingly on Africa.

Following the decision to reduce the number of country offices and staff in sub-Saharan Africa, AIDAB has turned to Australian NGOs to handle some bilateral food aid on its behalf. While this arrangement provides a means of ensuring that food aid is more likely to reach poor and hungry people for whom it is intended, there is the danger of exceeding the capacity of these organizations by asking them to manage food shipments on a larger scale than that to which they have been accustomed, and to do tasks for which they may not be appropriate. Alternatively, AIDAB could increase the use of the services of other food aid agencies with professional experience or combine its food aid inputs, and funds accruing from food aid sales, with those of other donors in co-financing projects and programmes in African countries. AIDAB's co-operation with WFP in Africa has shown the mutual benefits that could be forthcoming by drawing on the services of WFP to a greater extent, and by pursuing co-financing opportunities with food or locally generated funds.

More attention is now being given to the effective use of funds accruing from the sale of Australian food and commodities in recipient countries. This can add to the impact of food aid for development. It is realised that these funds represent a valuable resource, the use of which should be more carefully planned, managed and evaluated.

The future directions of Australian food aid may be influenced by a number of factors relating to how allocated funds are programmed and their use planned and managed. Australia's food aid is financed from an annual budget. This gives rise to a number of problems in ensuring that the resources allocated are used optimally. Multi-annual commitment of food aid resources would help in overcoming these problems as well as in facilitating more effective planning and use of resources in developing countries.

There are a number of other problems. Prices for wheat (the largest single commodity component in Australian food aid) are set in US dollars, as the Australian Wheat Board considers AIDAB to be an export outlet. All freight rates are also quoted in US dollars. This creates problems related to exchange-rate movements. Secondly, the annual budget cycle corresponds to the financial year, which in Australia is July to June. However, food aid commitments are not determined until September each year, before the harvest. At this time of year, commodity prices are high and food commodities used in the food aid programme are in short supply. The annual budget cycle also creates pressures when entering into transactions with Australian suppliers during the second half of the financial year to move commodities in order to avoid the lapsing of budget allocations.

These and other aspects of the Australian food aid programme are now being reviewed.

References

AIDAB (1979) *Food Aid to Sri Lanka: a Review of the Australian Program.* Canberra.
AIDAB (1982) *Food Aid to Bangladesh: a Review of the Australian Program.* Canberra.
AIDAB (1983a) *Food Aid to Ethiopia: a Review of the Australian Program.* Canberra.
AIDAB (1983b) *Food Aid to Egypt: a Review of the Australian Program.* Canberra.
AIDAB (1984) *Food Aid to Tanzania: a Review of the Australian Program.* Canberra.
Jackson, Gordon (1984) *Report of the Committee to Review the Australian Overseas Aid Program.*
    (Gordon Jackson Chairman). Canberra.

Appendix Table 10.1 Australia: Cereal food aid deliveries ('000 tons – in grain equivalent)

	1987	1988	1989	1990	1991	1987–91 Average
Total:	284.3	422.2	309.7	357.6	288.6	332.5
By food aid channel:						
– Bilateral	185.8	218.0	178.3	221.6	90.8	178.9
– Gvt-to-Gvt	177.9	201.6	162.5	189.7	72.5	160.8
– through NGOs	8.0	16.4	15.8	31.9	18.2	18.1
– Multilateral	98.5	204.2	131.4	136.0	197.8	153.6
By food aid category:						
– Emergency Relief	71.6	88.7	94.7	104.2	46.6	81.2
– Project	140.5	257.0	133.1	155.6	221.9	181.6
– Agr./Rural Development	99.7	215.5	126.0	151.1	186.6	155.8
– Nutrition Intervention	35.0	32.7	0.5	1.5	21.3	18.2
– Food Reserve	–	–	–	0.2	–	–
– Other Development Project	5.8	8.8	6.7	2.8	13.9	7.6
– Non-project (Programme)	72.3	76.5	81.8	97.8	20.1	69.7
By region:						
– Sub-Saharan Africa	107.6	95.6	75.2	71.9	60.5	82.2
– North Africa/Mid-East	58.4	86.2	54.1	80.7	12.6	58.4
– Asia and Pacific	118.4	240.0	170.3	184.4	213.5	185.3
– Latin America and Caribbean	–	0.3	10.2	1.5	1.9	2.8
– Europe	–	–	–	19.1	–	3.8

Source: WFP/INTERFAIS Database

Appendix Table 10.2 *Australia: Non-cereal food aid deliveries ('000 tons)*

	1987	1988	1989	1990	1991	1987–91 Average
Total:	4.8	4.4	7.7	3.0	4.8	4.9
By food aid channel:						
– Bilateral	1.3	–	2.3	1.0	2.9	1.5
– Gvt-to-Gvt	1.3	–	2.3	0.3	–	0.8
– through NGOs	–	–	–	0.6	2.9	0.7
– Multilateral	3.5	4.4	5.4	2.0	1.9	3.4
By food aid category:						
– Emergency Relief	1.2	1.9	0.3	1.1	3.3	1.5
– Project	3.6	2.5	5.4	1.9	1.5	3.0
– Agr./Rural Development	2.2	1.3	2.1	1.9	0.1	1.5
– Nutrition Intervention	0.8	0.7	1.0	–	1.2	0.7
– Other Development Project	0.7	0.5	2.3	–	0.3	0.8
– Non-project (Programme)	–	–	2.0	–	–	0.4
By region:						
– Sub-Saharan Africa	2.5	2.4	1.8	1.7	3.3	2.3
– North Africa/Mid-East	–	–	1.7	–	–	0.3
– Asia and Pacific	1.3	2.1	2.2	0.2	1.5	1.4
– Latin America and Caribbean	1.1	–	2.0	1.1	–	0.8

Source: ibid.

11 Canada

Reassessing Food Aid's Roles
for Food Security
& Structural Adjustment

As a major food producer and exporter, especially of wheat, Canada has been involved in the provision of food aid for 40 years. During that period, Canadian food aid policies and programmes have been subjected to a number of internal reviews and assessments, particularly at the time of the world food crisis of the early 1970s and after the World Food Conference of 1974. There have been important changes in the structure of the food aid programme and its administration, a new focus on the efficiency and effectiveness of development and emergency food aid, and an emphasis on evaluation and accountability. These elements were confirmed in Canada's new strategy for official development assistance in 1988.

As in other countries, economic recession has forced the government to scrutinize budget allocations closely and to assess its aid further in terms of its developmental impact. Canada's ODA as a percentage of GNP decreased from 0.52 in 1978 to 0.44 in 1990. Food aid dropped from 18% of ODA to 12% over the same period. However, Canada remains the world's largest food aid donor on a per capita basis.

While food aid enjoys a certain comparative advantage in Canada's ODA, its value will continue to be assessed in comparison with other forms of aid. The relative performance of the various channels through which food aid is provided will also be subject to continuous review.

Background

The specific objectives of Canada's food aid have been defined as increasing the quantity of food available in food-deficit countries, accelerating the pace of development by freeing foreign exchange and generating domestic resources for investment, providing supplementary food to nutritionally vulnerable groups and offering basic subsistence during emergency relief and rehabilitation operations.

Canada's food aid budget reached an all-time high of C$436 million in 1987. Since then, it has declined and is currently about C$400 million. Annual budget allocations are generally reviewed upwards in the course of the fiscal year (April to March) in the light of increasing requests for emergency food aid. Food aid is the third largest component in Canada's ODA after the bilateral (non-food aid) programme and financial contributions to the international financial institutions. Canada's commitment under the 1986 Food Aid Convention is to provide a minimum of 600,000 tons of cereals (in wheat equivalent) annually, compared with 495,000 tons under the 1967 and 1971 FACs. The volume of Canadian food aid increased appreciably during the 1980s. In 1990/91, Canadian cereals food aid amounted to over 1.1 million tons, almost double its minimum FAC commitment. On average, between 1984/85 and 1990/91, Canada shipped over one million tons of cereals a year as food aid.

Canada has established a policy guideline of providing at least 25% of its food aid by value in the form of non-cereal commodities. In tonnage terms, wheat, wheat flour and maize have accounted for 90% of its food aid shipments but in value terms cereals have accounted for about two-thirds of the food aid budget in recent years. The non-cereal commodities in the food aid basket are vegetable oil, pulses, skim milk powder and fish products.

In the 1970s and early 1980s, about 60% of the food aid in value terms was chan-nelled bilaterally. In the last few years, near half (49%) has been channelled multi-laterally through WFP, and about 45% through the bilateral programmes. In the early 1980s, food aid provided through NGOs accounted for between 2% and 4% of total food aid, rising to 6% in 1991. A major shift in the programme has been the increasing allocation of resources for emergencies. While during the period 1983-9 emergency food aid represented about 27% of the food aid budget, it currently represents more than 40%.

In March 1988, the government launched a new policy framework for ODA, *Sharing our Future*. This document recognizes food aid as a valuable and flexible development resource which can be used to support development priorities such as poverty alleviation, food security and structural adjustment. In support of these new policies, a framework paper was prepared to assist country desk officers in deter-mining whether food aid is an appropriate resource in supporting structural adjust-ment programmes in food-deficit developing countries. The paper outlines a number of issues including the potential disincentive effects of food aid on agricultural policies or prices, the existence of an explicit or implicit food security strategy, the accept-ability of Canadian food commodities, the possibility of mitigating the short-term costs of adjustment for the most seriously affected groups and the co-ordination of CIDA's action with that of other donors. It also covers additional programming ques-tions like programme or targeted food aid, the establishment or not of counterpart funds, annual or multi-year commitments.

Furthermore, criteria for the allocation of the bilateral food aid budget have been elaborated in order to ensure the most effective use of this resource. These criteria refer to the level of need, assessment of the agricultural policies and the absorptive capacity of the recipient country, the efficient use of food aid as a development resource and its integration with CIDA's overall developmental programme in a recipient country. A growing demand for food aid coupled with important budgetary constraints has emphasized the need for such criteria in order to maximize the developmental impact of bilateral food assistance.

Food Aid Administration

Canada's food aid programme is not based on separate legislation but is part of the overall responsibility of providing development assistance through the budget of the Canadian International Development Agency (CIDA). This agency established a Food Aid Co-ordination and Evaluation Centre (FACE) in 1978. In the past, food aid was

not fully integrated into Canada's bilateral aid programme. Following the establishment of FACE, a more integrated approach has been developed and implemented.

The government establishes ODA levels, of which food aid forms a component, on
a three-to-five year basis as part of its overall Policy and Expenditure Management
System. These 'strategic planning figures', which are established on advice from CIDA
following extensive consultation with interested government departments, provide the
basis for the elaboration of annual budgets and for allocation decisions among the
three food aid channels – bilateral, multilateral and non-governmental.

The level of Canadian food aid each year is expressed in dollar terms. As the
food aid programme is approved and administered on an annual basis, activities
related to the delivery of approved allocations must be completed inside the fiscal
year or funds will lapse. Exceptions to this rule are bilateral multi-year agreements
and the two-year pledges to WFP and the IEFR, which permit a 10% carry-over into
the next fiscal year. All food aid budgetary allocations are subject to the appropriation
of funds by Parliament and to the same scrutiny and accountability as any other
federal expenditure.

FACE has overall responsibility within CIDA for the food aid budget, policy and
programme development, the co-ordination of activities, the provision of services
to bilateral project officers and the evaluation of food aid. This responsibility is
shared with three geographical branches (Africa, Asia and the Americas), the Special
Programmes Branch (which administers funding to NGOs), and the Procurement
Division, which is responsible for commodity procurement and transportation. Food
aid is subject to the procurement procedures of the federal government. Food commodities are purchased either through the Department of Supply and Services or directly
from federal or provincial marketing agencies. FACE initiates and co-ordinates the
presentation of submissions to the Treasury Board for food aid, monitors food aid
commitments and disbursements, and co-ordinates bilateral budget reallocations
during the fiscal year.

The bilateral channel   Priority is given to low-income, food-deficit countries, particularly those in which Canada has continuing ODA programmes. These countries are
chosen in accordance with Canadian foreign policy objectives and developmental and
humanitarian considerations. In general, this channel is used for programme food aid
for sale on local markets.

Ocean shipping costs are normally paid by Canada, although beneficiary countries
may choose to meet these costs and use their full dollar allocations for the purchase
of Canadian food. Internal costs for storage and distribution in the recipient country
are not normally paid by Canada, but exceptions are usually made in emergency
situations.

There has been an increasing trend for wheat to be channelled through Canada's
bilateral programme and wheat flour through multilateral programmes, reflecting
their different programme and project aid orientations. Relatively small proportions
of skim milk powder are channelled bilaterally; increasing amounts are being supplied through NGOs. Fish products are provided both multilaterally and bilaterally.
Vegetable oil has remained most prominent in bilateral programmes.

In the early years, a large proportion of Canadian bilateral food aid went to Asia,
while supplies through multilateral and NGO channels were directed more towards
Africa and Latin America. The share of Africa in the bilateral food aid programme
increased steadily from 30% in 1983 to about 60% in 1991. In that year, Asia received
29% and Latin American and the Caribbean 12%. Major recipients of bilateral food

aid have included Angola, Bangladesh, Ethiopia, Ghana, Jamaica, Mozambique, Pakistan and Sudan.

Bilateral food aid is provided as a direct commodity transfer from Canada to an organization or agency designated by the beneficiary government. This has usually been done as grant programme aid on an annual basis, although since 1982-3 multi-year allocations have been made to selected countries that have made a policy commitment to increase their food production.

Most bilateral food aid is sold internally by the recipient government and the counterpart funds generated are used to support development projects. Each bilateral food aid commitment is subject to a separate 'Memorandum of Understanding' with the recipient government. It generally includes a usual marketing requirement (UMR) that normal levels of commercial imports of the food commodities provided will be maintained in addition to those supplied as food aid. The Department of External Affairs consults with other food exporting countries, in conformity with the Consultative Subcommittee on Surplus Disposal (of FAO), to determine the UMRs of countries receiving Canadian bilateral food aid. The Grain Marketing Bureau of Agriculture Canada also co-ordinates Canada's dealings under the International Wheat Agreement, which includes the FAC.

The multilateral channel   Canada has traditionally been a strong supporter of the multilateral approach in international co-operation and has been a major supporter of multilateral food aid, particularly through WFP. It has also played an important role in stimulating inter-donor co-ordination to improve the effectiveness and efficiency of food aid both within the forum of the CFA and elsewhere.

Canada supported the establishment of the IEFR in 1975 and has been a consistent contributor to it. These contributions have been used mainly to provide food commodities produced in Canada, although authority has also been obtained to use cash contributions to purchase food in developing countries. Canada has responded speedily to WFP's appeals for cash to help the Programme co-ordinate emergency food aid operations and improve logistics in sub-Saharan Africa, and has also provided cash for storage and transportation to facilitate emergency food aid operations.

The bulk of Canadian multilateral food aid has been provided to WFP, with smaller amounts supplied through UNRRA and UNBRO. Canada has been the second largest contributor (after the US) to WFP since its inception. For the 1989-90 biennium, it contributed US$266 million to WFP's regular resources, US$8 million to the IEFR, US$6.6 million to protracted refugee operations and US$1.5 million for non-food items.

An Interdepartmental World Food Programme Committee was established in 1963 (comprising representatives of CIDA and of the Departments of External Affairs, Finance, Fisheries and Oceans and Regional Industrial Expansion and chaired by Agriculture Canada) to facilitate decision-making with respect to the multilateral channel of Canada's food aid. This Committee is required to advise the government on the proposed programme and budget of WFP, to review, evaluate and analyse WFP activities, to prepare position papers for the CFA, and to facilitate communication with WFP. The administration of Canada's contribution to multilateral food aid is a shared responsibility between CIDA and the Minister of Agriculture, who is responsible for announcing the level of the Canadian biennial pledge to WFP and the IEFR, for approving the levels of food aid commodities to be provided, for approving WFP shipment requests before forwarding them to CIDA, and for reporting to WFP on the use of the Canadian pledge.

Multilateral channelling of a significant part of Canada's food aid is seen to offer possibilities that complement its bilateral programme, such as the maintenance of links with countries in which Canada has no development assistance programme and the opportunity to contribute to development projects or emergency operations that are beyond the capacity of a single donor. Multilateral assistance is also seen as being immune to national, commercial and political interests and, therefore, able to help developing countries make economic adjustments that are difficult domestically but necessary for economic and social progress.

As part of a close working relationship, representatives of Canada and WFP meet annually to determine the composition of the Canadian commodity pledge to the Programme and to co-ordinate WFP operations and Canada's bilateral food aid programme. The need to disburse Canadian commodity pledges to the Programme within a single fiscal year has posed problems; because of the Canadian climate, the St Lawrence Seaway is closed in the winter months, restricting the transport of commodities. A special procedure has been devised, however, to avoid the lapsing of unused annual pledges.

Canada makes extensive use of WFP services for its bilateral food aid programme, mainly in the form of monitoring and reporting on its bilateral food aid in certain beneficiary countries. The Programme has also provided overland transport services to some landlocked countries. More extensive, integrated services have also been provided by WFP for Canada's bilateral food aid in Bangladesh and Bolivia.

The non-governmental channel   Since 1976, Canada has provided food aid through NGOs that have direct contacts with people in developing countries. Although the volume is limited, this is considered an especially effective channel because of its flexibility, particularly in the context of the continuing crises in sub-Saharan Africa, for both project and emergency food aid.

Food aid provided through Canadian NGOs takes two forms. First, skim milk powder has been provided to supplement feeding programmes for vulnerable groups, including those in refugee camps. Costs of transportation and distribution are assumed by the NGOs. The second form is through a facility known as the Canadian Foodgrains Bank (CFB). The CFB was launched by the Mennonite Central Committee in 1976 to meet emergency food aid needs, and is currently an umbrella facility encompassing 10 Canadian NGOs. The CFB receives three sources of support: food donations, cash contributions and CIDA funding. CIDA funds about 80% of the total food procurement and shipment.

The CIDA contribution is used to help pay for the purchase of grain and for handling, storage and shipment costs but does not cover the costs of distribution to beneficiaries in the recipient country. Canadian farmers can contribute grains through arrangements with the Canadian Wheat Board or they can make a gift of grain directly to the CFB. Contributions are tax-deductible. Volunteers also provide help in cleaning, bagging and preparing grain for shipment.

The concept of the CFB has caught the imagination of Canadian farmers to such an extent that it has grown rapidly in recent years. In the fiscal year 1990-91, it shipped a total of 58,000 tons of wheat, oil, pulses, maize and flour to 13 food-deficit countries. Africa received 89% of the total shipment and the remainder went to Latin America.

When a need is perceived, the CFB can respond by using the extensive network of NGOs to make an assessment and devise the most appropriate distribution arrangement, frequently by using NGOs on the spot. The response can take several forms, including direct shipment from Canada or borrowing stocks from nearby sources that are subsequently replenished from the CFB. WFP has provided shipping and monitoring services for the CFB. Considerable savings in ocean transport costs have been made for the participating NGOs through consolidated shipments with WFP consignments to common destinations.

Issues for the Future

Canada's development assistance is budgeted in financial terms, with food aid as one element. Canada's comparative advantage as an agricultural exporter, and the agricultural and broad public constituency that has traditionally supported the food aid programme, have made food aid an important part of its ODA. Nevertheless, the trade-offs between food aid and other forms of ODA are clearly established, and its impact is constantly assessed in comparison with other forms of assistance.

With the world market price of wheat determining the dollar value of Canada's FAC contribution and with a growing demand for food aid, particularly for emergencies, CIDA recognizes that new criteria are needed to allocate food aid among countries and channels. This has been particularly evident as the programme emphasis has shifted from Asia and Latin America to Africa.

Commodity composition of Canada's food aid   CIDA is adopting a more pro-active approach to suppliers to ensure that the medium-term commodity needs of the food aid programme are known. CIDA has also discussed arrangements with the Canadian Dairy Commission aimed at reducing the cost of the fortification of skim milk powder with Vitamin A to the standard set by the World Health Organization. Other issues being explored include the potential for the increased use of cornmeal and pulses, the feasibility of encouraging production of special food preparations for emergency situations, and improved packaging. While Canada has financed some transportation and local purchase operations, especially of coarse grains in Africa, these did not become a significant part of food aid programming during the 1980s.

The channelling of food aid   Bilateral programme food aid can address the need for balanced growth and structural adjustment in recipient countries. Multilateral food aid, mainly through WFP, has been directed through projects that have contributed towards employment and income generation, the building of development infrastructure and improved nutrition in developing countries. The relative cost-effectiveness of both channels and their management and decision-making capabilities will have an important influence on the proportions of food aid that will flow through them in future years.

The NGO channel represents a small part of Canada's overall food aid programme. The NGOs distribute food through local organizations, often with religious affiliations, in recipient countries where they have well-established networks and an ability to reach certain target groups. The NGOs are conscious of the dangers of over-stretching themselves and of creating an imbalance among their financial, technical and food aid resources. They prefer to retain their independent identity and to avoid becoming surrogates of the Canadian Government's food aid programme. They feel that their food aid programmes should expand only in accordance with their absorptive capacity to deliver project food aid effectively to low-income and malnourished groups in recipient countries.

Development and emergency assistance   The African food crisis of 1984-6 high-lighted the important difference between developmental and emergency food aid. While CIDA does not consider it appropriate to assign a fixed proportion of its food aid to each category, it has adopted the practice of other donors and WFP in categorizing its food aid as either developmental or for emergencies.

Priority is given to ensuring immediate and adequate food deliveries to save lives. CIDA is also aware, however, that if the food shortages in Africa are perceived only as emergencies attributable to unfavourable weather, rather than as problems which are largely man-made, relief assistance will be provided rather than developmental aid designed to get at their root causes. Moreover, if emergency food aid is provided more readily than developmental food assistance, it could penalize countries that are making serious efforts to achieve agricultural and rural development.

CIDA has decided that developmental food aid should be largely programmed bilaterally through multi-year allocations to countries and multilaterally through WFP. Its bilateral allocations will be concentrated on those countries that have developmentally sound policies and programmes in place for their food and agricultural sectors, or are making a serious commitment to introduce such measures; where Canada has the capacity to supply commodities that meet their needs; and where Canada has the capacity to administer its assistance effectively. At the same time, CIDA has strengthened its capacity to respond to food emergencies.

Multi-year programming   The authority to make multi-year commitments, that was first granted to CIDA in 1981, has been one of the most positive steps taken to enable food aid to be used for development. Multi-year commitments facilitate inter-donor co-ordination and improve administrative efficiency and the timeliness of food aid. Experience has shown that such commitments have made the policy dialogue with recipient countries more effective. Furthermore, governments in developing countries are more willing and able to make significant policy adjustments if they know they will receive food aid throughout the period of change. Multi-year commitments also bring food aid into line with other types of Canadian development assistance and facilitate their integration. A potential drawback in multi-year programming is that it could reduce budgetary flexibility if it were extended to more countries.

Policy dialogue   Canada is engaged in a dialogue with a number of countries in an endeavour to relate its assistance to overall national policies and programmes. It seeks to have discussions with officials who are directly involved in establishing national priorities. CIDA recognizes that the policy dialogue can be a delicate long-drawn-out process of give and take that calls for a consistent policy on the part of donors as well as recipients with respect to economic development in the country concerned, and that in most cases the dialogue will work best when all donors co-ordinate their efforts. CIDA has undertaken to integrate its policy discussions into the broader international setting in such fora as the World Bank consultative groups and UNDP round tables.

Funds from food aid sales   Canadian policy since the early 1950s has required funds to be established by recipients from the sale of bilateral food aid and other commodity aid. These funds can be used to provide local currency components and support for development projects and programmes agreed between the recipient governments and Canada. Under appropriate conditions, the funds not allocated to specific projects or programmes within a reasonable time can be released to the recipient government to provide support for general development.

CIDA believes, however, that a flexible approach is required as the need for, and the possibilities of monitoring, these funds vary among recipient countries. It is recognized that the case for these funds is stronger when structural adjustment is planned in countries that have had weak macroeconomic policies, or in those countries that have been short of funds to meet the local costs of Canadian-assisted projects. Priority in the use of the funds is given to broadly defined agricultural development projects supported by Canada. It is considered that this priority gives most assurance that Canadian food aid will not act as a disincentive to improvements in local agricultural production.

To ensure consistency, control of the funds is linked to CIDA's country or regional programme review process. An indicative list of projects or uses to which the funds may be allocated is included as an annex to the memorandum of understanding or loan agreement concluded with the recipient government. Accountability for disbursements from the funds rests with the recipient government. CIDA is responsible, however, for the planning and monitoring of the funds and for compliance with established policies and procedures.

Canada is experiencing budgetary constraints in its aid programme coupled with competing demands for its assistance. The challenge remains to maximize the developmental and humanitarian impact of its food aid, whether it is channelled bilaterally, multilaterally or through NGOs.

Appendix Table 11.1 *Canada: Cereal food aid deliveries ('000 tons – in grain equivalent)*

	1987	1988	1989	1990	1991	1987–91 Average
Total:	1299.2	1319.9	826.8	953.1	1211.4	1122.1
By food aid channel:						
– Bilateral	767.0	616.8	399.6	529.2	628.2	588.2
– Gvt-to-Gvt	751.6	562.7	364.9	492.6	616.7	557.7
– through NGOs	15.4	54.1	34.7	36.6	11.5	30.5
– Multilateral	532.2	703.1	427.3	423.9	583.2	533.9
By food aid category:						
– Emergency Relief	224.1	331.9	200.4	223.0	251.9	246.3
– Project	883.5	696.8	554.5	567.9	842.8	709.1
– Agr./Rural Development	763.3	548.9	314.6	468.3	625.4	544.1
– Nutrition Intervention	116.5	30.7	23.3	19.0	82.6	54.4
– Other Development Project	3.8	117.2	216.6	80.6	134.8	110.6
– Non-project (Programme)	191.6	291.2	71.9	162.3	116.7	166.7
By Region:						
– Sub-Saharan Africa	264.4	367.1	267.7	267.8	287.1	290.9
– North Africa/Mid-East	125.7	220.4	126.0	145.3	255.5	174.6
– Asia and Pacific	866.0	658.6	344.4	439.4	546.6	571.0
– Latin America and Caribbean	43.1	73.7	88.8	67.8	121.2	78.9
– Europe	–	–	–	32.9	1.0	6.8

Source: WFP/INTERFAIS Database

Appendix Table 11.2 *Canada: Non-cereal food aid deliveries ('000 tons)*

	1987	1988	1989	1990	1991	1987–91 Average
Total:	124.4	157.6	56.2	88.2	58.1	96.9
By food aid channel:						
– Bilateral	99.2	116.6	20.8	56.0	17.7	62.0
– Gvt-to-Gvt	98.3	111.2	17.0	37.1	16.2	55.9
– through NGOs	0.8	5.4	3.8	18.9	1.5	6.1
– Multilateral	25.2	41.0	35.3	32.1	40.4	34.8
By food aid category:						
– Emergency Relief	7.1	45.6	26.4	40.5	33.8	30.7
– Project	62.9	75.1	22.9	30.6	22.4	42.7
– Agr./Rural Development	52.6	58.3	10.1	3.4	7.0	26.3
– Nutrition Intervention	5.6	8.3	2.4	2.0	3.2	4.3
– Other Development Project	3.4	7.5	9.5	25.1	12.1	11.5
– Non-project (Programme)	54.4	36.8	6.9	17.2	1.9	23.4
By Region:						
– Sub-Saharan Africa	21.8	39.6	32.6	32.4	31.9	31.7
– North Africa/Mid-East	3.8	4.5	3.3	2.1	5.3	3.8
– Asia and Pacific	77.7	64.7	2.3	9.1	1.8	31.1
– Latin America and Caribbean	21.1	48.7	17.9	40.2	19.0	29.4
– Europe	–	–	–	4.3	0.1	0.9

Source: ibid.

12 EC The European Community

Growing Pains

The European Community and its member states are collectively the second largest source of food aid in the world. The EC first provided food aid in 1968 after becoming a signatory to the first Food Aid Convention the previous year. However, that aid represents only a small proportion of food production, exports and stocks in EC member states, and proportionately less on that reckoning than that from other major donors. It has, therefore, been possible to provide substantial additional amounts of food aid since 1989, first to Eastern Europe and then to members of the Commonwealth of Independent States (CIS), the republics of the former Soviet Union, as well as to mount special programmes for sub-Saharan Africa.

This chapter focuses on 'Community action' within the EC food aid programme, implemented by the Commission in Brussels, rather than 'national action' carried out by member states individually. Some reference is made to national action, however, to show the totality of food aid provided and the relationships between the two types of action. Two companion case studies of Germany (Chapter 13) and the Netherlands (Chapter 14) provide complementary perspectives on national action.

The EC and its member states, as a signatory to every Food Aid Convention since 1967, have collectively pledged the second largest minimum annual contribution, currently 1.67 million tons of grain (in wheat equivalent). The Community has pledged resources to the World Food Programme regularly since 1968, and has been a consistent contributor to the International Emergency Food Reserve since it first came into operation in 1976. It also channels food aid through other UN organizations (UNHCR, UNBRO and UNRRA), the International Committee of the Red Cross, the League of Red Cross Societies, and NGOs normally registered in its member states.

There has been a certain tension between the use of food aid as a means of disposing of the Community's burgeoning food stocks and as a significant part of EC development assistance. Since the beginning of the 1980s, a series of Community regulations and policy resolutions have stressed the developmental use of food aid as a flexible resource, and the need to devolve responsibility for its programming and mobilization to those directly concerned with development assistance in the EC Commission.

Evolving Policy Framework

The current framework for the Community's food aid policy and management is based on the EC Council regulation 3972/86 of 22 December 1986 (*OJ* L370/1, 30 December 1986). This regulation represented an important milestone in a long sequence of actions designed to enhance the developmental effectiveness of EC food aid. It brought together, and reiterated, a number of important policy objectives expressed in previous regulations, communications and resolutions. In the latter half of 1989 and the first half of 1990, the Council of Ministers adopted another resolution providing a more detailed commentary on the 1986 regulation.

The main objectives of this policy and management regulation are:

– to integrate food aid more fully into the totality of the Community's development assistance;
– to integrate EC food aid as completely as possible into the development policies and programmes of recipient countries; and
– to make EC food aid management more efficient by strengthening and widening the Commission's decision-making and implementation functions.

According to the regulation, the objectives of EC food aid are to promote food security in recipient countries and regions; to raise the standard of nutrition of recipient populations; to help in emergencies; to contribute toward the balanced economic and social development of the recipient countries; and to support recipient countries' efforts to improve their own food production. Priority is given to projects and programmes that promote this last objective.

Under the 1986 regulation, food aid is to be allocated primarily on the basis of an objective evaluation of real food needs, with economic considerations also taken into account. Where EC food aid is provided in support of a development programme spread over a number of years, it may be committed on a multi-annual basis. Normally, EC food aid is reserved for the poorest countries and is linked, if necessary, with the implementation of annual or multi-annual development projects, sectoral actions or development programmes related to the food sector. While the bulk of EC direct cereal food aid is provided for balance of payments and budgetary support, the aid may be contributed directly to such projects, actions or programmes, and funds generated from the sale of EC food aid may also be used. Where the food aid is sold, the sale price must be set in such a way as not to disrupt the domestic markets of recipient countries. Priority is given to immediate consumption needs but EC food aid may also be granted to enable reserve stocks to be built up in recipient countries.

The management, procurement and delivery of EC food aid was separated from the management of the Community's Common Agricultural Policy under the 1986 regulation. This was a major step which allowed EC food aid to be more efficient and better adapted to the needs of recipient countries than in the past. The integration of EC food aid more fully into the development strategy of recipient countries and its packaging with other development co-operation have been a major concern for the Community since the beginning of the 1980s. For example, a regulation was adopted by the Council of Ministers in June 1984 on implementation of 'alternative operations', allowing the Community to substitute financial and technical aid on a grant basis for part or all of food aid allocated to a particular country when it would be counter-productive to continue to supply food aid. This facility has been particularly useful for developing countries with marked fluctuations in food production, as in sub-Saharan Africa during and after the recent food crises. A major emphasis in EC food aid policy since

1982 has been on 'food strategies' (see later in this chapter). The 1986 framework regulation and subsequent EC Council resolutions as well as the third and fourth Lomé Conventions have reinforced this approach.

Planning and Decision-making

The EC Commission, the EC Council of Ministers and the European Parliament have interacting roles with respect to food aid.

The Commission has two major roles: initiating Community action, and implementing the budget as well as decisions taken by the Community. As regards food aid, the Commission prepares the basic budget proposals, taking into account the financial guidelines set by the Community, and presents recommendations on the basis of which apportionments are decided. It also proposes new or modified regulations and prepares documents that form the basis for discussions with member states. It assumes overall responsibility for the execution of the Community action part of the EC's food aid programme in accordance with the decisions of the relevant Council of Ministers after consulting member states through the EC Food Aid Committee. This Committee, which is chaired by the Commission, examines all food aid allocations for recipient countries and agencies, and co-ordinates Community and national food aid operations. The Commission also decides on emergency food aid action and takes measures required to speed up the provision of such aid, but the precise modalities are unclear following the establishment of a new EC Humanitarian Assistance Office (ECHO). Within the Commission, direct responsibility for food aid rests with the Directorate-General for Development (DG VIII), which includes a Food Aid Unit.

The Council of Ministers is the decision-making body. Concerning food aid, in addition to the role it plays in the budgetary process, the Council, according to the regulation of December 1986, apportions the cereals aid provided under the FAC between the Community and national operations; apportions national cereals operations under the FAC among member states; determines the countries and organizations to which food aid may be supplied on an annual or multi-annual basis; and lays down general criteria for covering the cost of transporting food aid beyond the port of loading. It also takes major political decisions on food aid policies as well as on special food aid programmes, such as the Special Plan for Africa in 1991 and the Special Food Aid Programme in 1992, both being additional food aid programmes proposed by the Commission in response to the urgent problems facing African countries.

The European Parliament is responsible for approving the Community budget, which includes provision for food aid. It also provides opinions on food aid policy matters and takes an active interest in various issues with respect to food aid implementation, which often result in strong support for the Commission's initiatives on food aid.

The fourth Lomé Convention and Council resolutions and regulations seek to enhance coherence between EC food aid and the overall development objectives of recipient countries. Desk officers in DG VIII for African, Caribbean and Pacific (ACP) countries that receive EC assistance under the Lomé Convention, act as focal points in this regard. Until the decision in December 1992 to transfer responsibilities for non-ACP developing countries (excluding China) from the Directorate-General for External Affairs (DG I), desk officers in DG I acted as focal points for those countries in co-ordination with the Food Aid Unit in DG VIII.

The Directorate-General for Agriculture (DG VI) arranges for the mobilization of

EC food aid consignments. The Budget Directorate-General (DG XIX) carries responsibility for setting overall budgetary ceilings within the EC Commission and negotiates with the various directorates with regard to their respective allocations. The role of monitoring overall performance is carried out by the European Court of Auditors. The Director-General for Financial Control (DG XX), however, monitors financial performance on a regular basis and performs internal audits.

In retrospect, the Council regulation of December 1986 can be seen as marking a significant step in clarifying planning and decision-making procedures for the Community food aid programme as well as devolving increased responsibility to the Commission for its implementation.

Flow, Direction and Uses of Food Aid

Development assistance from the EC and its member states was 0.50% of GNP in 1989-90 compared with the average for all DAC/OECD countries of 0.35. Food aid normally accounts for about a fifth of the total value of all EC official development assistance commitments, a higher proportion than for any other donor. The total quantity of EC food aid is small, however, in comparison with the aggregate food production, exports and stocks of the EC member countries. And the cost of storage of EC food stocks has been significantly higher than total outlays on EC food aid.

Budgetary resources   The EC finances its food aid programme out of annual commitments from its development aid budget. The food aid budget for 1991 amounted to about 627 million ECU, accounting for slightly more than 1% of commitments under the total Community budget. In addition, the EC provides development resources through its extra-budgetary facilities, the European Development Fund (EDF) and the European Investment Bank (EIB). Budgetary and extra-budgetary resources together amounted to 4,360 billion ECU in 1991, about 16% of which was allocated for food aid.

Within the food aid budget itself, the greatest share of resources is allocated for the procurement of commodities, with dairy products historically claiming the largest portion, although it was declining in the 1980s. With the special programmes for Africa in 1991 and 1992, cereals now dominate procurement. Transport costs are also covered by the Community, in almost all cases up to the port of unloading or to the final destination. Allocations for transportation doubled in the mid-1980s in response to the needs of developing countries, particularly for landlocked countries and those affected by drought and civil war in sub-Saharan Africa.

Levels and composition of food aid   Largely as a result of the Community's decision to augment the level of its commitments under the 1980 FAC, EC and member states' food aid in cereals steadily increased to almost double the levels of the early 1970s. In 1991, EC Community action cereal food aid deliveries alone to developing countries were over one and a half million tons (in grain equivalent), about 13% of global deliveries. There has been a significant reversal of the relative proportions of EC Community and national action cereal food aid contributions under the Food Aid Conventions. For the first FAC of 1967, a ratio of Community and national actions of 29:71% was agreed within the EC. The share of Community action in the minimum contribution was subsequently increased to 55% following the 1980 and 56% under the 1986 Convention.

In practice, the EC and its member states have regularly exceeded their annual minimum commitments under the FAC. Significant fluctuations have occurred largely because of problems associated with the Community budgeting on a calendar year basis, while FAC commitments, made in physical quantities, relate to the crop year running from July to June. Delays have also been encountered in finalizing annual food aid allocations under the Community action programme. Fluctuations in food aid deliveries can have a beneficial effect for recipient countries if they are counter-cyclical in nature, that is, where allocations and shipments are relatively insensitive to short-run international price movements. However, they can introduce an element of unpredictability in EC food aid and, therefore, create negative planning and other effects in the longer term. The Community has taken steps to restructure operational procedures with a view to improving timeliness and overall efficiency.

The EC is a major provider of non-cereal, especially dairy, food aid. In 1991, it provided over 323,000 tons. The downward trend in the supply of dairy products since 1982 is in response to widespread criticism, especially within the European Parliament and by the EC Court of Auditors, with the general realization that it is difficult to use dairy products in a cost-effective way as food aid. The reduction is also a clear illustration of the growing consensus within the EC regarding the use of food aid as a resource genuinely attuned to the needs of development rather than as a conduit for surplus disposal. Dairy products have been increasingly provided in support of development projects rather than as programme aid, mainly because of the greater opportunities to use such products constructively, for example, in dairy development through multi-lateral organizations or NGOs.

An emerging feature of EC food aid, which is in part related to the greater emphasis on development concerns, is the introduction since 1983 of an increasing volume of other non-cereal commodities, such as vegetable oil, beans, sugar and fish, in addition to the traditionally predominant supplies of cereals and dairy products. In particular, the EC has replaced butter oil with vegetable oil in instances where oil is for use in cooking rather than in the reconstitution of milk.

Direct and indirect food aid   EC food aid flows through two main channels referred to as 'direct' and 'indirect'. Direct food aid is that which is provided to recipient countries by the EC itself. Indirect food aid is that portion of EC food aid channelled through international and non-governmental organizations.

Initially, a large proportion of EC food aid shipments were channelled *directly* in the form of cereal food aid. Direct food aid has accounted for about three-quarters of total EC food aid. In recent years, however, a growing share has been channelled *indirectly*. In 1991, a third was provided directly and two-thirds indirectly in value terms. Within the EC's indirect food aid, resources have been channelled largely through WFP, UNHCR, the International Committee of the Red Cross (ICRC), the League of Red Cross Societies (LRCS) and NGOs. WFP alone received about a quarter of EC dairy food aid, reflecting the increasing use of this resource as project aid.

Resources allocated to WFP   The EC and its member states together contributed over one-third of WFP resources for the biennium 1989/90. The EC co-operates with WFP in five ways. First, it has made voluntary pledges to WFP's regular resources since 1969. A distinct feature of these pledges has been the predominance of the proportion made in commodities; the cash component for transportation was 19% in 1991. This stems from the way in which the EC makes its pledges, both in respect of the volume of high value products allocated and regulations limiting untied cash contributions.

The cash element, apart from purchasing food in developing countries, covers transport and associated costs of the food pledged, with only a limited sum to cover other expenditures. This does not meet the objective in WFP's General Regulations, which envisages a two-thirds to one-third ratio between pledges in commodities and in cash respectively in the aggregate. EC commodity allocations to WFP have consisted largely of cereals, including wheat from EC member countries or other cereals purchased in developing countries; dairy products, for which the EC remains an important source, despite reductions; and significant quantities of pulses and vegetable oil in recent years.

Secondly, the EC has contributed to the IEFR since its inception in 1976. It has contributed both commodities and cash for triangular transactions and local purchases in developing countries. The EC was the second largest contributor (after the United States) in the biennium 1989-90, providing US$31 million. The commodity contributions have consisted mainly of grain, with relatively smaller quantities of pulses, skim-milk powder, sugar, vegetable oil and butter oil. Thirdly, the EC has been a strong supporter of WFP's protracted refugee operations, providing US$31 million during the biennium 1989-90.

Fourthly, the EC provides grants to WFP for non-food items and logistical support in emergencies. The contribution for non-food items in the biennium 1989-90 was US$1.5 million. Fifthly, since 1982 the EC has asked WFP to provide services for the purchase, transportation, supervision and monitoring of its bilateral food aid, especially, although not only, for countries in sub-Saharan Africa.

Non-governmental organizations   NGOs represent a significant channel for the EC indirect food aid programme. NGO-EC co-operation involves a number of organizations and developing countries. An NGO wishing to receive EC food aid for use in its own operations must fulfil three essential criteria: its headquarters must generally be in one of the EC member states; its statutes must incorporate the provision of humanitarian assistance as a major objective; and it must have a proven record of success in distributing food aid effectively in developing countries. In addition, EC guidelines for NGOs include provisions requiring, among other things, that increasing attention should be given to food aid to food-deficit countries, and that priority should be given to rural development projects, particularly those that promote food self-sufficiency programmes and social welfare projects. NGO programmes supported with EC food aid have, therefore, focused largely on rural development and welfare-oriented activities in support of hospitals and schools. Since the crises of the mid-1980s, NGOs have become a major channel for EC emergency aid, particularly to countries of sub-Saharan Africa affected by war and drought.

A co-ordinating body for NGOs in EC member states, known as EuronAid, was established in December 1980 to provide logistical and financing services to NGOs using EC food aid in their relief and development programmes. EuronAid has a current membership of 20 NGOs but provides services to all NGOs requesting its services, whether members or not. In 1991 it handled some 515,000 tons of EC food aid. EuronAid also enhances NGO co-ordination, serves as a forum for discussion on ways of effectively helping people in need in developing countries, and helps in developing a common policy for generally improving their standard of living. EuronAid is funded by a levy on shipments and contributions by member agencies.

Sales and free distribution   EC direct food aid is provided through two modalities: grant programme food aid, involving the sale of commodities provided, as budgetary or balance of payments support, with the generated funds being used for development activities; and project food aid, involving the free distribution of commodities to target groups in, for example, school feeding or FFW programmes.

Sales account for the bulk of EC direct food aid in most recipient countries. In many cases, the proceeds from the sale of commodities have been used to provide local cost support to development activities assisted by EC financial aid, mostly in agriculture and rural development. For ACP countries that receive assistance under the Lomé Convention, this means that there is greater scope for food aid becoming developmentally linked with EDF-supported projects and programmes under Lomé indicative plans. In non-ACP countries, food aid often constitutes a major proportion of the Community's total development assistance, both in terms of the food provided and funds generated through food aid sales.

The programming, management and use of funds generated from the sale of commodities provided as food aid have encountered difficulties in a number of countries, as documented in special and annual reports of the EC Court of Auditors. There have sometimes been serious lags between the receipt and sale of food aid commodities and the transfer of funds into special accounts. Another problem relates to the prices at which EC food aid commodities have been sold, especially in countries where food prices are highly subsidized. Progress is being made in resolving these problems. All EC direct food aid should be valued at world market prices and the equivalent amount transferred to an EC special account normally not later than three months after delivery of the food consignment.

A small number of recipient countries have EC-assisted food aid programmes that involve direct, free distribution to beneficiaries. For example, a large free distribution programme was implemented in Ethiopia, where food aid was used in a labour-intensive FFW programme for soil and water conservation. WFP provided services for monitoring EC food aid in this programme. Similarly, the Community is providing large amounts of food aid for FFW and vulnerable group development in Bangladesh, for which WFP provides monitoring services.

Regional and country distribution of direct EC food aid   The continent of Africa overtook Asia as the largest beneficiary of direct EC cereal food aid in the late 1970s. Latin America and the Middle East, apart from Egypt, have consistently received small proportions of direct EC food aid, averaging between 2% and 5% of total shipments in recent years. A small number of countries, including Bangladesh, Egypt and India, have received a high proportion of direct EC development food aid. Severely affected countries in Africa, such as Ethiopia, Mozambique and Sudan, have been major recipients of direct EC emergency aid. A large number of countries, including most ACP states, have received small allocations of direct assistance. In 1991, a Special Programme for Africa was launched, with contributions from the Community and member states, underscoring the continued priority for this region. The programme consisted of an additional 600,000 tons of emergency food aid in cereals, two-thirds from the EC as a whole and the remainder from EC member countries individually. The Community action has been covered by a special budget of 140 million ECU for the supply of commodities and their transportation to final destinations, and 12 million ECU as additional logistical support. In 1992, a further special programme of approximately double the scale of 1991 was agreed in response to drought and other acute problems in the region.

Since 1989 the EC has also provided substantial programme aid to Eastern Europe and the republics of the former Soviet Union. This aid has been organized by External

Relations (DG I), outside the regulatory framework of EC food aid to developing countries. Funding was initially provided under the Community's agricultural budget. This aid is part of the effort of the group of 24 countries (G24) which the Community was also handed responsibility for co-ordinating. The EC also made humanitarian food aid allocations to countries of the former Soviet Union and Central and Eastern Europe in 1991 with a total value of 289 million ECU. This amount was budgeted for over and above food aid allocations to developing countries.

Programming of assistance Beginning with the third Lomé Convention in 1985, specific attention has been given to the more integrated programming of all EC development assistance, including food and other non-Lomé aid, concentrating assistance on a few development sectors. Most ACP countries have chosen to concentrate aid on supporting a rural development sector strategy aimed, in the majority of cases, at greater food security or self-sufficiency. The EC considered that the results of this approach to aid programming were encouraging and that the challenge was to bring the same qualitative improvements into the implementation stage. This would require that cohesion of assistance, including food aid, is maintained. A programme rather than a project-based approach would be required, with projects becoming components of programmes. This would not exclude, however, the funding of isolated projects and programmes; the arrangement should be flexible enough for adjustments to be made in the course of implementation. Accordingly, the fourth Lomé Convention in 1990 emphasizes the targeted use of funds generated from the sale of food and other commodity assistance, for example, in financing expenditures in the health and training sectors.

The EC is one of the few donors to have a major regional development assistance instrument. The fourth Lomé Convention sets out detailed regional criteria to encourage ACP states to enlarge and intensify their joint development efforts so that they can take the form of tangible co-operation, even regional integration. Regional programming was already well advanced in some regions that had regional co-operation structures.

Food strategies Food strategies have received major emphasis in EC food aid policy. This concept involves the packaging of food aid with other forms of EC development assistance to assist the food and agriculture sector in developing countries in the context of an agreement or donor-recipient dialogue on policy reform. Policy and investment focus is given to the agricultural sector and development assistance is planned on the basis of a sectoral programme, rather than for individual projects.

Since 1982, the EC has supported the implementation of pilot food strategies in a number of countries in sub-Saharan Africa, to which food aid has provided important support. The EC Council of Development Ministers considers that the adoption of food strategies can result in a better integration of food aid with financial and technical assistance and that, despite difficulties and weaknesses, the food strategy approach can be considered suitable for more general application. A gradual extension of this approach was therefore envisaged, although in practice progress has been rather slow.

Dairy development EC dairy food aid (skim-milk powder and butter oil) is being used to assist recipient countries in the development of their own dairy industries, although levels of dairy aid are gradually being reduced. By far the largest development project assisted by EC food aid has concerned the development of the dairy industry in India, with co-financing from the World Bank (see Chapter 3). Another example of EC food aid for the development of integrated dairy development is in China.

Triangular transactions   Changes in EC food aid policy regulations have made provision for purchases of food in exporting developing countries for use as food aid in other developing countries through triangular transactions. The objectives are to provide commodities more suited to the food habits of consumers, to speed up the supply of emergency aid and to strengthen food security. This provision has thereby enhanced the flexibility of EC food aid programming, while further delinking supplies from dependence on EC export availabilities. Such transactions have been carried out mainly within sub-Saharan Africa. Cash for triangular transactions has also been provided to international agencies, including WFP, and to NGOs, especially to speed up delivery in emergency situations. In 1991, EC triangular operations involved 350,000 tons of food commodities at a cost of 125 million ECU. They were carried out mainly in China, Uganda, Turkey, Pakistan, Zimbabwe and Argentina for supply to Ethiopia, Sudan, Somalia, Mozambique and Angola.

Alternative operations   Alternative or substitute operations aim to provide financial and technical aid when the changing food supply situation of a country makes it no longer appropriate to provide food aid. They aim to improve self-reliance in food through increasing food and agriculture production in the recipient country. The cash provided in place of food aid, as well as funds generated from the sale of EC food aid, can be used to cover both external and local expenditures, including maintenance and operating costs.

In 1988, two Council regulations were adopted on the implementation of storage programmes and early warning systems and on the execution of co-financing for the purchase of food products or seeds by international bodies or NGOs, thus broadening the scope of EC food aid.

Emergency aid   The Commission can take quick emergency action to help governments and people facing serious unforeseen difficulties as a result of natural disasters. Member states are simply informed of the action taken. In the case of man-made disasters, however, emergency assistance can be provided only after consulting member states by telex, giving them 48 hours to raise any objections.

The 1986 framework regulation defines an emergency qualifying for EC assistance as 'an exceptional situation in which famine, or an imminent danger thereof, poses a serious threat to the lives or health of the population in a country which is unable to cope with the food shortfall using its own means and resources'. The Commission must ensure that priority is given to the mobilization of food aid for emergencies. Emergency assistance is limited to a period not exceeding four months.

EC emergency food aid is financed from the Community's food aid development budget. In addition, a supplementary reserve has been set up to cover exceptional emergency food needs. Under the third and fourth Lomé Conventions, special allocations have been made for mostly non-food emergency aid. This aid may be integrated into national indicative programmes in order to prepare the execution of reconstruction or rehabilitation operations. Aid may also be granted to ACP states taking in refugees or returnees to meet acute needs not covered by emergency aid and to implement longer-term projects and action programmes aimed at food self-sufficiency.

In response to the widely recognized need to ensure closer integration of different aspects of emergency aid, the EC established ECHO in March 1992 with global responsibilities for humanitarian assistance. The rationale for this office is to enhance the speed and efficiency of all EC emergency operations involving both food and non-food resources. The office is also expected to improve co-ordination among EC member states and to facilitate co-operation with other donors, international organizations and NGOs. The implications for future EC food aid were not initially made clear.

Issues for the Future

The future level, composition and direction of EC food aid may be influenced by a number of factors. Some of the main concerns may be briefly outlined as follows.

The EC food aid programme is a large undertaking. A clear mandate exists to operate the programme effectively and efficiently in the interests of developing countries. While considerable attention has been given since the beginning of the 1980s to the policy and programming aspects of EC food aid in order to make it a flexible instrument for development, applied efficiently and pragmatically, equal attention is required for its effective implementation.

The Food Aid Unit at EC headquarters in Brussels, and the capacity of EC country delegations, need to be strengthened. Food aid has complex effects that require careful analysis on a country-specific basis. To the extent that food aid is effectively integrated into the mainstream of EC development assistance instead of being handled as a separate and parallel action, the workload could be reduced. This would also give greater coherence to the EC's total development assistance programme and would ensure complementarity among the different aid instruments.

Capacity and coherence can be increased by strengthening co-ordination not only among the EC's Community and national food aid programmes, but also between these and the food aid programmes of other donors and organizations. Most of the EC member states' individual national programmes are so small that they can make only marginal contributions to development in the recipient countries as individual entities. Thus, greater cohesion among them, in concert with EC Community action, would increase their effectiveness. Closer cohesion at the country level between the EC Community and national food aid programmes and those of other donors would also lead to increased capacity and effectiveness.

Greater cohesion with other food aid donors could also increase the EC's capacity to enlarge its food aid programme. In this context, agreement has been reached with WFP to examine how the two organizations might work more closely with governments in selected countries in assessing needs, identifying priorities and programming and implementing a coherent plan for food aid.

The Maastricht Treaty on Political Union signed in February 1992 by EC member states includes a chapter on development co-operation. This chapter provides the first explicit statement in a legal framework of objectives and the relationships between Community and national developmental co-operation activities. Follow-up to the treaty in terms of closer co-operation between the member states is envisaged, which could eventually have far-reaching implications for future EC food aid.

A major problem of EC food aid has been the short planning horizon with its continued emphasis on annual programming through a cumbersome process of implementing regulations. Provision, however, has been made for multi-annual programming. The limited experience of the EC and the experience of some other food aid donors have shown that it is possible to devise a programme of multi-annual commitments on a forward rolling basis, within an annual budget system. Such programmes provide a guaranteed flow of food aid for specific development objectives and support recipient governments in their endeavours to implement policy reforms and adjustment measures. They are particularly important for project food aid.

Efforts to improve the planning, management and use of funds obtained through the sale of EC food aid in recipient countries also need to be continued and pursued more systematically in order to enhance their contribution to development.

EC Council regulations in the 1980s permitted the increased used of triangular transactions and the provision of financial and technical assistance in place of food aid through alternative operations. Particular attention now needs to be given to the adoption by donors, including the EC and WFP, of a common code of conduct for such operations.

Lastly, there is the question whether the large increases in total EC food aid resulting from programmes for Eastern Europe and the former Soviet Union will have longer-term implications or will prove to be only a temporary phenomenon. These developments have shown the capacity of the EC to provide far higher levels of food aid than were previously supplied during the two decades since shipments began in 1969. This could augur well for meeting the increasing needs of developing countries for food aid, co-ordinated with financial and technical assistance.

Appendix Table 12.1 *EC Community action: Cereal food aid deliveries[a] ('000 tons – in grain equivalent)*

	1987	1988	1989	1990	1991	1987–91 Average
Total:	1284.1	1547.0	1451.8	2306.1	1886.0	1695.0
By food aid channel:						
– Bilateral	1097.7	1277.8	1262.8	1929.4	1381.4	1389.8
– Gvt-to-Gvt	1054.2	1169.2	1164.3	1664.6	893.9	1189.2
– through NGOs	43.4	108.6	98.6	264.9	487.5	200.6
– Multilateral	186.4	269.2	189.0	376.7	504.5	305.2
By food aid category:						
– Emergency Relief	317.8	451.8	403.4	519.8	877.9	514.1
– Project	188.8	281.5	179.2	257.7	264.2	234.2
– Agr./Rural Development	78.0	160.0	110.9	119.4	177.3	129.1
– Nutrition Intervention	105.3	84.2	33.5	16.7	12.2	50.4
– Food Reserve	–	3.5	6.7	12.0	–	4.4
– Other Development Project	5.6	33.7	28.0	109.6	74.7	50.3
– Non-project (Programme)	777.4	813.7	869.2	1528.5	743.9	946.6
By region:						
– Sub-Saharan Africa	374.3	688.4	425.2	664.6	977.5	626.0
– North Africa/Mid-East	351.9	296.1	297.7	141.7	250.9	267.7
– Asia and Pacific	482.2	511.5	397.6	282.1	233.3	381.3
– Latin America and Caribbean	75.7	50.9	56.8	67.9	50.8	60.4
– Europe	–	–	274.4	1149.7	373.5	359.5

[a] Excluding food aid provided by individual EC member states in their national action programmes.

Source: WFP/INTERFAIS Database

Appendix Table 12.2 *EC Community action: Non-cereal food aid deliveries*[a] *('000 tons)*

	1987	1988	1989	1990	1991	1987–91 Average
Total:	158.0	267.0	193.2	233.3	395.7	249.5
By food aid channel:						
– Bilateral	103.8	190.8	129.0	156.4	299.6	176.0
– Gvt-to-Gvt	84.5	143.5	99.8	105.5	195.1	125.7
– through NGOs	19.3	47.3	29.3	51.0	104.5	50.3
– Multilateral	54.2	76.3	64.2	76.8	96.1	73.5
By food aid category:						
– Emergency Relief	43.3	91.8	48.3	85.3	168.0	87.3
– Project	71.4	114.4	107.9	84.6	75.4	90.8
– Agr./Rural Development	32.7	52.5	69.6	32.2	31.4	43.7
– Nutrition Intervention	29.3	35.0	24.1	24.6	21.1	26.8
– Food Reserve	1.8	2.2	0.8	2.6	–	1.5
– Other Development Project	7.6	24.7	13.4	25.2	22.9	18.8
– Non-project (Programme)	43.4	60.7	37.0	63.4	152.4	71.4
By region:						
– Sub-Saharan Africa	59.5	86.9	47.4	83.7	120.9	79.7
– North Africa/Mid-East	23.0	45.6	36.0	34.1	43.4	36.4
– Asia and Pacific	31.3	96.7	60.6	33.1	38.7	52.1
– Latin America and Caribbean	44.2	37.9	36.6	29.3	32.2	36.1
– Europe	–	–	12.5	53.1	160.5	45.2

[a] Excluding food aid provided by individual EC member states in their national action programmes.

Source: ibid.

13 Germany[1]

An EC Member State
National Programme:
Issues of Parallel Responsibility

Germany is the third largest free market economy and the fourth largest source of official development assistance in the world. Germany itself was a major recipient of food aid until the early 1950s. Since 1959 it has been a food aid donor. It is now both the largest single food aid donor in Europe and the largest contributor to the European Community's food aid programme. It has made contributions regularly to WFP, the IEFR and the Food Aid Convention since their inception.

Germany's ODA has not kept pace with the rate of expansion of its economy, however, despite strong public opinion in favour of larger resource transfers to developing countries (especially the poorest among them) and frequent appeals from well-known and respected German NGOs. During most of the 1980s, while German ODA increased by less than 6% in real terms, GDP increased by over 14%. ODA disbursements of US$6,320 million (at current prices) in 1990 represented 0.42% of Germany's GNP, above the weighted average for DAC member countries of the OECD of 0.35%, but well below the UN target of 0.7%, which the German Government recognizes as a figure for orientation purposes.

Since 1970, Germany's GDP at constant prices has grown at twice the rate of its agricultural sector. In the late 1980s, the agricultural sector actually shrank, while GDP expanded by over 15%. The agricultural sector's contribution to GDP has therefore fallen to around only 2%. The production of most of the country's basic food commodities does not reach domestic consumption levels and has to be supplemented by imports.

About one-third of Germany's ODA is channelled multilaterally through the UN system and through the aid programmes of the European Community. The share of food aid in Germany's ODA has ranged between 5% and 10% in recent years.

---

[1] This paper considers the food aid experience of the former Federal Republic of Germany only. Although the former Democratic Republic of Germany also had an overseas aid programme, this largely consisted of technical assistance and only relatively small amounts of food aid were supplied. The balance of German food aid policies and programmes for developing countries has, therefore, not been noticeably altered as a result of German reunification.

Development Co-operation

New policy guidelines for German development assistance were adopted in 1986. The broad aims and principles of development assistance policy were defined as: combating hunger and poverty, thereby benefitting the poorest sections of the populations in developing countries; assisting the development of viable national economies and social diversity to enable developing countries to progress under their own momentum; and promoting regional co-operation among countries and their integration into the world economy. German development assistance policy is focused primarily on helping the poor to help themselves, through their own institutions and organizations, particularly in sub-Saharan Africa.

The policy guidelines give sectoral priority to: food security and rural development, the main objective of German development assistance, in order to help developing countries, especially in sub-Saharan Africa, to feed themselves; protection of the environment; improvement of energy supplies; promotion of education and training; and population activities, linking family planning with improvements in living conditions. The guidelines stress that in all sectors women must receive special consideration in the planning and implementation of projects and programmes. Since the circumstances and needs of developing countries differ, the guidelines underline that it is not possible to give each sector equal priority. Agreement is therefore reached with each country separately as to where deficiencies are most acute and how the country concerned and German assistance can contribute towards their removal.

Of the measures to increase agricultural production, special emphasis is given to helping small farmers by supplying equipment and building up efficient marketing systems, and to agricultural research. For such measures to be successful, it is stressed that there should be land ownership or long-term leases and that marketing and pricing policies should offer incentives for agricultural production. To halt the rural exodus to urban areas, development of the entire rural area is recommended by creating an efficient social and economic infrastructure embracing public health and education, transport, water and energy supply. Considerable importance is given to small crafts and trades, rural extension services and self-help organizations.

The policy guidelines note that food aid can be given to help overcome shortages in food supply. They observe that the suggestion that food aid can be limited to short-term measures because it is said to hamper food production in the recipient country or because of negative effects on consumers has proved to be unrealistic, at least in a number of African countries. The government will continue to provide assistance under the FAC. Efforts will still be made to limit the potentially harmful side-effects of food aid and to ensure that it serves the purposes of development policy. As far as possible, therefore, the food needed will be procured in developing countries. Germany supports the incorporation of food aid into food security programmes through FFW, the establishment of national reserves and the expansion of storage and distribution capacities as well as the development of comprehensive food production strategies, especially in countries with structural deficits.

Evolving Food Aid Policy

As in a number of other donor countries, early German food aid consisted of bulk supplies shipped mainly to meet emergencies in developing countries, with little consideration given to how it was used or to accountability. Since the mid-1970s, however, strong emphasis has been placed on increasing people's participation in self-help efforts and on influencing the use of the resources provided through the accompanying provision of technical assistance.

Two distinct regional approaches have been adopted in using food aid. In the Sahelian countries of West Africa, the establishment and management of food security reserves was promoted from about 1975, an approach initially stimulated by FAO's food security assistance scheme. The process of using food aid to build up security stocks has now largely been completed. During the 1980s, measures to adjust the economies of many Sahelian countries began to be implemented within the context of structural and sectoral adjustment lending programmes of the IMF and the World Bank. The original concept of food security reserves managed by parastatal marketing organizations was, therefore, adapted and integrated into the restructuring of national cereal markets, taking into account the necessary policy changes.

In Central and South America, so-called 'integrated food security programmes' have been implemented, starting with Honduras in 1975. The original objectives were based on the experience of German-financed emergency assistance in the region in the early 1970s, namely to achieve an adequate level of subsistence for marginal groups by improving conditions for agricultural production, protecting agricultural potential and integrating poor farmers into the market economy. The strategy was to involve the active participation of the target groups in self-help activities through their own organizations and institutions, using labour-intensive technologies. Activities which received aid were to be based on requests received from the groups themselves and not imposed on them.

A resolution was adopted by the German Parliament in December 1987 on 'Food security in regions affected by hunger'. This resolution urged the German Government to increase efforts to purchase food in surplus-producing developing countries for use as food aid. Efforts already undertaken in this regard are being continued, wherever possible and economically feasible, to comply with the resolution. In 1988, 35% of the volume of German cereal food aid and 44% of the volume of non-cereal food aid provided bilaterally were obtained in developing countries, especially in sub-Saharan Africa.

Co-ordination and harmonization of procedures for food aid management and deliveries have been intensified with other donors. Co-operation in food security policy and programmes has also been strengthened with other bilateral donors as well as with organizations such as the EC Commission, FAO, the World Bank and WFP. In the regional context of the Sahel, co-operation has been increased with members of the Club du Sahel and the Secretariat of the Permanent Interstate Committee for Drought Control in the Sahel (CILSS).

An important policy paper setting out concepts and principles for the planning and implementation of food aid and food security projects was completed in November 1989 (BMZ, 1989). It observed that food aid and food security measures can be deployed either as independent instruments or as preparatory or supplementary measures, in co-ordination with financial or technical assistance. It noted that food aid can contribute to satisfying basic human needs, if provided on time and in a form appropriate to the consumption habits of the beneficiaries and to the production possibilities of the recipient country. Integrated into comprehensive aid programmes, food aid can also contribute to achieving food security. If handled carefully, food aid can cushion the adverse effects of structural adjustment programmes.

The paper noted that, although food aid had special importance for low-income food-deficit countries, it was a highly controversial form of development co-operation.

If deployed incorrectly, it could hamper genuine solutions to problems, hinder local production and result in undesirable changes in consumer behaviour, thereby creating dependence. When food aid was provided not as a grant but as a credit, it could also worsen the debt situation of developing countries.

Nevertheless, the policy paper viewed food aid as an instrument to overcome food bottlenecks. The aims of food aid were defined, in accordance with the objectives laid down for the EC food aid programme, as: promoting food security of recipient countries and regions; raising the nutritional status of beneficiaries; and contributing to balanced economic and social development in recipient countries. Different types of food aid measures could be applied depending on whether the aim was to achieve food security in the short or longer term, or to prevent food insecurity from occurring. Those measures included:

(i) *Emergency food aid*: In response to disasters and to alleviate unforeseen or exceptional food shortages or nutritional deficiencies in developing countries, this type of food aid could be either sold through normal market channels or, where the afflicted population has insufficient purchasing power, distributed in the short term free of charge.

(ii) *Refugee and displaced person programmes*: For refugees, free distribution of food, feeding programmes or FFW, ideally in combination with self-help measures, were considered to be imperative. Food was provided free of charge to displaced persons.

(iii) *'Regular' food aid*: This type of aid represented a contribution toward covering a structural food deficit that a recipient country was unable to eliminate either from its own production or through commercial imports. It was a form of balance of payments assistance or programme aid, and was not project-related.

(iv) *Preventive measures as disaster relief, and to help overcome short-term supply bottlenecks*: These measures involved the establishment and management of national buffer stocks and support in the preparation of a database for the formulation of a cereal market policy. In addition to the provision of food aid for buffer stocks, measures also included financial assistance to improve and expand storage facilities and to set up early warning systems, and technical assistance and training in stock protection and management, the establishment of market and supply information systems, and co-ordination of food aid received from a number of sources.

(v) *Integrated food security programmes*: Such programmes involved a combination of food aid (generally from local sources) with financial and technical assistance to provide extension services, materials and equipment. The target groups were the poor and malnourished in rural as well as urban areas.

(vi) *Additional measures*: The range of instruments has been extended in recent years to include a combination of FFW and cash-for-work, inputs-for-work, equipment-for-work and food-for-training.

The policy paper also remarked that bilateral food aid to overcome chronic, longer-term food insecurity was concentrated essentially on the same low-income food-deficit countries as bilateral financial and technical assistance. It was considered essential, therefore, that food security projects involving food aid should form an integral part of bilateral co-operation programmes involving all forms of German aid, as food aid is seen as an additional resource to promote economic development. Similarly, this principle applied to German participation in the programmes of multilateral agencies.

In the case of structural adjustment programmes involving food aid, it was considered most important to co-ordinate financial and food assistance at the time of programme planning and preparation, to harmonize the conditions under which aid was provided, and to make a multi-year commitment of food aid as well as financial assistance. Food aid could be used to mitigate the adverse effects of adjustment on the poor through public works programmes or, if appropriate, short-term feeding programmes. Funds from the sale of food aid commodities could also be used to support national budgets for education, training and health which, as experience had shown, could be adversely affected by structural adjustment measures.

The policy paper stressed that the objective of food aid as a development instrument must be for such aid to become superfluous within a process of self-sustained economic development in developing countries. This required three conditions: increased efforts on the part of the developing countries themselves; optimal deployment of food aid in recipient countries; and a change of donor attitude so that food aid was not merely regarded as an instrument for solving their own problem of agricultural surpluses.

Since 1973, the German Government has submitted to Parliament, usually at two-year intervals, reports on its development assistance policy. Initially, Parliament's response through its resolutions emphasized the use of food aid in cases of natural disasters and other emergencies, urging that such assistance should not weaken incentives for local food production. In general the developmental nature of food aid seems to have been given only secondary consideration.

The relationship between food security and food availability, on the one hand, and measures designed to combat poverty, encourage production for self-consumption and generate additional purchasing power, on the other hand, were specifically mentioned in a resolution passed by Parliament in May 1986. In the mid-1980s a series of Parliamentary resolutions also called for a clearer definition of EC emergency and regular food aid, and their relationship; clarification of the criteria for the selection of countries to receive food aid from the Community; priority for procurement of the food commodities in developing countries themselves for use as food aid, and only in exceptional cases from the EC market; improved control systems for food aid distribution; and an evaluation of the EC's experience with food aid.

The German Parliament has pursued procurement of food in developing countries for use as food aid with particular perseverance, as seen, for example, in its December 1987 resolution on 'Food security in regions affected by hunger'. A resolution in November 1990 called upon the EC to make greater efforts to draw on available surpluses in a number of African countries through triangular transactions and local purchases, and to move away from indirect budgetary assistance and sales of food commodities from the EC that could act as a disincentive for domestic food production. The resolution called for an EC food aid policy based less on member countries' interests and more on humanitarian and development assistance policy criteria.

Food Aid Administration and Budget

Efforts have been made to co-ordinate and rationalize the assignment of responsibilities within the government's development assistance administration, but it remains relatively complex. Five public agencies are involved: three federal ministries in Bonn; the Federal Office for Agricultural Market Regulation (BALM), with headquarters in Frankfurt; and the German Agency for Technical Co-operation Ltd (GTZ) at Eschborn near Frankfurt.

The Federal Ministry for Economic Co-operation (BMZ) has responsibility for defining policy, planning and co-ordination of the government's entire bilateral and multilateral development assistance programme. BMZ also acts as a lead agency in the interministerial decision-making process. It receives and makes decisions on requests for food aid and concludes agreements on the provision of such aid. A BMZ representative heads German interministerial delegations that conduct negotiations with food aid recipient countries and WFP.

BMZ comprises three departments: one essentially for assistance channelled bilaterally, another for aid provided through multilateral agencies, and a third primarily for general administrative and personnel matters and co-operation with Germany's public and private institutions. The implementation of food aid falls within the multilateral department, despite the rather large component of Germany's bilateral food aid.

The Federal Ministry for Food, Agriculture and Forestry (BML) is consulted by BMZ on food aid matters. It is responsible for the procurement of commodities that BMZ recommends should be supplied. The advisory role of BML on individual requests to BMZ for food aid is considerably facilitated by an annual food aid allocation exercise conducted by BMZ in consultation with BML during which tentative earmarking of food assistance in response to anticipated requests is discussed.

The Foreign Office (AA) has a special budget line for *ad hoc* contributions for strictly humanitarian relief assistance in response mainly to sudden natural disasters or accidents caused by technical failure that require immediate life-saving or life-preserving interventions. The funds allocated for this purpose can be increased, if necessary, by using unspent allocations from other AA budget lines or other federal resources.

Special efforts are made to ensure rapid approval of humanitarian assistance. The AA may call upon the support services of the Federal Ministry of Transport and/or the Federal Ministry of Defence, to facilitate the fast movement of relief assistance. The AA keeps a small stock of relief items readily available at Cologne/Bonn airport. Usually, however, it draws from stocks of the German Red Cross or other German NGOs working in the affected area, or authorizes the nearest German embassy to carry out local purchases on its behalf.

The AA's role in the processing of requests for food aid financed by BMZ is similar to that of BML. The AA is included in the consultation process leading to the establishment of an annual food aid allocation plan; and BMZ seeks AA's views whenever an individual request for food aid is examined.

The Federal Office for Agricultural Market Regulation (BALM) is a federal agency acting under BML's supervision. BALM is essentially responsible for the implementation of the EC's agricultural market directives in Germany. It is charged, *inter alia*, with the regulation of nearly all basic food commodity markets and, for emergency assistance, with the establishment and management of food stocks for human and livestock consumption.

It is responsible, on BML's behalf, for the procurement of cereal commodities in EC markets for use in Germany's bilateral food aid programmes (including those implemented with the assistance of the NGO community) and in WFP-assisted projects implemented with regular resources pledged by Germany. It issues EC-wide tenders for competitive bidding, arranges for quality control of the commodities supplied, if necessary through its own laboratories, and arranges for shipment to the designated loading port. BALM is not usually involved in the procurement of cereal commodities for WFP's emergency operations, as it is BMZ's policy to provide cash resources for this purpose to enable WFP to purchase cereals in, or close to, the developing country afflicted.

The German Agency for Technical Co-operation Ltd (GTZ) is the channel for technical assistance financed by BMZ. It also administers German bilateral food aid provided within the framework of food security programmes. GTZ has the legal status of a limited liability company; it is not a government department or public agency but is owned by the Federal Government. This semi-autonomous status allows it to retain a certain independence. It has over 1,000 staff, with technical teams and officers working in a number of developing countries on development projects supported by Germany.

GTZ plays a complementary role similar to that of BALM concerning BMZ-financed development food aid channelled through WFP. It is responsible for the procurement of non-cereal commodities as part of WFP's regular resources pledged by the Government.

Processing of food aid requests   Food aid allocations are made in response to requests from governments of developing countries, German NGOs and international aid organizations (mainly WFP and the UNHCR). The criteria used in deciding on a request are primarily (i) food requirements (emergency and structural deficits); (ii) per caput income; and (iii) the existence of especially needy population groups. Other criteria also include: the balance of payments position of the requesting country; the expected economic and social impact, the cost of the measures proposed; the self-help potential of the target group to be supported; the policy commitment of the country concerned to increase food security, taking into account its agricultural structure, food consumption habits and socio-cultural factors.

Information required for determining the type and scope of food aid interventions is mainly obtained from WFP, FAO, UNHCR, the German embassies in the countries concerned, NGOs and the government authorities in developing countries. Special attention is given to monitoring the food supply situation in some 35 developing countries that regularly require emergency aid. The German embassies in these countries are required to provide information annually on this subject. Another important source of information is provided through the food security programmes implemented by GTZ. Particular attention is given to consultation and co-ordination with international aid agencies and other major donor countries in the developing country and at their headquarters. While co-ordinated action has been strengthened, it is recognized that there is room for further improvement in this regard.

Implementation of the various types of bilateral food aid measures is carried out in several ways. Emergency aid is provided through German NGOs, WFP or GTZ-implemented food security programmes. Food aid for refugees is normally handled by WFP in co-operation with UNHCR; German NGOs may also be called upon. Regular bilateral food aid supplies are handled through BALM or GTZ or through WFP's bilateral services. Project-related food aid is mainly handled by GTZ, directly or through sub-contractors, by German NGOs or through WFP's bilateral services.

Food aid budget mechanism   Budgetary provision for German food aid, which is treated separately from, and additional to, other forms of German ODA, is included in three independent titles of the federal budget. Cereal food aid is provided through the budget line 'Promotion of food security programmes in developing countries within the framework of the Food Aid Convention'. This is used in the first instance to fulfil Germany's minimum annual obligation under the FAC and for the establishment of buffer stocks through the purchase of local staples in recipient countries. Support measures can also be financed to some extent, such as those that ensure effective use of the food aid provided and enhance the recipient countries' own efforts in the food sector. The cereals mainly provided are wheat, maize, sorghum, millet and rice.

For non-cereal food aid commodities, the budget line is 'Promotion of food security programmes in developing countries'. This budget provision is used primarily to finance measures that help developing countries implement food security programmes and improve nutritional status through, for example, FFW activities. Financial support is also provided through this budget line for emergency and relief measures, especially those of German NGOs and international organizations.

German annual voluntary contributions to WFP's regular resources are financed under a separate budget line.

Flow, Direction and Use of Food Aid

Germany's food aid programme consists of the usual three main components: bilateral assistance, multilateral channelling and NGO programmes. In addition, Germany participates in the EC food aid programme, which, in 1991, accounted for about two-thirds of Germany's food aid in net value terms. About 15% was channelled multilaterally and about 10% was made available through German NGOs.

Bilateral food aid An increasing proportion of German bilateral food aid is acquired in developing countries through triangular transactions and local purchases. Germany has not provided programme food aid for undifferentiated budget support since 1980. When bilateral food aid is monetized, the funds generated are designated for specific purposes, in particular for FFW programmes.

German bilateral food aid has three main elements. Around 60% is used in emergency and refugee operations. Some 20% is linked to development projects implemented by GTZ or German NGOs, mostly for use in food security programmes implemented with GTZ assistance. Two types of food security programmes have been implemented. Cereal market policy programmes have been carried out in sub-Saharan Africa, mainly in the Sahelian countries of West Africa. The objectives of these programmes have been: strengthening the effectiveness and efficiency of national cereal marketing boards by establishing national security reserves; introducing market information systems; assisting in the formulation of a cereals market and price policy; improving logistics; introducing measures to reduce post-harvest losses; and conducting training programmes at various management levels. Cereal food aid has been provided primarily to assist in the establishment of national food reserves and, when monetized, to purchase local materials and equipment.

The second type, known as integrated food security programmes, have been implemented in Cape Verde, China, Guatemala, Haiti, Honduras, Indonesia, Kenya, Peru and Somalia. The main objective of this type of programme has been to enable the beneficiaries to improve their nutritional status and to secure their subsistence by increasing and diversifying agricultural production; mobilizing self-help potential; giving special attention to the promotion of women's groups; identifying alternative off-farm income sources; improving health facilities and public hygiene; strengthening physical infrastructure; and conducting training programmes. Food aid from the cereals and non-cereals budget lines has been monetized and the proceeds used for: the procurement of local food to support FFW and food for training activities; the purchase of local equipment and materials to provide incentives for work; financing operational costs; payment of local experts and support staff; and, to a smaller extent, the provision of cash in cash-for-work activities.

In both types of food security programme, food aid is provided together with financial and technical assistance as a package of development aid. Evaluations of such programmes have shown that while they have been successful in improving the infrastructure and increasing agricultural production, they have not always or automatically improved the nutritional status of beneficiaries. The health and nutrition sectors have often not received the necessary attention. Food security programme concepts have now been redesigned, with greater emphasis on base-line surveys and monitoring and evaluation systems.

The third element of German bilateral food aid, which accounts for some 20% of the total, has consisted of complementary measures to improve the efficiency and effectiveness of food aid, such as assistance for improving storage, stock management and transportation. A small proportion has been monetized to help meet the local costs of technical assistance programmes implemented by BMZ.

Multilateral food aid   German multilateral food aid provided through UN organizations has been channelled through WFP and UNHCR. As well as making voluntary pledges to WFP's regular resources in every year since the inception of WFP's operations in 1963, Germany has contributed both commodities and cash to the IEFR since 1977 and has provided non-food items and services to WFP for large-scale emergency operations. Germany has made use of WFP's expertise and experience for the purchase, transportation and monitoring of German bilateral food aid to Bangladesh, Lebanon, Nepal and countries in sub-Saharan Africa. Overall, Germany was WFP's fourth largest donor during the biennium 1989–90, providing US$98 million.

Germany has channelled about a fifth of its multilateral food aid in the 1980s through UNHCR in the form of both cereals and non-cereal commodities.

EC food aid programme   Germany contributes some 65% of its total food aid to the EC Community action food aid programme. Its contribution is assessed as amounting to 29% of the total programme. Its combined minimum annual contributions to the Community and national action components of the total EC food aid programmes currently amount to a total obligation under the FAC of about 453,000 tons (in wheat equivalent). Germany has regularly exceeded its minimum annual obligations under the FAC. In addition, it contributes to the non-cereals EC Community action food aid budget.

Non-governmental organizations   NGOs play an important role in German emergency and development assistance. They act as a channel for aid flows financed by the federal and state governments and the EC Commission, in addition to providing assistance from their own resources, and they have considerable influence on the media and public opinion. Their importance in the area of food aid is reflected by the fact that some 30% of the BMZ-funded food aid was channelled through them in 1991, slightly more in tonnage terms than was supplied to WFP's regular programme and the IEFR.

The four NGOs providing food aid are the German Red Cross, German Agro-Action, and the organizations of the Catholic and Protestant churches, Caritas and the Social Service Agency of the Evangelical Church. All of them tend to view food aid essentially as an emergency relief resource, and the German public sees them as a natural channel for this type of assistance. The latter two NGOs specialize in emergency assistance, while their two sister organizations providing development assistance (Miserior and Bread for the World) generally do not include food aid in their programmes.

The German NGOs formulate their own food aid programmes independently of direct government influence. All aim to purchase as high a proportion of food commodities as is economically feasible in the aid recipient countries themselves, or in the same region.

Future Scope and Directions

Some of the main factors likely to influence the future scope and direction of German food aid may be summarized as follows.

Concern has been expressed that the momentous events in Eastern Europe and the former Soviet Union, leading to the reunification of Germany, could lead to a re-direction of German ODA away from developing countries. However, the government has indicated that the large increases in aid to Eastern Europe, as well as investment in East Germany, will not lead to a decline in its commitment to assist developing countries. Investment by the private sector in developing countries could decline for some time, however, owing to the considerable need for investment in modern equipment and infrastructure in East Germany and neighbouring Eastern European countries. NGOs involved in development assistance have called for a cutback in budget appropriations to the Ministry of Defence in view of the decreasing tensions between Eastern and Western Europe and for a commensurate increase in funds for assistance to developing countries.

The future of German food aid, compared with that of other elements of German ODA, will depend to a large extent on the perceptions and results of such aid, especially since Germany is not confronted with the pressures of surplus production of food commodities and, as a matter of policy, increasingly seeks to provide cash for food purchases in developing countries. In the past, there has been strong pressure to use food aid only in emergencies, but attitudes are slowly changing as experience has shown that, carefully used, food aid can be an effective resource in the attack on poverty and hunger. This view has been explicitly stated in official development assistance policy.

Particular concerns have been expressed about the need for greater co-ordination of food aid among donor countries and agencies, especially in recipient countries. Better integration of food aid into the national plans and programmes of developing countries and into the development assistance programmes of German ODA is also being sought. More stress is also being placed on the monitoring and evaluation of food-assisted projects and programmes as well as on a greater knowledge of the people and communities to be assisted. Germany is looking to WFP to play a greater role in improving food aid co-ordination and integration.

Apart from emergency assistance, the development sectors likely to receive priority attention in the use of future German food aid are: nutrition improvement for marginal groups through integrated food security programmes; increased agricultural and food production; and structural and sectoral adjustment with particular focus on the social costs for the poor. At the same time, concern has been expressed that more food aid should be used to address the growing problems of the urban as well as the rural poor, especially through integrated urban-rural development programmes.

Drawing on the experience of other food aid donors and agencies could also result in broadening the application of food aid to other development sectors, including those priority areas identified in the 1986 development assistance policy guidelines, namely, environmental protection, promotion of education and training, and support to women in development.

Reference

BMZ (Federal Ministry for Economic Co-opration (1989). *Food Aid and Food Security Programmes as an Instrument of Development Co-operation*. Policy Paper (English-language version). Bonn, December.

Appendix Table 13.1 *Germany: Cereal food aid deliveries[a] ('000 tons – in grain equivalent)*

	1987	1988	1989	1990	1991	1987–91 Average
Total:	228.1	307.8	219.2	314.2	178.4	249.5
By food aid channel:						
– Bilateral	128.1	183.6	127.4	203.1	127.3	153.9
– Gvt-to-Gvt	119.4	154.3	94.0	120.2	74.1	112.4
– through NGOs	8.7	29.3	33.4	82.9	53.2	41.5
– Multilateral	100.0	124.2	91.8	111.1	51.1	95.6
By food aid category:						
– Emergency Relief	88.2	164.4	118.0	212.1	117.2	140.0
– Project	105.5	79.4	83.2	89.8	59.2	83.4
– Agr./Rural Development	80.5	38.4	41.4	48.8	42.0	50.2
– Nutrition Intervention	10.8	20.8	11.9	5.7	9.7	11.8
– Food Reserve	10.9	17.8	–	13.7	–	8.5
– Other Development Project	3.3	2.4	29.9	21.6	7.5	12.9
– Non-project (Programme)	34.4	64.0	18.0	12.4	2.0	26.1
By Region:						
– Sub-Saharan Africa	120.6	205.4	92.7	187.1	117.9	144.7
– North Africa/Mid-East	0.2	14.8	15.0	15.6	1.1	9.3
– Asia and Pacific	93.8	58.4	86.9	106.1	47.6	78.5
– Latin America and Caribbean	13.5	29.1	24.7	5.4	8.7	16.3
– Europe	–	–	–	–	3.0	0.6

[a] Excluding Germany's assessed contribution to the EC Community Action food aid programme.

Source: WFP/INTERFAIS Database

Appendix Table 13.2 *Germany: Non-cereal food aid deliveries* [a] *('000 tons)*

	1987	1988	1989	1990	1991	1987–91 Average
Total:	35.8	64.2	50.9	53.3	42.7	49.4
By food aid channel:						
– Bilateral	7.9	33.1	20.5	17.0	19.5	19.7
– Gvt-to-Gvt	6.1	23.0	9.1	0.9	1.7	8.2
– through NGOs	1.8	10.2	11.4	16.1	17.2	11.5
– Multilateral	27.9	31.0	30.3	36.3	23.2	29.7
By food aid category:						
– Emergency Relief	21.1	36.8	30.7	37.2	23.7	29.9
– Project	14.7	17.1	20.2	16.1	19.0	17.4
– Agr./Rural Development	6.8	11.2	5.8	6.5	9.1	7.9
– Nutrition Intervention	1.5	1.9	5.7	5.0	3.8	3.6
– Food Reserve	1.9	–	–	–	0.3	0.4
– Other Development Project	4.5	4.0	8.6	4.6	5.8	5.5
– Non-project (Programme)	–	10.3	–	–	–	2.1
By Region:						
– Sub-Saharan Africa	14.2	37.7	33.0	41.2	29.0	31.0
– North Africa/Mid-East	3.4	10.0	7.2	5.2	5.9	6.4
– Asia and Pacific	13.0	12.4	3.2	3.4	3.8	7.1
– Latin America and Caribbean	5.2	4.1	7.5	3.5	4.0	4.9

[a] Excluding Germany's assessed contribution to the EC Community Action food aid programme.

Source: ibid.

14 Netherlands

An EC Member State National Programme:
Financing Food & Development

Food aid dates back to the beginning of Dutch development co-operation in the mid-1960s. In the first decade, up to the mid-1970s, the emphasis was on the use of domestic agricultural surpluses in developing countries facing food shortages. Dairy products constituted an important part of the aid programme. During the second half of the 1970s, more attention was given to the demand side of the food problem. The share of grain in Dutch food aid expanded during this period at the expense of dairy products. However, the emphasis remained on meeting food deficits. From the beginning of the 1980s, food aid was increasingly viewed as a development instrument; in addition to humanitarian considerations, new goals were formulated of providing balance of payments and budgetary support. During this period, food aid as programme aid was given high priority. Moreover, Dutch policy was increasingly geared towards the policies of multilateral and international organizations. Concepts proposed by WFP, FAO and the World Bank provided an impulse for Dutch aid policy. The original, primarily bilateral, aid programme gave way to multilateral aid, on the one hand, and aid channelled through NGOs, on the other.

Different interpretations have been given to the integrated approach to food aid as a development instrument. In the early 1980s, food aid was integrated into food strategies, the main goal being to increase food self-sufficiency. In the second half of the decade, this food strategy concept was not pursued. But serious food shortages recurred in a number of developing countries, leading to renewed emphasis on large-scale food aid supplies. The one-sided nature of the food strategy, with its emphasis on production and food availability, was criticised. Undernourishment was seen as a problem not just of supply but also of purchasing power. The concept of food security, therefore, began to play an important role. The introduction of structural adjustment programmes further boosted interest in the demand side of aid programmes. The austerity measures implemented within this framework hit the weaker groups of society particularly hard and food aid was seen to have an important role in mitigating the social cost of adjustment measures for the poor.

A central policy objective of Dutch development co-operation is poverty allevia-tion, in the context of which a main aspect is seen as achieving food security. In general terms, the government's aid policy envisages enabling all people at all times to have access to enough food to lead a healthy and active life either through their own production or by being able to buy what they need. Reducing the dependence of developing countries and vulnerable groups on external assistance is a key element of that policy.

Food aid supplied within this food security policy framework is regarded as supporting a sustained improvement in the food situation of developing countries. However, the government regards food aid as only one of a number of ways of promoting food security. Its provision is determined on a case-by-case basis and is compared with other aid alternatives, such as whether it may be more appropriate and effective to provide infrastructural and logistical support or agricultural inputs. Providing food aid from local production in developing countries is favoured whenever this is possible. Food aid forms a relatively small but stable component of Dutch development assistance. There is no separate budget for food aid. Pledges to WFP, as one of the contributions to United Nations voluntary funds, are financed out of the budget for multilateral development co-operation. Emergency food aid is financed through the emergency and humanitarian assistance. Bilateral food aid can be financed from either country allocations or regional funds.

Only a small part of Dutch food aid is provided bilaterally on a government-to-government basis. The major part is channelled in voluntary pledges through WFP, in the assessed national contribution to the EC's Community action food aid programme and through Dutch NGOs. The Dutch have therefore played an active role in advocating effective and innovative uses of food aid not only in their own bilateral aid programme but also in international co-operation and have proposed or supported initiatives for improving food aid policies and programmes in intergovernmental bodies and at international meetings.

Development Co-operation

The Netherlands is one of the few countries to have achieved and maintained a high proportion of its GNP as official development assistance. It is also one of the largest aid donors in per capita terms. The government decided as early as 1976 to allocate 1.5% of net national income to development assistance and has adhered to this target ever since. This target placed ODA at approximately 1% of GNP, well above the UN target of 0.7% set by the United Nations. In 1991, ODA amounted to US$2,621 million, representing 0.94% of GNP, and is generally untied.

The country's commitment to development co-operation enjoys wide support from all sectors of Dutch society and has been maintained by successive coalition governments. Two factors may help to explain this. First, the Dutch economy has traditionally been extremely open, geared toward commerce and trade. A strong orientation towards the outside world has been the basis of, as well as a necessary condition for, sustained Dutch economic development. Secondly, Dutch society is characterized by a high degree of popular participation and self-determination. Local communities are directly involved in running their own affairs through a multitude of groups, committees and associations. In the past, local communities not only financed their own activities and services in the social sector but also supported missionary work overseas through public subscriptions.

Similarly, local groups are involved in development activities. The extensive network of NGOs and groups throughout the Netherlands has had an important influence on development co-operation policy and funding and in mobilizing public contributions in times of emergency. For example, a fund-raising campaign for Africa in

November 1985 raised 100 million guilders within 24 hours. In more recent years, single campaigns have raised less, but their frequency has increased. The Netherlands pursues a policy of involving various sectors of Dutch society in the aid programme on the principle that it is not a matter for government ministries alone. Increasing use has been made of the private sector and social organizations, among which Dutch NGOs play a prominent role.

In 1991, a quarter of Dutch ODA was provided through non-bilateral channels, of which about 30% was supplied through UN agencies, the World Bank group and the EC, and 9% through various regional banks and funds.

A high proportion of bilateral aid is directed toward low-income countries. Continuous efforts are made to improve its quality and efficiency. Particular importance has been attached to donor co-ordination in recipient countries through the co-financing of development projects and a sectoral approach to the provision of aid.

Evolution of Food Aid Policies

The people of the Netherlands have traditionally been concerned particularly with issues relating to hunger and malnutrition, partly as a result of their own acute suffering at the end of the Second World War in 1944/5. This 'hunger awareness' has been a major catalyst for Dutch development assistance, with a principal objective being to tackle the structural causes of hunger and poverty in developing countries.

Food aid was referred to in the earliest Dutch policy statements on development assistance in the 1950s within the context of this fundamental concern with the problems of hunger and poverty and the right to food. A policy document at that time stated that food aid constituted a combination of an increased market outlet for surplus agricultural products and the need for food in developing countries. By the time WFP was established in 1961, however, it was recognized that the solution to food deficits in developing countries lay not in planned surplus production in the developed countries but in efforts to increase local food production. When the first Dutch Minister for Development Co-operation presented a policy paper on development assistance to Parliament in 1967, it was stressed that food aid should be handled very carefully so as not to disturb local markets or international trade. The government welcomed the establishment of WFP as the first systematic attempt to use food surpluses for developmental purposes through multilateral channels which could appropriately address, and avoid, the potential problems of creating disincentives to local production and disrupting international markets.

This preference for multilateral aid, as well as for channelling food aid through NGOs with a sound knowledge of the local situation in developing countries, has been an enduring feature of Dutch food aid policies. The government initially supplied food aid through NGOs in the 1960s. This collaboration was formalized in 1970 when a programme for 'Dairy aid through private organizations' was started with the objective of providing dairy products as food aid to vulnerable groups of mothers and children. Two years later, this programme was extended to include other commodities. From 1973, cash was also used for purchasing food in developing countries for food aid rather than providing commodities from the Netherlands, although the availability of domestic agricultural surpluses also had an influence on food aid policy.

The period from 1975 to 1981 was characterized by an evolution in policy from the incidental provision of food aid towards the development of a sectoral programme of assistance in which food aid was given a more consistent and longer-term dimension. Following the World Food Conference of 1974, the government strongly supported a structural approach to the world food problem in response to the crisis of the early 1970s. Dutch food aid commitments doubled between 1974 and 1976. In 1977, an extra budget line was created in the Dutch development co-operation programme for bilateral food aid, in addition to the existing budget lines for food aid through WFP, the European Community, NGOs and the Dutch contribution to the Food Aid Convention.

The government emphasized, however, that other parallel efforts were needed to increase food production in the developing countries, and in 1979 it decided to make food aid more development-oriented. A new budget line was created that financed not only traditional food aid but also other activities to promote food production. A special unit was created to manage a new sectoral programme for 'food aid and food production' and to promote a sectoral approach, thereby centralizing the highly fragmented responsibilities that existed among a number of units handling Dutch ODA.

A major policy document on 'Food production and nutrition programmes', presented to Parliament in 1981, stressed that Dutch food aid should be provided within an integrated approach, covering all aspects of the food system, through a multi-annual programme of assistance to a selected number of countries. The concept of 'food strategies', developed by the World Food Council, was strongly supported. Criteria for selecting countries to support these food strategies included willingness of the recipient government to formulate an integrated food policy, and the possibility of donor co-ordination and regional co-operation. Between 1981 and 1985, emphasis was placed on providing assistance for the formulation and implementation of food strategies that allowed the funding of a number of activities other than food aid operations. In 1982 and 1983, it was stated that no bilateral food aid would be provided out of the sectoral programme since sufficient aid was being provided through multilateral channels, the EC and NGOs. The sectoral programme, renamed 'Food production, nutrition, food security and food aid', was part of the sectoral assistance programme for rural development. In response to the food crisis in Africa, however, the decision not to provide additional food aid beyond current international obligations was reversed in 1985 and bilateral food aid was reinstated. The new bilateral food aid budget was intended to finance not only food aid, including the use of food produced in developing countries through local purchases and triangular transactions, but also agricultural inputs, logistical support, local transport and distribution. A shift toward programme food aid was also apparent.

While food aid in the period up to 1985 was strongly related to the implementation of food strategies, that approach has now been replaced by the concept of food security. Dutch food aid policy continues to be based on a sectoral approach, linked increasingly to structural adjustment efforts and the policy dialogue between recipient governments and donors aimed at achieving food security in assisted countries. Food aid is therefore provided within the broader context of programmes that seek to increase local food production, achieve food security, improve nutrition and generally support rural development. Major food aid policy objectives include:

• helping in the structural adjustment process through the provision of food aid to the most vulnerable groups and by helping to change food policies with the aim of increasing local food production, thereby reducing commercial imports;
• increasing the use of food produced in developing countries through local purchasing and triangular transactions;

- continuing support to WFP in the implementation of rural development projects in which food aid is an important and effective input;
- monetizing food aid to generate funds for rural development activities;
- using cash assistance in place of food aid when it is more appropriate and when the food supply situation of a developing country is such that food aid is not required.

The Netherlands is a strong supporter of programmes to restructure cereal markets and integrate food security activities. Programmes to restructure regional cereal markets are considered to offer an enabling framework for co-ordinating support for food production, processing and distribution as well as for food imports and food aid. The Netherlands attaches much importance to establishing a mechanism for continuous dialogue between governments and donors on recipient countries' food security policies.

The Dutch have stressed that structural adjustment programmes should not be undertaken without incorporating food security measures, and that more attention should be given to the social dimensions of the economic adjustment process. They consider that the importance of local food production and processing and access to food by the poor has not been sufficiently taken into account in many current structural adjustment programmes.

The need for flexibility in the provision of food aid has been stressed on many occasions. Flexibility between the different modalities of food aid, between food aid and other forms of aid and the provision of additional cash resources are considered essential for the effective use of food aid. Nutrition programmes and initiatives to improve the nutritional status of vulnerable groups in developing countries are also being assisted, and support to improve household food security has been given much emphasis. The government considers that in most cases supplementary feeding should be based on locally available foods. As the weaning age is considered an extremely vulnerable period in a child's life, specific attention is given to projects directed towards improving the availability of low-cost, locally produced weaning foods. Collaboration has been established with WFP in this field.

International Food Aid Policy Concerns

The Netherlands has been a strong supporter of WFP from its inception, reflecting the preference given to providing food aid through multilateral channels. In the biennium 1989-90, it was the sixth largest donor to the WFP regular programme, providing US$66 million. This commitment, together with the fact that assistance to food production, food security and rural development figures prominently in Dutch development co-operation, has motivated the government to host international conferences and *ad hoc* consultations and to take a number of important policy initiatives in intergovernmental fora. An international seminar on food aid was held in 1983 to mark the twentieth anniversary of the start of WFP's operations.

Particular concern has been expressed about the need to formulate a stricter definition of emergencies in order to achieve a better use of emergency food aid. The government has proposed that the term 'emergency' should refer to an unpredictable event that causes sudden and acute food deficits in defined areas or groups requiring immediate distribution of free food, for a short period of time, to the afflicted population.

The government has pressed consistently for improved co-ordination among bilateral donors and multilateral agencies through a policy dialogue with recipient governments at country level. It considers that food aid could constitute an important means for fostering such co-ordination, with WFP playing a more active role. Co-ordinated action could also build up the institutional capacities of developing countries and result in the operation of early warning systems, particularly in Africa, on which the government considers there should be a greater concentration of effort.

The Netherlands provides about a third of its pledge to WFP's regular resources in the form of cash: 60% of its commodity pledge is available in cash for purchases of food in developing countries. With regard to food purchases in the Netherlands, no agreement is sought to buy specified commodities and WFP is free to buy according to what is required by developing countries. The only condition is that the prices at which commodities are purchased in the Netherlands are competitive. The Dutch have urged other donors to be similarly flexible in their contributions to WFP.

Dutch contributions to the IEFR and to protracted refugee operations supported by WFP can also take the form of cash. Similarly, the Dutch advocate a more extensive use of swap arrangements whereby WFP and other food donors exchange the food commodities they provide for other food commodities in a developing country. The Dutch have also set an example to other donors by providing WFP with an untied annual contribution equivalent to US$2.5 million for non-food items required for WFP-assisted development projects. In addition, an annual contribution of US$3.6 million is also provided in cash to WFP to improve the quality of the projects it supports.

Strong Dutch support for WFP has been based especially on the view that as a multilateral agency it is in a better position than bilateral food aid programmes to address issues such as the potential effects of food aid on market displacement and its disincentive to local food production.

The government has also been at the forefront of a number of other innovative initiatives in food aid. For example, within the European Community it has initiated the delinking of food aid from the Common Agriculture Policy to enhance the developmental impact of EC food aid. The government also initiated discussion in the Consultative Sub-committee on Surplus Disposal on modifying the concept of 'usual marketing requirements' to take food aid requirements as a starting point rather than maintaining commercial import levels.

Dutch NGOS and Food Aid

Dutch NGOs have played an important role in the evolution of the Netherlands' food aid policies and programmes. About 6% of ODA is made available annually to Dutch NGOs from the development co-operation budget through a special budget line. Private donors provide additional funds. In addition, Dutch NGOs raise a considerable amount through subscriptions from the general public for development assistance to developing countries. NGOs also submit additional requests for emergency food aid and a considerable part of bilateral emergency food aid provided by the government is channelled through NGOs.

The government also gives support to NGOs designed to improve the nutritional status of vulnerable groups. The NGO programme for food and nutrition improvement provides assistance to a large number of small-scale projects, implemented by counterpart institutions in the developing countries. In these projects, supplementary feeding is only one option in a range of activities aimed at improving the nutritional status of vulnerable groups. Food supplements are almost exclusively locally produced commodities.

Food Aid Flows

From its inception, food aid has been provided from a variety of sources within the Dutch aid budget. Furthermore, food aid is looked on not as an end in itself but as one of the resources that can contribute to food security. It can therefore be used interchangeably with other forms of development assistance, such as agricultural inputs, in food security programmes.

In absolute terms, the value of Dutch food aid was reasonably stable throughout the 1980s. In relative terms, however, its share of total ODA declined from 10% at the end of the 1970s to 4.5% at the end of the 1980s. In virtually no other DAC/OECD country was this relative decrease so sharp.

During the 1980s, the largest part (about a third) of Dutch food aid was channelled through WFP. Slightly less (about 31%) was accounted for by assessed contributions to the EC's food aid programme. A declining share has been provided on a government-to-government basis; about 28% in the first half of the 1980s, but only 15% in the second half of the decade. In contrast, an increasing share of Dutch food aid has been channelled through NGOs, reaching 19% in the latter part of the 1980s.

During the 1980s, about 44% of Dutch food aid went to countries in sub-Saharan Africa, 26% to the Asia and Pacific region, 19% to Latin America and the Caribbean and about 11% to the Middle East and North Africa. The major recipient countries were Bangladesh, Ethiopia, Mali, Mozambique and Sudan.

Almost half of this was provided as project assistance, reflecting the fact that the major part of Dutch food aid was channelled through WFP and NGOs, organizations that used food aid to support project activities. The share of programme food aid also increased to about 27% in the second half of the 1980s in line with the policy to use food aid to support structural adjustment programmes. The proportion of Dutch food aid for emergencies is highly sensitive to requirements: it fell sharply to about a quarter during the late 1980s from about 43% in the early 1980s, as there were fewer disasters in sub-Saharan Africa. But it has increased again in the early 1990s in response to the serious and widespread recent disasters in Africa.

Triangular transactions and local purchases have become an important feature of Dutch bilateral food aid. In the late 1980s, about half of the local purchases were carried out by WFP on behalf of the Government, largely in sub-Saharan Africa, mainly to expedite deliveries during emergencies. Purchases have been made to support development activities including FFW in India, the restructuring of cereals markets in Senegal and Mali, and the food banks programme in Mozambique. Purchases have also been made in one developing country to reimburse food loans obtained in another that were used for food aid.

The commodity composition of Dutch food aid, which initially reflected the structure of Dutch agriculture, has been progressively modified to reflect recipient needs. Livestock products constitute about two-thirds of the value of total agricultural production in the Netherlands. Arable farming has declined to about 9% and self-sufficiency rates for cereals are low. Agricultural exports amount to about a quarter of the total value of exports. The official food aid budget is only 0.5% of the value of agricultural exports; food aid commodities procured in the Netherlands represent only 0.24% of the value of agricultural exports. The importance of food aid for the

Dutch economy is thus negligible. The policy position of Dutch agro-industry is that development co-operation should be directed towards increasing purchasing power in developing countries to permit increased commercial imports rather than towards lobbying for increased food aid.

Almost 60% of the food aid budget was spent on cereals and dairy products during the 1980s, with a declining expenditure on the latter category of commodities. Other products, including oils, fats and canned foods (beef/chicken/fish), accounted for one sixth of Dutch food aid. More than a quarter of food aid funds were used mainly to supply equipment and technical assistance for project implementation and improved logistics for relief operations as well as for agricultural inputs (fertilizer, seed, tools) for increasing food production in the recipient countries.

For the biennium 1989-90, the Netherlands was the sixth largest donor to WFP's regular resources, with a total pledge equivalent to about US$66 million. The Netherlands also made additional pledges to WFP's regular resources during the biennium, contributions to the IEFR (US$3.3 million), to non-food items (US$8.9 million) and to protracted refugee operations (US$1.3 million). It has also been a regular user of services provided by WFP for its bilateral food aid programme including the purchase and transport of commodities and the monitoring of their use.

Food Aid Administration

Food aid is financed out of a development co-operation budget administered within the Ministry of Foreign Affairs under a Minister for Development Co-operation. There are different budget lines from which food aid can be financed, including one for the Dutch obligation to the EC food aid programme. The various budget lines are managed by separate units within the Ministry of Foreign Affairs without a co-ordinating mechanism.

There has always been close co-operation between the Ministry of Foreign Affairs and the Ministry of Agriculture, Environment and Fisheries on all aspects of Dutch food aid. The latter Ministry is responsible for the procurement and quality control of food commodities obtained in the Netherlands for the food aid programme through its Government Food Procurement Agency.

The number of staff dealing with food aid in both ministries is very small, reflecting the preferred use of multilateral channelling of food aid. Staff managing other budget lines in the Ministry of Foreign Affairs also play a role in the administration of food aid. Nevertheless, this aid is considered separately from financial and technical assistance in Dutch ODA and has not been fully integrated into the Netherlands' country development assistance programmes.

Quality control of food commodities procured in the Netherlands has been the subject of close and continuous attention. An established principle is that food aid commodities must be subjected to the same quality tests as those required for the domestic market. The nutritional value of food aid commodities is also closely examined and often adjusted to the needs of the beneficiaries. For example, since the beginning of the 1970s, all dried skimmed milk supplied as food aid for direct feeding is vitaminized using a process developed in the Netherlands and tested for a shelf life of at least six months after shipment.

The attention given to the formulation of food aid policies in the Netherlands and in international fora has not been matched until recently by vigorous appraisal and implementation of food aid programmes and operations and by a clear accountability of transactions. Food aid has not been given any special identity but is regarded as one of a number of ways to achieve developmental objectives. Reporting and monitoring have been undertaken by staff not specialised in food aid. Accountability suffered for a number of reasons, not least because of the fragmentation of the financing of food aid through a number of separate budget lines, which changed frequently over time.

Steps have now been taken to ensure proper accountability. The Ministry of Agriculture, Environment and Fisheries is involved in accounting and monitoring of Dutch food aid deliveries. Within the Ministry of Foreign Affairs, an information system has been introduced to provide a better insight into food aid allocations from different budget lines.

Future Issues and Concerns

Food security in the developing countries will remain an important policy concern in Dutch development assistance policy, including the various roles that food aid can play in the process of structural and sectoral adjustment, with due attention to the effects of adjustment on food security and on the social condition of the poor. It is considered that the immediate problems of hunger, malnutrition and poverty among vulnerable groups should be addressed through better targeted programmes. Furthermore, the inter-relationship between emergency and development assistance, particularly in countries and regions with recurring disasters, requires more rigorous definition and use of emergency assistance so that it does not undermine efforts towards achieving sustained development.

More consideration could also be given to other factors, such as enhancing the roles of women in development, environmental protection and the construction and improvement of rural infrastructure. The use of food aid to help meet recurrent as well as initial development costs in developing countries could be further explored.

The future level of food aid will depend on the perceived level of needs. The Netherlands is obligated to provide food aid under the FAC and to contribute to the EC's Community action food aid programme. Public opinion remains strongly in favour of helping the poor in developing countries to overcome hunger and poverty. But there have been strong criticisms of the counter-productive effects of inadequately planned and delivered food aid.

The government has pressed consistently for flexibility in food aid and has adopted such an approach to increase the efficiency of food aid. It would also like to restrict the free distribution of food aid in emergencies. Food aid should be monetized wherever possible. The provision of cash wages in employment schemes could help to increase beneficiaries' purchasing power.

High priority has been given to establishing arrangements in developing countries for close and continuous dialogue among donors and between them and government officials. The Netherlands looks to WFP to play a leading role in helping to foster and strengthen co-ordination in donors' food aid policies and programmes and between food aid and financial and technical assistance. It welcomes the co-ordinating role WFP now plays in large-scale emergency operations and would like to see that role extended to the use of food aid for development at the national level.

There has been strong public support in the Netherlands for the increasing share of bilateral food aid channelled through NGOs in recent years. This is based on the view that NGOs have the closest contact with, and the best appreciation of, the problems of poor people and communities in developing countries. The extent to which more food aid can be channelled through NGOs will be determined, *inter alia*, by the financial and technical resources they can also acquire and by the capacity of their counterpart organizations in developing countries to handle more aid. These constraints are likely to be felt more acutely as NGOs endeavour to transfer the focus of their programmes from relief to reconstruction, rehabilitation and development.

In order to be effective, it is emphasized that food aid needs to be brought into the mainstream of the planning and programming of development assistance. Therefore, the Dutch have discontinued the practice of having a separate budget line for food aid. It is also appreciated that monitoring and evaluation systems should also be built into the aid programme. This would not only improve accountability but assess the impact of food aid along with that of other forms of assistance, and adjust and improve the design and implementation of future aid programmes.

In a document on Dutch aid policy for the 1990s (Ministry of Foreign Affairs, 1990), it is stated that the food security focus of the 1980s will be continued. In this context, the Netherlands will press for greater flexibility in food aid so that (i) the supply will always be based on the food situation in each developing country, and (ii) a larger proportion is made available in the form of money for the purchase of food in developing countries or for the financing of 'cash-for-work' programmes. As part of structural adjustment programmes geared toward achieving food security, assured food aid support should be provided that would take the form of imported food only when critical food shortages occurred.

An evaluation of Dutch food aid carried out by the Operations Review Unit of the Ministry of Foreign Affairs, published in 1991, focused on sub-Saharan Africa (Ministry of Foreign Affairs, 1991). It concluded that in many cases food aid, especially programme food aid, did not reach the most vulnerable groups. It tended to change traditional eating habits, acted as a disincentive to local food production and led to greater dependence. Partly as a result of subsidized food imports, substitution of imports for domestic food had been accelerated and markets for locally produced traditional foods reduced. Subsidized food imports, combined with adverse domestic policies, such as over-valued exchange rates, had also reduced the incentive to process traditional foods to make them more acceptable to urban and high-income households. The evaluation recommended that food aid as a development resource, particularly through FFW, should therefore be subject to a critical review, and that the Dutch Government should urge the European Community to substitute financial assistance for a significant part of food aid supplied in the form of European agricultural surpluses.

The evaluation's findings concerning emergency food aid were generally more positive, although it noted that efficiency could be improved. Donors and authorities in afflicted countries often postponed action until people were faced with the immediate threat of starvation. Storage and distribution capacities in most African countries were inadequate to cope with large-scale emergency food aid operations. The evaluation concluded that in many instances a more gradual supply of relief food was possible and preferable.

References

Ministry of Foreign Affairs, Directorate-General International Co-operation (1990). *A World of Difference*. The Hague.

Ministry of Foreign Affairs, Development Co-operation (1991). *Food Aid and Development: Evaluation of Dutch Food Aid with Special Reference to Sub-Saharan Africa, 1980–89*. Summary Evaluation Report. The Hague, July.

Appendix Table 14.1 *Netherlands: Cereal food aid deliveries[a] ('000 tons – in grain equivalent)*

	1987	1988	1989	1990	1991	1987–91 Average
Total:	176.7	101.9	32.1	114.2	141.8	113.3
By food aid channel:						
– Bilateral	47.5	35.0	12.2	73.9	76.6	49.1
– Gvt-to-Gvt	43.1	32.8	11.2	72.4	72.9	46.5
– through NGOs	4.4	2.2	1.0	1.5	3.7	2.6
– Multilateral	129.2	66.9	19.9	40.3	65.2	64.3
By food aid category:						
– Emergency Relief	60.0	66.1	7.7	42.7	89.8	53.3
– Project	112.6	25.8	22.4	47.7	47.0	51.1
– Agr./Rural Development	82.8	22.7	8.8	19.1	34.9	33.7
– Nutrition Intervention	5.2	0.4	0.8	5.5	5.1	3.4
– Food Reserve	4.5	2.2	3.0	6.7	–	3.3
– Other Development Project	20.1	0.4	9.9	16.5	7.1	10.8
– Non-project (Programme)	4.1	10.0	2.0	23.8	4.9	9.0
By region:						
– Sub-Saharan Africa	73.4	89.0	26.5	85.3	74.4	69.7
– North Africa/Mid-East	4.4	2.2	0.3	–	0.1	1.4
– Asia and Pacific	96.5	8.9	0.4	23.8	63.2	38.6
– Latin America and Caribbean	2.4	1.8	4.9	5.1	4.0	3.6

a Excluding the Netherland's assessed contribution to the EC Community Action food aid programme.

Source: WFP/INTERFAIS Database

Appendix Table 14.2 *Netherlands: Non-cereal food aid deliveries[a] ('000 tons)*

	1987	1988	1989	1990	1991	1987–91 Average
Total:	21.5	44.1	11.3	15.5	20.5	22.6
By food aid channel:						
– Bilateral	9.4	23.7	2.5	7.8	14.7	11.6
– Gvt-to-Gvt	8.3	22.9	0.9	6.4	14.1	10.5
– through NGOs	1.1	0.9	1.5	1.5	0.6	1.1
– Multilateral	12.1	20.4	8.8	7.7	5.8	10.9
By food aid category:						
– Emergency Relief	2.4	10.2	1.8	3.5	4.5	4.5
– Project	16.8	33.6	9.0	6.9	4.7	14.2
– Agr./Rural Development	6.8	8.8	3.6	3.1	0.8	4.6
– Nutrition Intervention	7.8	15.4	1.9	0.8	2.4	5.6
– Food Reserve	–	4.9	–	–	–	1.0
– Other Development Project	2.3	4.6	3.5	3.0	1.5	3.0
– Non-project (Programme)	2.3	0.3	0.5	5.1	11.4	3.9
By region:						
– Sub-Saharan Africa	6.1	20.8	7.1	12.3	16.5	12.6
– North Africa/Mid-East	4.8	6.4	2.0	2.1	1.0	3.3
– Asia and Pacific	2.5	14.4	0.6	0.8	2.5	4.2
– Latin America and Caribbean	8.0	2.5	1.7	0.3	0.5	2.6

[a] Excluding the Netherland's assessed contribution to the EC Community Action food aid programme.

Source: ibid.

15 Japan

Evolving Food Policies
of an Agricultural Importing Country

Japan has evolved from being a major recipient of food aid after the Second World War to becoming one of the world's largest food aid donors, despite being a major food-importing country. It has also been a consistent supporter of WFP from its inception in 1963, a signatory to the four successive Food Aid Conventions and a contributor to the IEFR since 1978. Yet relatively little is known about Japanese food aid.

The philosophy underlying Japan's economic co-operation with developing countries is born out of its own development efforts since the Second World War. It has placed particular emphasis on assisting the self-reliant efforts of the developing countries themselves to achieve economic and social development and on promoting the welfare of their people and the stability of their livelihoods, as a major contribution to international peace and security.

A major element of Japan's grant aid programme is assistance aimed at increasing food production in developing countries. Japan considers that the most important factor for solving food shortages in developing countries is the self-reliant efforts of these countries themselves. Since fiscal year (April to March) 1977, Japan's grant aid programme has contained a separate budget item specifically entitled 'aid for increased food production', which includes the major food aid budget. Aid has been considerably increased under this item, which has made a major contribution to increasing food production, especially in Asia. At the beginning of the 1990s, this budget item accounted for more than a fifth of all Japan's grant aid. About half went to the provision of agricultural inputs such as fertilizers, insecticides and farm machinery, and half to food aid.

Background

Japan is committed to substantial increases in its official development assistance. Between 1970–71 and 1989–90, it increased its ODA over three-fold in real terms, from 11 to 19% of the total ODA provided by the DAC members of the OECD, the major donor countries. Japan's ODA as a percentage of GNP increased from 0.23% in 1978 to 0.32% in 1991, close to the average for DAC/OECD countries of 0.34%, although only half of the UN target of 0.7%.

Japan has given strong support to the multilateral approach to aid provided through the UN system. The annual share of multilateral aid averages a quarter to a third of its total ODA, largely as contributions to the international financial institutions. Japan is among the top donors to most of the UN organizations it supports. It recognizes three merits in channelling aid through multilateral institutions: political neutrality; a facility for conducting policy dialogue and for supporting policy reform in recipient countries; and the expertise and information accumulated by UN organizations that can be used by donor countries.

The Japanese Government has stressed the need to improve the effectiveness and efficiency of its economic co-operation programme. It has sought to strengthen its appraisal and implementing system, to reinforce co-ordination between ODA and private enterprise, to expand its evaluation activities and to promote co-operation with other donor countries and international organizations.

Japan's ODA has been provided in various areas including agricultural and rural development, the energy sector, human resources development, and the promotion of small and medium-sized private enterprises. It concentrates not only on infrastructural development but also on meeting the basic human needs of the poor. A large proportion goes to low-income and least developed countries. A specific feature of Japanese economic co-operation has been concern for the problems of sub-Saharan Africa, and efforts have been made to expand its ODA in that region since the late 1970s. A concomitant development emerging from the African food crises of the mid-1980s has been the strengthening of co-operation with and among NGOs. Although they have only recently been involved, the assistance of Japanese NGOs has increased markedly in recent years. The government has also been assisting NGOs by providing information and subsidies and encouraging closer co-operation among them.

Food Aid Administration

Japan's food aid programme is funded from three budget lines in its ODA. The first relates to its multilateral food aid, which is entirely channelled through WFP's regular programme and the IEFR. This constitutes about a tenth of total Japanese food aid, and it is administered by the UN Bureau in the Ministry of Foreign Affairs.

The second budget line is managed by the Economic Co-operation Bureau in the Ministry of Foreign Affairs under the bilateral grant aid programme which accounts for about 90% of Japan's food aid. Until 1983 budget allocations were also made for long-term, credit-financed food aid loans, administered by the Food Agency in the Ministry of Agriculture, Forestry and Fisheries. While all food aid administered by the Ministry of Foreign Affairs is drawn from the budget allocations of the *grant* element of Japan's ODA, the budget for these so-called 'rice loans' was provided from the ODA *loans* element.

Bilateral grant food aid   Requests for bilateral grant food aid are appraised primarily by the Grant Aid Division of the Economic Co-operation Bureau in the Ministry of Foreign Affairs in accordance with established operational criteria. Appraisal involves consideration of factors such as the food shortages in recipient countries, the level of food production, imports and exports of food commodities, food aid provided by other donor countries, the domestic economic and social situation, balance of payments conditions and the overall relations with Japan.

Requests that are considered acceptable are included in a draft plan for the allocation of food aid to each recipient country. The plan is worked out by the Grant Aid

Division within the framework of Japan's Food Aid Convention commitment. The recipient government concludes contracts with Japanese suppliers for the purchase and transportation of food in accordance with stipulations contained in notes exchanged between the Japanese Government and the government of the recipient country. Purchase and delivery of Japanese bilateral grant food aid are carried out by Japanese private traders, with pricing and other detailed terms of transactions determined between the recipient government and the Japanese trader. Regarding grain, the trader is normally a member of the Grain Importers Association, which consists of the major traders and is responsible for all Japanese grain imports and exports. In the case of canned fish, the traders are members of the Tuna Packers Association of Japan or the Marine Packers Association.

Contributions to WFP Japan's contributions to WFP are primarily administered by the UN Bureau in the Ministry of Foreign Affairs. When the Bureau decides the composition of food aid in kind under the regular pledge to WFP, it obtains information on domestic food production from the Ministry of Agriculture, Forestry and Fisheries. The price and quantity for the purchase and delivery of domesticly produced food aid is determined by the government in consultation with the WFP Secretariat. The government indicates the trader for the delivery of the food, who is asked to deliver the commodities to the port of the recipient country in accordance with WFP's instructions. Normal WFP procedures have been applied for commodities purchased through triangular transactions.

Administration of rice loans Japan's rice loans used to be managed by the Food Agency in the Ministry of Agriculture, Forestry and Fisheries in co-operation with the Ministry of Foreign Affairs. The potential impact of such loans on international trade was taken into account so that they did not adversely affect commercial transactions.

Food Aid Dimensions

Food aid has been a relatively small, but significant, element in Japan's ODA since 1963. In 1979-83 it accounted for an average of over 6% of ODA but for only just over 1% of ODA in the period 1984-88. Japan has contributed consistently to the regular resources of WFP since the inception of its operations in 1963. Japan's bilateral food aid programme started in 1968 as a result of its becoming a member of the FAC the previous year. Japan has contributed regularly to the IEFR since 1978. Food aid was provided bilaterally in the form of long-term rice loans in the periods 1970-74 and 1979-83.

In the past, domestic production and stocks of rice had a significant effect on the level, composition and form of Japan's food aid. Food aid deliveries peaked in the early 1970s and early 1980s when rice stocks reached record levels. Food aid in the form of long-term rice loans also increased significantly during these periods.

Since then, in order to reduce rice stocks but to retain self-sufficiency in rice, the government has implemented a policy of restricting production by providing incentives to farmers to take rice out of cultivation and by providing subsidies to diversify crop production. As a result, rice stocks have fallen considerably and no new rice loan commitments have been made since 1983. Since then, a policy has been implemented of procuring all Japanese food aid in rice from developing countries, in particular from

Thailand and Pakistan, through triangular transactions. Relatively modest quantities of fish products have also been provided since 1975, representing a small proportion of Japanese production and exports.

Bilateral food aid   As already noted, some 90% of Japan's food aid has been provided bilaterally in recent years. This assistance has been supplied out of Japan's commitment to the FAC. Japan has been a signatory to all four FACs. Its minimum annual obligation under both the 1980 and 1986 FACs has been 300,000 tons, currently making it the tied fourth largest contributor.

Expanding triangular transactions: As already indicated, triangular transactions are the main source of Japan's food aid in cereals. Rice has been purchased in Thailand and Pakistan. Increasing consideration is also being given to the purchase of other cereals in sub-Saharan Africa to facilitate inter-regional co-operation, save transport expenses and better match food consumption habits in recipient countries.

Transport costs: Japan pays all transport costs associated with supplying its food aid to the least developed countries and 50% of the costs for other countries. For land-locked countries, it pays the costs to the frontier station or to other designated delivery points. Various kinds of grant aid have also been extended for improving transport and storage capacity in recipient countries.

Counterpart funds: Cereal food aid provided bilaterally for development purposes either directly from Japanese stocks or through triangular transactions, has been sold mainly in the recipient countries. The recipient country undertakes to deposit in local currency an amount equivalent to at least two-thirds of the yen disbursement paid for the purchase of the commodities. This is deposited in a special account and used for economic and social development purposes, including food production, after consultation between the authorities of the country concerned and Japan.

Recipient countries: Until the late 1970s, the major part of Japan's bilateral food aid, in common with other parts of its ODA, went to countries in Asia. Asian countries, in particular Thailand, Bangladesh and Pakistan, remain by far the largest recipients. However, following improvement of the food situation in many Asian countries and the crisis in Africa, there has been a significant geographical redistribution of its aid since the early 1980s. About 30 countries now receive Japanese bilateral food aid, including a large number in sub-Saharan Africa.

Given its relatively short experience in providing aid to Africa, the government has considered it important that, in the implementation of its economic co-operation programme, it should take into account African conditions and the aid policies and experience of other donor countries and international organizations. It has endeavoured to take a comprehensive approach to aid for African agricultural development. Aid at the grass-roots level is also being strengthened by increasing the presence of Japanese volunteers and by supporting NGOs working in Africa. Japan is also encouraging and participating in aid co-ordination initiatives for African countries.

Food aid loans: Major recipients of long-term, credit-financed rice loans made during periods of large domestic rice stocks in 1970–74 and 1979–83 included the Republic of Korea, Indonesia and Bangladesh in Asia, and Tanzania, Madagascar, Mozambique, Sierra Leone, Kenya and Mali in Africa. The terms and conditions governing such loans included repayment within 30 years with a grace period of either five or ten years. There was a 2% interest rate for loans during the grace period and 3% thereafter. It was stipulated that such loans should not interfere with normal international commercial trade in rice.

Aid to refugees: About half of Japan's bilateral food aid is allocated for refugees. This aid has been channelled mainly through the multilateral organizations, WFP and UNRRA. Wheat, rice, dairy products and hard biscuits have been supplied through these organizations. Assistance through WFP has been primarily for UN Border Relief Operations along the Thai-Cambodian border, for Afghan refugees in Pakistan and, more recently, for refugees in Africa. Assistance to Palestine refugees has been provided through UNRRA.

Multilateral food aid   All Japanese multilateral contributions in food aid are made to WFP. Its pledges are announced in US dollars and made available in yen for the purchase of commodities from Japan as well as from other countries. About a third of its pledges have been provided in cash, to meet the transportation and administrative costs of delivering food aid to recipient countries. For the 1989-90 biennium, Japan pledged US$29 million to WFP's regular resources.

Japan has also made small, but increasing, contributions to the IEFR in US dollars. For the 1989-90 biennium, its contribution was US$8 million. These contributions have enabled WFP to purchase commodities in developing countries for the victims of natural disasters and for refugees in developing countries and to pay for related transport and administrative costs, and for internal transport, storage and handling expenses in the least developed countries. In addition, Japan provided US$33 million for protracted refugee and displaced people operations supported by WFP.

Japan also contributes to WFP for the purchase of essential non-food items needed for WFP-assisted development projects, including transport and storage items, small tools and equipment and canteen and cooking implements for institutional feeding programmes. US$2 million was provided for the 1989–90 biennium.

A significant element in the relationship between Japan and WFP has been the Programme's provision of services for the Japanese bilateral food aid programme. WFP has made its expertise and experience available for the purchase of commodities, partly in developing countries, and their shipment to recipient countries. About half of total Japanese food aid was provided in this way in 1992.

Food aid through NGOs   The provision of food aid and associated non-food items by Japanese NGOs is a relatively recent development, principally in response to the food crises. In Japan, as in other industrialized countries, the public responded generously to appeals initiated by NGOs and supported by the government to assist Africa in the mid-1980s.

In 1985, a number of NGOs provided funds to WFP for the purchase of food in developing countries for use as food aid to seriously affected African countries and for non-food items, especially trucks and vehicles urgently required to distribute food to the most needy people. About 600 million yen were contributed to WFP by Japanese NGOs, the first occasion on which such contributions were made.

Issues for the Future

Japan is committed to increasing its ODA substantially. However, the level of its food aid is likely to remain a relatively small part of its ODA in the immediate future. Japan has been a strong and consistent supporter of multilateral assistance provided through the UN system. Although it has provided resources to WFP from the outset, its ranking among donors to the Programme has been lower than to other multilateral organizations where it is among the top contributors. Instead, more use is made of the expertise and experience of WFP through bilateral services to help Japan with the implementation of its bilateral food aid programme.

Food aid has been primarily regarded in Japan as short-term relief assistance, although its longer-term benefits through triangular transactions are also recognized. The different functional forms of food aid as a broad-based and versatile investment resource for development could be more fully taken into account in providing this form of assistance to recipient countries. More information on the various forms of food aid, for example, as an income transfer to poor people, as an incentive for community action, as a releaser and creator of funds through different ways of monetization, as balance of payments support, and as a support to structural and sectoral adjustment polices and programmes, could help facilitate the development of a broader range of food aid programmes than has been pursued in the past.

There has been considerable scope and opportunity for Japan's food aid to be more effectively linked to the financial and technical elements of its aid programme in a comprehensive approach to helping developing countries. Its main food aid budget item is listed with aid to increase food production in the developing countries in the grant aid programme. This budget item is now being used in line with financial and technical assistance provided from other parts of the economic co-operation programme in order to enhance agricultural and rural development in the developing countries in mutually reinforcing ways.

An example may be taken from Japan's triangular transactions in food aid. While such transactions can serve to stimulate food production in the developing countries where food is purchased, they can also be used to address the attendant problems of food management. In this context, the problems of food marketing, logistics and pricing policies for producers and consumers could be addressed. Japan's financial, technical and material assistance to a country could thus be brought together to support both food production and management improvements in developing countries.

As the number of countries receiving Japanese bilateral food aid has increased, the focus of that aid has shifted to Africa in response to the food crises in that region. Japan's experience in Africa is relatively new and, as with other donors, its individual contribution in relation to overall needs is limited. The impact of Japan's food aid to Africa could be strengthened by drawing on the expertise and experience of other organizations in providing its assistance.

Other measures to improve the effectiveness of Japan's food aid programme include further strengthening the appraisal of requests, a training programme for the officers involved, and fostering closer policy dialogue with developing countries.

Appendix Table 15.1 *Japan: Cereal food aid deliveries ('000 tons – in grain equivalent)*

	1987	1988	1989	1990	1991	1987–91 Average
Total:	561.2	518.1	450.3	457.3	438.0	485.0
By food aid channel:						
– Bilateral	543.5	509.2	428.3	440.9	258.0	436.0
– Gvt-to-Gvt	543.5	508.5	428.3	440.9	248.5	433.9
– through NGOs	–	0.8	–	–	9.6	2.1
– Multilateral	17.6	8.9	22.0	16.2	180.2	49.0
By food aid category:						
– Emergency Relief	160.0	218.5	293.9	207.4	290.4	234.0
– Project	6.7	7.1	10.9	16.6	23.8	13.0
– Agr./Rural Development	0.6	1.2	8.7	11.1	14.0	7.1
– Nutrition Intervention	–	5.3	–	1.2	2.4	1.8
– Food Reserve	5.0	–	–	–	–	1.0
– Other Development Project	1.1	0.6	2.2	4.2	7.4	3.1
– Non-project (Programme)	394.5	292.6	145.5	233.0	124.1	238.0
By region:						
– Sub-Saharan Africa	179.5	181.4	128.9	94.9	155.9	148.1
– North Africa/Mid-East	28.4	33.0	21.3	0.2	18.6	20.3
– Asia and Pacific	337.3	250.0	289.5	203.5	247.6	265.6
– Latin America and Caribbean	16.1	53.7	10.6	5.6	15.0	20.2
– Europe	–	–	–	153.1	1.2	30.9

Source: WFP/INTERFAIS Database

Appendix Table 15.2 *Japan: Non-cereal food aid deliveries ('000 tons)*

	1987	1988	1989	1990	1991	1987–91 Average
Total:	3.9	6.4	16.0	5.2	8.8	8.1
By food aid channel:						
– Bilateral	0.7	2.1	2.0	1.6	3.5	2.0
– Gvt-to-Gvt	0.6	2.1	2.0	1.6	2.0	1.7
– through NGOs	0.2	–	–	–	1.5	0.3
– Multilateral	3.2	4.3	14.0	3.5	5.3	6.1
By food aid category:						
– Emergency Relief	1.6	2.0	9.6	1.6	2.8	3.5
– Project	2.3	3.0	6.4	3.5	4.9	4.1
– Agr./Rural Development	1.4	2.0	3.5	3.1	3.3	2.7
– Nutrition Intervention	0.1	0.2	0.5	0.1	0.3	0.3
– Other Development Project	0.7	0.8	2.3	0.4	1.3	1.1
– Non-project (Programme)	–	1.4	–	–	1.2	0.5
By region:						
– Sub-Saharan Africa	2.7	5.1	5.8	3.0	4.1	4.2
– North Africa/Mid-East	–	–	2.1	–	0.7	0.6
– Asia and Pacific	1.2	1.0	6.3	2.2	1.2	2.4
– Latin America and Caribbean	–	0.2	1.7	–	1.4	0.6
– Europe	–	–	–	–	1.4	0.3

Source: ibid.

16 Sweden

The Problems of Good Policy

The guiding principles of Sweden's development co-operation with developing countries are to promote: the growth of per capita resources within recipient countries; social and economic justice and equity; economic and political independence; and the democratic and social development of their societies. A target of 1% of GNP was established for Sweden's official development assistance in the late 1960s, significantly above the target set by the UN of 0.7%. Subsequently, there were progressive increases in development assistance, and the 1% target has been attained, making Sweden one of the biggest donors in *per caput* terms. Sweden has given strong and consistent support to international solidarity through the UN system. A substantial proportion of Swedish aid, especially its food aid, has been provided through multilateral channels, primarily through WFP. Sweden has played a leading role in stimulating co-operation among countries in developing progressive aid policies in the UN and other fora.

Assisting low-income countries unable to improve their own situation is a major motivating force behind Sweden's development assistance policy. A main objective of the country's aid is to help raise efficiency in the productive sectors of the recipient countries' economies, with priority being given to agricultural and rural development. The humanitarian impulses of Sweden's aid policies are also strong, as shown in its special assistance programmes to provide emergency relief and its particular interest in schemes designed to combat hunger and malnutrition and to promote women's participation in the development process.

As in other donor countries, however, the economic recession has forced the government to scrutinize national budget allocations closely. Sweden's ODA has been relatively unaffected. Low projected growth in production and income, and the unfavourable impact of net changes in exchange rates, however, have led to a situation where even attainment of the 1% target will not result in an increase in development assistance in real terms. Increased attention is being given, therefore, to an evaluation of aid provided through multilateral as well as bilateral channels, to increase its quality, efficiency and effectiveness.

During the 1980s there were conflicts in the aims of agricultural policies with respect to production levels, income distribution, and efficiency in the use of national resources. Consumers were hit by severely rising food prices and decreasing real incomes, developments which caused a decrease in the consumption of some food-stuffs. This led to the creation of large surpluses of agricultural products at the same time as inflation and high interest rates caused economic problems within Swedish agriculture and threatened the economic survival of newly established farmers. A parliamentary Commission on Food Policy established in the spring of 1983 made proposals for a comprehensive national food policy whose main objectives included securing the country's food supplies in times of peace as well as during national emergencies; the provision of high quality products at reasonable retail prices; and a living standard for Swedish farmers comparable to that of wage-earners in other sectors.

During the late 1970s and early 1980s Sweden's agricultural sector generated only a small proportion of the country's GDP, which was growing faster than agriculture's contribution to it. As a result, agricultural employment in Sweden declined at a time when overall employment was increasing. Although agriculture is thus playing a declining role in the Swedish national economy, it has generated increases in the output of certain basic agricultural commodities that have exceeded the country's domestic requirements. As a result, there have been substantial surpluses, a large proportion of which have been exported. However, Swedish food aid has historically formed only a small part of the country's ODA (about 4% in value terms). Food aid in wheat and vegetable oil, the two commodities dominating Sweden's 'food aid basket', has also been modest in relation to national production and commercial exports of these products.

Since the mid-1970s, almost 80% of the country's food aid has been channelled multilaterally through WFP, by means of pledges to WFP's regular resources and through contributions to the Food Aid Convention and to the International Emergency Food Reserve. Multilateral aid has grown faster than bilateral food aid and foreign assistance as a whole. For the 1989–90 biennium, Sweden was the sixth largest donor to WFP, providing over US$89 million, of which over US$52 million was pledged to WFP's regular resources, US$15.3 million for protracted refugee operations, US$14.8 million for the IEFR and US$7.2 million as non-food items.

Until the mid-1980s, about a fifth of Sweden's food aid was provided bilaterally, mainly to 18 so-called 'programme countries' on which other types of bilateral development assistance have also concentrated. This food aid primarily represented emergency assistance supplied to meet the recipient countries' needs, arising out of natural or man-made disasters. Subsequently, this bilateral aid has declined sharply to very low levels in the early 1990s.

Sweden has also supplied small quantities of canned fish, fish protein concentrate and vegetable oil each year as a contribution to WFP's regular resources. Its annual contribution to the FAC amounted, from 1974–5, to 35,000 tons of wheat (in wheat equivalent), increasing to 40,000 tons a year under the 1980 FAC. Since the beginning of the IEFR in 1975, Sweden has consistently made a contribution of 40,000 tons of wheat (in wheat equivalent) each year, and since 1978–9, an average annual quantity of 1,500 tons of vegetable oil.

A small part of Swedish food aid has also been made available, on an *ad hoc* basis, through NGOs. This has been mainly intended to provide humanitarian relief in emergency situations and to reduce the effects of acute food shortages.

Food Aid Administration

The Swedish public administration distinguishes to a high degree between, on the one hand, responsibilities for policy, legal and budget matters and, on the other hand, responsibilities for day-to-day operations and supervision over the actual implementation of decisions. The Ministry of Foreign Affairs, in particular its Department for International Development Co-operation comprising a multilateral aid and a bilateral aid division, deals with the policy, legal and budgetary aspects of Sweden's development assistance, including food aid. The Department is also the focal point for all issues concerning multilateral assistance, the implementation of which rests with international organizations.

The Swedish International Development Authority (SIDA) is mainly responsible for the implementation of the country's bilateral development co-operation programme. Matters relating to food aid are handled in four of SIDA's eleven divisions: the Procurement Division, which purchases food aid commodities and non-food items on behalf of the Ministry of Foreign Affairs; the Area Division, which supervises the implementation of bilateral food aid programmes in individual countries; the Agricultural Division, which carries out technical scrutiny of agricultural and rural development projects; and the Health Division, which examines the nutritional aspects of food aid.

The Ministry of Foreign Affairs is responsible for liaison between the government and WFP. The Ministry of Agriculture is also closely involved in food aid matters. Issues concerning WFP are discussed regularly by representatives of the two ministries. An advisory group for certain food policy related matters, chaired by a representative of SIDA and attended by both SIDA and Ministry of Foreign Affairs' representatives, reviews requests for food aid funded from bilateral country programmes. SIDA is assisted in technical and nutrition matters by consultants at the International Rural Development Centre of the Swedish Agricultural University of Uppsala, and the Department of Nutrition at the University of Uppsala. An advisory group on emergency assistance, chaired by SIDA and consisting of representatives of the Department for International Development Co-operation and of the Swedish Red Cross, reviews requests for such aid.

The two most frequently purchased commodities in Sweden's 'food aid basket' to WFP are wheat/wheat flour and vegetable oil. Wheat is obtained from the Swedish Grain Trade Association, a parastatal organization that buys the country's surplus grains and handles their export. Whenever wheat flour is provided, the wheat purchased by SIDA's Procurement Division is milled by the Swedish Flour Milling Association. Vegetable oil extracted exclusively from rape seed produced in Sweden is purchased from Karlshamns Oljefabriker, a firm owned by the Swedish Co-operative Union and Wholesale Society, a strong consumer co-operative movement.

SIDA's Procurement Division has also obtained a large variety of non-food items, such as trucks, trailers, tyres, a mobile vehicle workshop and milk cans. Tenders are issued to obtain offers from a large number of competing firms. The companies awarded purchase contracts are not necessarily Swedish.

Sweden has consistently provided one-third of its pledges to WFP's regular resources in cash to defray the costs of transport and administration of food aid. The commodities shipped from Sweden have been carried on vessels obtained by WFP through open, international tender.

Major Characteristics of Sweden's Food Aid

Certain strong features of Sweden's food aid programme have developed over the years. These may be summarized as follows:

Multilateral focus: Ideological and pragmatic reasons have influenced Sweden's approach towards a division of labour between Swedish government agencies and WFP. A tradition of confidence and faith in the UN system as a forum for international co-operation and solidarity is deeply rooted in Swedish society. This attitude is reflected in the consistent support that WFP has received from Sweden since its inception. The government has also laid emphasis on the importance of food aid being demand- rather than supply-determined and the provision of food aid in accordance with an internationally agreed set of criteria quite independent of political considerations. The policies and priorities adopted by the CFA and WFP have sustained Sweden's confidence in the multilateral approach to food aid.

The government has consistently recognized the benefits of economies of scale and burden-sharing in the implementation of food aid programmes. Rather than embarking on a costly training of headquarters and field staff and the development of its own food aid administration on a large scale, it regards tax income as being used more effectively by making it available to WFP in the form of commodity and cash resources. Swedish bilateral food aid is supplied as bulk shipments to only a small number of 'programme countries', whereas multilaterally channelled resources are distributed for the benefit of a considerably larger number of countries in a co-ordinated manner and without the need to establish additional field offices. On the other hand, Sweden has been able to draw upon the specialized skills and knowledge of WFP staff, including its field staff assigned to both Swedish 'programme countries' and countries where only WFP maintains a presence.

Forward planning: Sweden was one of the first donor countries to adopt forward planning of food aid, both to facilitate effective planning of its use and to provide assurance of a continuing supply over several years to the recipient countries. The Ministry of Foreign Affairs has devised a formula of a three-year, firm/indicative, rolling commitment within the government's annual budget proposals. There have been difficulties in applying the formula during the recession but the advantage of foreseeable pledges has been maintained by keeping a floor for annual commitments for each of the three years of the cycle.

Flexibility and stability: Two-thirds of Sweden's contributions to WFP have consistently been provided in the form of commodities, while one-third has been made available in cash to defray WFP's costs for shipping and for technical, administrative and programme support. Any portion of the Swedish pledge that remains unused at the end of each budget year (July to June) is automatically carried forward and added to the resources allocated for the following year, thus increasing WFP's flexibility in calling forward commodities provided by Sweden.

The government has also demonstrated a high degree of flexibility in the selection of commodities from the 'food aid basket'. They may be chosen freely by WFP in accordance with its own requirements in line with the government's principle that its contributions in kind should be determined by WFP's demand and not by Sweden's supply. This approach has helped to avoid delivery of inappropriate commodities and has permitted WFP to shift consignments of high-demand commodities at short notice. Moreover, the rapid processing of WFP's requests for consignments has enabled it to arrange for the prompt shipment of Swedish food contributions.

Swedish contributions to the FAC and IEFR are also channelled through WFP. As these contributions are made in physical, and not in value, terms they are insulated from the effects of commodity price rises.

Cash contributions: Sweden has consistently provided its cash contributions in a freely convertible currency, at the beginning of each fiscal year, and has fully adhered to the cash provisions related to commodity contributions to both the FAC and the IEFR to meet the full costs of transportation. The government has also made available additional cash resources from bilateral emergency assistance funds to help finance triangular transactions, for example, the purchase of maize in Zimbabwe for subsequent shipment to Mozambique and Tanzania for use as food aid.

Non-food items: Sweden has been one of the largest contributors of non-food items used in combination with WFP food aid to ensure the effective implementation of development projects and emergency operations. In addition, it has provided transport experts to act as logistics officers in key locations to help remove bottlenecks in the delivery of food aid in international, large-scale emergency operations.

A Special Unit for Disaster Relief, forming part of Sweden's Stand-by Force in the service of the UN, is also made available at the request of disaster-stricken countries and the UN. This unit has operated closely with WFP. The Unit assists in planning relief work in disaster areas, providing aid for survival, co-ordinating health care, implementing technical assistance for the provision of water and shelter and carrying out the transportation of supplies, including air transport of vitally needed equipment. It has operated in countries such as Algeria, Bolivia, Ethiopia, Ghana, Somalia, Uganda, the Lebanon, along the Thai/Kampuchea border and in Kampuchea itself.

Issues for the Future

A number of issues and concerns may have an influence on the future level and direction of Swedish food aid, some of which may be briefly summarized as follows:

Structural reform There has been disquiet over the possible longer-term counter-productive effects of food aid. The Prime Minister, speaking at FAO in Rome on the occasion of the Third World Food Day in 1983, in the context of recurring emergencies, drew attention to the fact that it may be easier for a country to issue a plea for emergency food aid than to come to grips with the situation that caused the need for that aid in the first place. Many countries that received such aid faced chronic food shortages rather than acute emergency situations. Food might be available in the countryside but it did not reach the cities because of, for example, low agricultural prices or insufficient marketing systems. By receiving food aid, countries postponed the difficult actions needed to improve the flow of food within their borders. Food aid should not be used to subsidize poor agricultural policies. The long-run objective was to increase food production in the poor countries themselves. The Prime Minister suggested that it was necessary to reach an understanding between donor and recipient countries that food aid should be phased out after a certain period. In this way, food aid – preferably project food aid – could act as a lever in helping farmers in developing countries to adopt the needed structural reforms.

Level and direction of food aid There has been a wide divergence of opinion in Sweden between those who favour a large increase in food aid and those who wish it to remain, at best, at its present level. Those supporting substantial growth are motivated mainly by humanitarian concerns or by self-interest. Others are influenced either by considerations of the opportunity costs of food aid in overall development aid budget allocations or doubts as to whether food aid represents an effective development resource. For them, the case for food aid remains fraught with uncertainties and contradictions and they ask for examples of its successful use for development.

Given this uncertainty, it has been suggested, especially by the Swedish NGO community, that food aid should be provided only in cases of genuine emergency. So far there has been no formal definition of what constitutes a situation qualifying for Swedish bilateral emergency food aid. However, the advisory group on emergency assistance verifies that the unforeseen need for food aid has arisen out of a natural or man-made disaster, that it represents a very particular case, and that the aid input is not intended as a mere relief for difficulties in the balance of payments position of the country asking for help.

Concern has also been expressed about the *modus operandi* of prolonged food relief assistance to refugees and displaced persons. Rather than providing them with handouts, it has been suggested that, to the extent possible and feasible, they should be employed in FFW programmes in either settlement or rehabilitation schemes and that food aid should also be supplied for their nutritional improvement, education and training. Consideration has also been given in situations of recurring emergencies to the incorporation of assistance for disaster prevention and preparedness, combined with the provision of relief aid.

Co-ordination of food aid and other forms of aid   Food aid is not considered in the mainstream of Sweden's development assistance thinking. There are both institutional and conceptual reasons for this. The bulk of Sweden's food aid is channelled through WFP, while its smaller bilateral food aid is provided in the form of emergency relief. The Swedish direct food aid input is not, therefore, considered to be a complementary aid resource in the formulation and implementation of the development assistance programmes conducted by SIDA.

On the other hand, increased co-operation is being sought at the recipient country level between Swedish bilateral aid programmes and WFP aid, not least in times of emergency.

Multilateral channelling   Sweden wishes food aid to be channelled through the multilateral system, primarily through WFP. It considers that WFP should increasingly be the primary multilateral source of food aid and its logistics. Bilateral food aid should be reduced in favour of multilateral food aid.

Sweden emphasizes that food as a form of aid must be carefully utilized. It is important to identify the situations and circumstances where food aid has a comparative advantage in terms of reaching its beneficiaries with the least possible negative side-effects, relative to other forms of co-operation (particularly financial aid). Food aid must be demand rather than supply driven.

In development projects, financial aid and food aid should be seen as two funding resources used towards a common development goal. There is therefore need for an integrated approach to development assistance, and thus also for close co-operation between WFP and UNDP. At the same time, the poverty focus of food aid, which at times may be difficult to attain in financial aid, should not be lost. This focus for development projects, where food aid is used as part of resourcing, should be oriented towards those in greatest need, primarily in food-deficit least developed countries.

Food aid plays an important part in emergency situations. Mechanisms should be established for this form of assistance reaching those in greatest need as quickly as possible. At the same time, emergency actions should seek to avoid creating a disincentive to local production and to long-term self-sufficiency. For these reasons, Sweden attaches great importance to co-operation between WFP and the other agencies involved in emergency response. The establishment of the Department of Humanitarian Affairs and its Inter-Agency Standing Committee in the United Nations is seen as a means of ensuring regular and systematic consultation, co-operation and co-ordination in complex emergencies.

The presentation of UN consolidated appeals is seen, *inter alia*, as a mechanism to attain inter-agency programming interaction and co-ordination and as a means to present to the international community a consolidated overview of needs, on the one hand, and of the scope and extent of the required UN response to a complex emergency, on the other.

Food aid and nutrition development Serious attempts have been made to address the problem of malnutrition in developing countries through the manufacture of special fortified food commodities for use in programmes designed specifically to improve the nutritional status of vulnerable groups. These commodities have been used in co-operation with WFP and NGOs but have not generally proved to be cost-effective, in part because of the lack of expert staff and funds to teach the recipients how to use them and integrate them into local diets. Swedish NGOs have concluded that it is more cost-effective to manufacture fortified commodities for supplementary feeding based on foods produced in the developing countries themselves.

Food aid logistics Sweden has contributed to the improvement of logistics in the flow of food aid commodities. Swedish transport experts and members of the Special Unit for Disaster Relief have provided valuable inputs in recipient countries. With the increasing flow of emergency food aid, it is likely that such support will continue to be required in the future, especially in sub-Saharan Africa.

Well-functioning systems for the procurement and despatch of food commodities have also been established. Further attention is being given to reducing the cost of packaging vegetable oil, as it represents a significant portion of the total cost per unit shipped.

Conclusions

Sweden has portrayed a number of very positive features in its food aid policies and programmes both through WFP, and bilaterally. In common with other major donors, however, various aspects of its food aid have been re-examined, partly as a result of the effects of the recession and partly because of a general desire to strengthen the developmental impact of its assistance.

It is perhaps worth noting that, in spite of a worsening economic situation during the late 1980s, annual opinion polls on the attitude of the public toward Sweden's development aid programme have indicated that the ratio of those who support the current or an increased level of aid has remained at over 70%. Such a positive attitude can to a large extent be explained by the strong traditional attitude of international solidarity in Sweden and by the quality of public information work carried out by Swedish NGOs.

Appendix Table 16.1 *Sweden: Cereal food aid deliveries ('000 tons – in grain equivalent)*

	1987	1988	1989	1990	1991	1987–91 Average
Total:	166.2	127.1	111.0	88.2	76.5	113.8
By food aid channel:						
– Bilateral	71.1	31.3	25.4	9.7	5.0	28.5
– Gvt-to-Gvt	71.0	26.8	25.4	0.9	5.0	25.8
– through NGOs	0.2	4.5	–	8.8	–	2.7
– Multilateral	95.1	95.8	85.6	78.5	71.6	85.3
By food aid category:						
– Emergency Relief	56.5	76.1	79.5	52.9	39.6	60.9
– Project	99.3	46.2	31.4	35.2	37.0	49.8
– Agr./Rural Development	44.5	23.1	7.7	31.3	16.8	24.7
– Nutrition Intervention	–	4.4	1.5	0.7	9.7	3.2
– Other Development Project	54.8	18.6	22.3	3.2	10.5	21.9
– Non-project (Programme)	10.4	4.8	–	–	–	3.0
By region:						
– Sub-Saharan Africa	67.2	58.0	55.7	49.5	56.1	57.3
– North Africa/Mid-East	21.3	13.6	29.4	10.8	16.4	18.3
– Asia and Pacific	77.7	54.0	25.3	27.8	4.1	37.8
– Latin America and Caribbean	–	1.4	0.6	–	–	0.4

Source: WFP/INTERFAIS Database

Appendix 16.2 *Sweden: Non-cereal food aid deliveries ('000 tons)*

	1987	1988	1989	1990	1991	1987–91 Average
Total:	34.7	39.7	28.9	15.9	31.0	30.0
By food aid channel:						
– Bilateral	19.9	20.1	16.0	2.3	2.0	12.0
– Gvt-to-Gvt	19.9	19.0	15.9	2.3	–	11.4
– through NGOs	–	1.1	0.1	–	2.0	0.6
– Multilateral	14.8	19.7	13.0	13.6	29.0	18.0
By food aid category:						
– Emergency Relief	6.6	11.0	3.6	3.9	16.2	8.2
– Project	9.6	17.5	15.5	12.0	14.9	13.9
– Agr./Rural Development	4.9	8.9	5.7	7.4	9.9	7.4
– Nutrition Intervention	2.2	3.7	1.5	0.9	1.8	2.0
– Food Reserve	–	–	4.4	0.1	–	0.9
– Other Development Project	2.5	4.9	4.0	3.6	3.3	3.6
– Non-project (Programme)	18.4	11.3	9.8	–	–	7.9
By region:						
– Sub-Saharan Africa	26.0	23.3	24.3	10.2	20.0	20.8
– North Africa/Mid-East	2.8	6.6	3.6	3.3	2.6	3.8
– Asia and Pacific	5.8	2.3	0.8	0.2	7.8	3.4
– Latin America and Caribbean	–	7.5	0.2	2.2	0.6	2.1

Source: ibid.

17 USA United States of America

Changing Priorities
in Promoting Development,
Humanitarian Relief & Agricultural Trade

Background

The provision of food aid by the United States was given a legal and institutional basis in 1954. Since then, the US has provided more than $44 billion in food aid to every quarter of the developing world. Although its share in the provision of global food aid has fallen as other donors have increased their food aid, it still provided more than half of all cereal food aid and just under half of all non-cereal food aid at the end of the 1980s.

This chapter focuses particularly on major changes that have been made recently in the legislation governing US food aid. However, it is useful to sketch in the background. US food aid originated in relief assistance provided to victims of natural disasters, famines and civil disturbances beginning in the early years of the nineteenth century. Large-scale food aid was provided to Europe after the First World War, and again after the Second World War, under the Marshall Plan, when more than a quarter of a total aid package of $13.5 billion consisted of food, feed and fertilizer. This and other assistance was a precedent for the programme food aid that was later to be supplied for balance of payments and budgetary support. Provision was made in the Agricultural Act of 1949 (Section 416) to use US surplus agricultural commodities as food aid, and other precedents were made, including the Mutual Security Acts 1951–4.

But it was the Agricultural Trade Development and Assistance Act of 1954 – which has become widely known by its number, Public Law (PL) 480 – that was to institutionalize and provide the legal framework for US food aid basically in the form that still endures. PL 480 marked a recognition that world food shortages and US surplus agricultural production could no longer be considered to be isolated and temporary occurrences. It established a relationship between US domestic agricultural interests and foreign aid that has shaped the country's food aid policies and programmes. The PL 480 programme continues to be authorized as part of an omnibus US farm bill that is passed every four or five years. It is financed from Department of Agriculture appropriations and has not been incorporated into the Foreign Assistance Act, which encompasses most other forms of US external assistance.

Food Aid Categories

The food aid programme as originally configured in PL 480 in 1954 was divided into three components, reflecting different interests and purposes.

Title I: Sales for foreign currency: This programme food aid, provided on concessional credit terms and sold in the recipient countries, permitted the use of the foreign (i.e. local) currencies, with the agreement of the recipient government, for eight purposes: (i) development of new markets for US agricultural commodities on a mutually benefiting basis; (ii) purchase of strategic and critical materials; (iii) procurement of military equipment; (iv) financing the purchase of goods and services for other friendly countries; (v) promotion of balanced economic development and trade among nations; (vi) payment of US obligations abroad; (vii) loans to promote multilateral trade and economic development; and (viii) financing international educational exchange. In negotiating agreements under this Title, reasonable precautions were to be taken to safeguard the usual markets of the US and to ensure that world agricultural commodity prices would not be unduly disrupted. Private trade channels were to be used to the maximum extent practicable. Special consideration was to be given to developing and expanding sustained market demand for US agricultural commodities. Resale or trans-shipment of the commodities to other countries or use for other than domestic purposes were prohibited. And maximum opportunity to purchase US surplus agricultural commodities was to be afforded.

Title II: Famine relief and other assistance: Not more than $300 million of food aid commodities was provided on a grant basis for emergency assistance to meet famine or other urgent relief requirements, through voluntary relief agencies (to the extent practicable) and intergovernmental organizations.

Title III: General provisions: Through these provisions commodities were made available to private voluntary organizations (PVOs) for distribution in the US and abroad. They also permitted the barter of food commodities for strategic materials and goods not produced in the US.

Evolving Food Aid Policy

The US Congress has periodically revised PL 480, reflecting changes in demand-supply relationships for US agricultural products and in the perceptions and objectives of development. These modifications have also been expressions of shifts in the relative balance of relationships among the parties involved in US farm and foreign policy, evolving views about the role of food aid, and different trends in countries' needs in the various regions of the developing world.

Of the many modifications or supplements to the original PL 480, the following deserve special mention. In 1959, PL 480 was renamed 'Food for Peace', a rhetorical recognition of the potential foreign policy dimensions of food assistance. The legislation was substantially modified in 1966, eliminating the requirement that the commodities used in the food aid programme had to have been designated as 'surplus'; including as an objective the use of food aid to combat hunger and malnutrition; emphasizing the need for recipient countries to expand their own agricultural production; and calling for the phasing out of local currency repayments in favour of long-term credit sales repayable only in dollars or convertible currencies.

Reflecting a greater interest in the use of food aid for broad-based development, PL 480 was amended in 1975 to limit to no more than 25% the amount of Title I food aid that could go to countries above a specified per capita income level; to establish minimum tonnage levels for Title II assistance; and to permit (i) sales for local currencies under the Title II grant programme and (ii) up to 15% of Title I credits to be turned into grants – provided in each case the generated funds were used for specified agricultural and other development purposes of particular benefit to the poor, including small farmers.

This growing emphasis on turning PL 480 into an instrument for broad-based, equitable development led in 1977 to the enactment of a new Title III, 'Food for Development' programme, permitting a part of Title I food aid to be provided under multi-year agreements to low-income countries wishing to pursue additional development-oriented policies and activities. The funds generated from the sale of the food by the recipient country, and in some cases the food itself, were used to support development activities, and repayment of the credits to the US was waived, effectively putting the food aid on a grant basis.

Under Title II, the authority of Section 206 was used mainly to move away from emergency feeding programmes toward more developmentally-oriented activities, through sale of food and use of the generated currencies, in the poorest countries, especially those experiencing recurrent food emergencies.

The Food Security Wheat Reserve Act of December 1980 established a wheat reserve of 4 million tons to supplement and complement the Food for Peace programme in times of emergency and to honour US commitments when food availability dropped or prices increased. A new freestanding 'Food for Progress Act' was passed in 1985 to provide multi-year commitments of food aid to countries that undertook to introduce or expand free enterprise elements in their agricultural economies through changes in commodity pricing, marketing, input availability, distribution and private sector involvement. It also mandated the US Government to monetize at least 5% of the value of non-emergency food aid commodities provided through PVOs.

The most recent major step in the long evolution of US food aid policy is embodied in the new legislation included as part of the Agricultural Development and Trade Act of 1990, which contains extensive revisions to the original and subsequently amended PL 480 legislation. The new Act is effective for five years from January 1991.

The 1990 Agricultural Development and Trade Act Greater emphasis is now placed on using food aid to promote food security, nutrition intervention and child survival programmes, privatization of agricultural marketing systems, and integration of food aid with other US economic assistance programmes. The Act states,

> It is the policy of the United States to use its abundant agricultural productivity to promote the foreign policy of the United States by enhancing the food security of the developing world through the use of agricultural commodities and local currencies accruing under this Act.

Food security is defined as 'access by all people at all times to sufficient food and nutrition for a healthy and productive life'.

Food aid commodities and local currencies accruing therefrom are to be used for five purposes: (i) combating world hunger and malnutrition and their causes; (ii) promoting broad-based, equitable and sustainable development, including agricultural development; (iii) expanding international trade; (iv) developing and expanding export markets for US agricultural commodities; and (v) fostering and encouraging the development of private enterprise and democratic participation in developing countries. Recognizing the increased global needs for food aid, the Act calls on the United States and other donor countries to increase their food aid, and encourages other advanced nations to make increased food aid contributions to combat world hunger and malnutrition, particularly through the expansion of international food and agriculture assistance programmes.

Changes have been made to the three PL 480 food aid categories in the new legislation.

Title I: Trade and development assistance: Programme food aid under this title is to be provided on concessional loan terms, as in the past, for developing countries with foreign-exchange shortages and with difficulties in meeting all their food import needs commercially. Priority is given to countries that: (i) demonstrate the greatest need for food; (ii) undertake measures for economic development to improve food security and agricultural development, alleviate poverty and promote broad-based equitable and sustainable development; and (iii) demonstrate potential to become commercial markets for competitively priced US agricultural commodities. Repayment can be made in dollars or local currencies at concessional rates over a period of between 10 and 30 years with a grace period of up to seven years. The local currency generated from the sale of Title I commodities may be used in the recipient country for various agricultural and trade purposes.

In response to the new legislation, the Department of Agriculture has issued new guidance on Title I programmes for its Foreign Agricultural Service Counsellors and Attachés. This places special emphasis on supporting development programmes that are broad-based, equitable and sustainable, and that enhance food security in particular. In fiscal year (October to September) 1991, the Department of Agriculture initiated agreements for Title I programmes totalling $442.8 million.

Title II: Emergency and private assistance programmes: These programmes continue to provide emergency relief and non-emergency food aid in support of development projects. The types of use include: addressing famine or other urgent or extraordinary relief requirements; combating malnutrition, especially in children and mothers; alleviating the causes of hunger, mortality and morbidity; promoting economic and community development; promoting sound environmental practices; and carrying out feeding programmes. Assistance under this title is provided mainly through PVOs, co-operatives and intergovernmental organizations such as WFP.

The commodities supplied under this title may be directly provided to needy people, sold, exchanged or distributed by other appropriate methods. A minimum volume of food aid has been established for this title of 1.925 million metric tons for FY 1991 (of which 1.45 million metric tons must be used for non-emergency purposes), increasing by increments of 25,000 metric tons a year to 2.025 million metric tons for FY 1995 (of which 1.55 million metric tons must be used for non-emergency purposes). In FY 1991, the US Agency for International Development provided $803.2 million of Title II food aid (emergency and non-emergency). Of that amount, $270 million (about one-third) or over 1 million tons was programmed by 18 PVOs and co-operatives in 62 countries.

Title III: Food for development: The most significant changes in the new legislation have been made in the Title III Programme. This is a programme now especially for 'least developed countries' defined as: (i) those countries that meet the low-income criteria established by the World Bank (an annual per capita income of $610 or less in 1991); or (ii) food-deficit countries characterized by high levels of malnutrition among significant numbers of their population (defined as those countries with daily per capita consumption of less than 2,300 calories that cannot meet their food security requirements through domestic production or imports owing to shortage of foreign-exchange earnings, and have mortality rates of children under five years of age in excess of 100 per 1,000 births). Priority is to be given to those countries that have greatest need; have the capacity to use food aid effectively; show a commitment to policies to promote food security and reduce hunger and malnutrition measurably; and have a long-term plan for broad-based, equitable and sustainable development.

Food aid commodities provided under this title may be directly distributed to needy people or sold. When sold, the local currency generated may be owned by the US or by the recipient government. In FY 1991, 14 Title III agreements were signed with a total value of $276.7 million of assistance involving 1.4 million tons of food aid commodities. For FY 1992, 56 countries were considered to be eligible for Title III food aid – 36 in Africa, 14 in Asia and the Near East and 6 in Latin America and the Caribbean.

Five major factors may be identified as being responsible for the far-reaching changes in US food aid policies and programmes enunciated in the 1990 Act:

- Enhancing food security, alleviating hunger and promoting nutrition intervention and child survival programmes are seen as major goals both as an organizing development principle and in recognition of the comparative advantage of food aid as a development resource for achieving these goals. (Food is regarded as being at the centre of the development process in most developing countries. A large proportion of the rural population works to produce it, and a high percentage of the total population spends a large part of earned income to acquire it. Food availability affects price regimes and inflation rates. Food, therefore, is a key resource and food aid donors are seen to be particularly well-placed to support equitable and sustainable development.)
- Emphasis is placed on private enterprise and on privatizing marketing and distribution as a way of transferring the successful agricultural experience of the US. (Most food aid currently flows through public channels. Increasingly, the choice between using public channels and private traders is seen to be a major issue in the provision of food aid, influencing significantly its impact on development.)
- Greater recognition is given to the different levels of development of developing countries, to their different prospects for development and trade and hence to the need to design appropriate kinds of food aid programmes for each category of countries.
- More flexibility and greater reliability are given to the provision and use of food aid, and emphasis is placed on its integration with other US economic assistance programmes. More food aid is provided on a grant basis. Food aid commodities may be directly distributed, sold or exchanged. When sold, the funds generated may be owned by the US or the recipient government, and under certain conditions are not required to be placed in a separate account. With allowance for exceptions, agreements under all titles must be on a multi-year basis. Provision is also made for debt forgiveness.
- Clarifying the roles of the various government units involved in the administration of the US food aid programme is an important goal of the new legislation. Previously, an inter-agency Food Aid Subcommittee of the Development Co-ordination Committee was charged with planning future allocations and overseeing negotiations with other countries and international bodies. The Subcommittee was chaired by the Department of Agriculture, and members included representatives from AID, the Office of Management and Budget (OMB) and the Departments of State and Treasury. Protracted discussions resulted from their different responsibilities and priorities. Under the new legislation, there is a clear

demarcation of responsibility. The Secretary of Agriculture has the implementing authority for Title I, while Titles II and III are implemented by the Administrator of AID. To ensure policy co-ordination, however, a Food Assistance Policy Council has been established by Executive Order, comprising senior representatives of the Departments of Agriculture and State, AID and OMB, to advise on appropriate policies, co-ordinate decisions on allocations and prepare an annual report on the programmes and activities implemented under the new legislation.

Trends in US Food Aid Since 1954

The major trends in US food aid of all kinds over the period 1956–88 may be summarized as follows:

Size of programme: The volume of US food aid increased rapidly in the first decade (1956–65) to reach a peak of almost 19 million tons in 1962. It declined sharply in the next decade to reach its lowest level of about 3 million tons in 1975, and has subsequently remained at between 5 and 8 million tons a year. In value terms (at current prices), the total annual cost of US food aid, which is determined by the level of food prices and the volume of shipments in any year, reached a peak of $1.6 billion in the mid-1960s, then decreased to its lowest level of $866 million in the mid-1970s, and rose again to a record $1.9 billion in the mid-1980s. In 1990 it was $1.6 billion.

Relative size of titles: Over the years, there have been changes in the proportions of food aid channelled through the various titles. During the period 1956–8, and 30 years later in 1986–8, over half of total shipments were channelled through Title I agreements. Title II donations and barter arrangements under the original PL 480 act accounted for over 40% of shipments in 1956–8. After the PL 480 barter programme was phased down, Title I shipments increased to almost 80% of deliveries in 1966–8. Greater allocations to Africa in the mid-1970s and mid-1980s in response to the major food crises of these periods resulted in increasing the proportion of Title II shipments. Shipments under Section 416 of the Agricultural Act of 1949, as extended and revised, accounted for about 15% of total shipments during 1986–8, but the amount provided has fluctuated markedly from year to year depending on the availability of surpluses.

Table 17.1 *US food aid: relative shares of different legislative titles, 1956–88 (% of three-year total shipment costs)* [a]

Year	Title I [b]	Title II	Barter [c]	Section 416
1956–8	57	20	23	0
1966–8	78	20	2	0
1976–8	70	30	0	0
1986–8	56	29	0	15

[a] Figures rounded.
[b] Includes Title III.
[c] Commodities were shipped under the PL 480 barter programme until 1969.

Source: Economic Research Service, US Department of Agriculture (USDA).

Tonnage provided under Title I has constituted the largest part of the US food aid programme and a significant part of US economic assistance. Recipient governments buy their Title I commodities directly from the private sector in the US. As credits provided under this bilateral concessional loan programme are denominated in dollar terms, the volume of food that can be purchased fluctuates with changing US commodity prices.

The Title II programme has been legislated on a tonnage basis since the mid-1970s and is obtained principally from government stocks. The commodities supplied are restricted to those the Secretary of Agriculture determines are in surplus in government-owned stocks. These stocks are managed by the Commodity Credit Corporation (CCC), which is government-owned and operated and was established in 1933 to stabilize, support and protect farm income and prices. It also helps to maintain balanced and adequate supplies of agricultural commodities and their orderly distribution.

Limited use could be made of the Title III programme as defined before the new 1990 legislation, largely owing to complex administrative procedures and the level of conditionality required. Under the previous Title III agreements, a Title I loan could be forgiven if all the local currency generated from commodity sales was used for specified development purposes. These agreements contained self-help measures designed to promote broad-based rural development, especially improving the production, storage and distribution of agricultural commodities and enabling the poor to participate actively in increasing food production through small farm agriculture. The self-help measures had to be additional to those the recipient country would otherwise have undertaken in the absence of foreign aid.

Food aid and agricultural exports: The proportion of food aid in the totality of US agricultural exports has declined appreciably since the early 1960s; whereas it accounted for a quarter or more of the value of total agricultural exports at that time, it was 6% or less during the 1980s. This has happened not because the value of food aid has declined, but because the value of commercial exports and of credit and guarantee and export enhancement programmes has increased considerably. In 1988, for example, the value of total US agricultural exports was $35.3 billion, of which over three-quarters was from commercial exports, 20% from credit and guarantee and export enhancement programmes, and only 4% was made up of food aid shipments.

Food aid shipments in grains and grain products, which averaged 13 million tons a year during the first 15 years after PL 480 was enacted, have varied between 5 and 7 million tons in recent years. These shipments, which accounted for over half of US agricultural exports in the mid-1950s and early 1960s, represented less than 10% in the 1980s. Food aid shipments of wheat and wheat products, which make up the bulk of US grain aid, averaged over 60% of total exports of those commodities in the first 18 years after PL 480 was enacted but fell to below 20% in the 1980s, having been largely replaced by feed grains and rice.

Share of world food aid: As the world's largest food aid donor, the US has provided a high proportion of global food aid in cereals. About three-quarters of the volume of world cereal food aid came from the United States in the early 1970s. This proportion fell to about half in the mid-1970s, increased to about two-thirds in the mid-1980s and fell again to just over half at the end of the 1980s. The US provided 47% of global non-cereal food aid at the end of the 1980s, but its share has fluctuated as availabilities have moved between surpluses and shortages.

The United States is the largest contributor to the Food Aid Convention of 1986. It has guaranteed to provide a minimum annual contribution of 4.47 million tons of

Table 17.2 *US food aid: commodity composition, 1956–88* [a] *(% of value of three-year total shipments)*

Commodity group	1956–8	1966–8	1976–8	1986–8
Grains	51	63	56	56
Grain products	4	9	17	13
Vegetable oils	8	8	11	16
Dairy products	13	7	5	5
Livestock and meat products	1	0	0	0
Oilseeds and meals	0	0	0	1
Fibres and fabrics	18	9	2	1
Blended products	0	1	6	4
Others	5	3	3	4

[a] Figures rounded.

Source: ibid.

cereals (in wheat equivalent), almost 60% of the aggregate minimum annual contributions of all signatories, irrespective of fluctuations in cereal production and prices. It has consistently supplied more than its minimum annual contribution and accounted for over 60% of total FAC shipments throughout the 1980s.

Commodity composition   The shares of commodity groups in the value of US food aid shipments over the period 1956–88 are shown in Table 17.2.

Grains and grain products have constituted between 55 and 73% of the total value of US food aid shipments, vegetable oils have doubled their share to 16%, while the share of other commodity groups has decreased or remained relatively small.

Grants and loans: The US is the only donor not providing bilateral food aid entirely on a grant basis. The grant portion of the programme has increased, however, from 42% in 1980 to 56% in 1990.

Destination: The regional distribution of US food aid shipments in value terms over the period 1956–88 has shown dramatic trends, reflecting the significant changes in the need for food aid that have taken place.

The PL 480 legislation initially responded to the needs of war-torn Europe after the Second World War. As those needs subsided, massive shipments were made to Asia, particularly to the Indian subcontinent, mainly in the form of Title I programme food aid. As domestic food production in Asia increased under the Green Revolution and large-scale famine conditions ceased, the proportion of US food aid to that region was reduced. At the same time, widespread food crises have resulted in an increased share

Table 17.3 *US food aid: regional distribution 1956–88* [a] *(% of three-year total shipment costs)*

Region	1956–8	1966–8	1976–8	1986–8
Africa	2	12	31	44
Asia	33	69	53	28
Europe	51	6	3	1
Latin America	8	9	9	26
Middle East	6	4	4	1

[a] Figures rounded.

Source: ibid.

Table 17.4 *US food aid: channels and uses, annual average value 1986–90* [a] *(US$ million)*

Programme category/channel	PVOs	WFP	Govt to govt	Total	Category % of total
Food for development	162.8	67.0	3.8	233.6	56.8
Maternal child feeding	77.4	20.0	0	97.4	23.7
School feeding	34.8	18.7	2.1	55.6	13.5
Pre-school feeding	4.0	0.3	0	4.3	1.0
Other child feeding	3.7	0	0	3.7	0.9
Food for work	42.9	28.0	1.7	72.6	17.7
Emergency aid	73.4	23.3	63.4	160.1	38.9
Refugee	5.8	19.6	39.2	64.6	15.7
Disaster	67.6	3.7	24.2	95.5	23.2
Relief and self-help	7.3	8.3	1.5	17.1	4.2
General relief	2.6	1.5	0.5	4.6	1.1
Self-help	4.7	0	1.0	5.7	1.4
Regular relief	0	6.8	0	6.8	1.7
Total	243.5	98.6	68.7	410.8	100.0
% by channel	59.3	24.0	16.7	100.0	100.0

[a] Figures rounded.

Source: Foreign Agricultural Service, USDA.

of US food aid going to Africa. An additional factor is that Egypt alone, the largest recipient of US food aid, accounted for more than 15% of total food aid shipments in 1986–8. The share of shipments to Latin America has also increased, reflecting unsteady growth in per capita grain production and a general worsening of the economic situation, exacerbated by high debt servicing.

Channels: All PL 480 Title I programme food aid is provided on a bilateral government-to-government basis. Title II project food aid has been provided through US PVOs and WFP as well as bilaterally. The average annual value of the Title II programme for FYs 1986–90 was $411 million. Of that total, 59% was channelled through PVOs, 24% through WFP and the remaining 17% provided government-to-government.

Title II assistance has been programmed under three categories: (i) food for development; (ii) emergency assistance; and (iii) relief and self-help. Under the first category, the largest part of food aid channelled through PVOs has supported maternal child feeding programmes, with a smaller amount going to FFW programmes. For WFP it has been the reverse. A significant amount of Title II food aid channelled through both PVOs and WFP has also supported school feeding programmes. While most of US emergency assistance through PVOs has gone to the victims of natural disasters, the bulk of US emergency food aid through the International Emergency Food Reserve (IEFR), administered by WFP, has been provided to refugees. Most of Title II food aid channelled on a government-to-government basis has been for emergency operations to meet natural disasters.

Of the Title II food aid channelled through PVOs in FY 1990, more than a third in value terms went to Africa, 27% to Asia, 25% to Latin America and 13% to the Near East. For WFP, 43% went to Africa, 31% to Asia, with the remainder shared almost equally between Latin America and the Near East. Most (70%) channelled on a government-to-government basis went to Africa.

Multilateral support: The US has been a strong supporter of multilateral food aid provided through the United Nations system. It was an early contributor to the United Nations Relief and Rehabilitation Administration (UNRRA) and has provided food aid through UNICEF and UNHCR. Most of its food aid provided multilaterally, however, goes through WFP. The US was a major force in the founding of WFP in 1961, providing over half of the total voluntary pledges made for its first three-year experimental period (1963–5). Since then, it has remained the largest single donor. The proportion of total pledges provided by the US to WFP's regular programme has fallen, however, as other donors have increased their contributions. The US has also made contributions to the IEFR every year since 1978. These have ranged between $25 million and $286 million at current prices, including contributions to protracted refugee and displaced person operations, and have represented between a quarter and a half of all annual contributions to the Reserve.

In recent years, US commodity pledges to WFP have consisted of 20 food items, the bulk of which has been in cereals and blended foods. The US is the only supplier to WFP of bulgur wheat, blended foods and soy-fortified products. Since 1986, three-quarters of all US PL 480 Title II commodities must be in the form of bagged, fortified or processed products, restricting the amount of whole cereals that can be provided. Under US cargo preference legislation, three-quarters of US food aid commodities must be shipped in US vessels. The US must also approve the supply of commodities to WFP-assisted emergency operations on a case-by-case basis. US contributions to the IEFR cannot be made in advance but must be made in response to individual requests for emergency aid. WFP has provided transport and monitoring services to the US, mainly in sub-Saharan Africa, for its bilateral food aid programme.

Food Aid Impact

This section synthesizes the main findings of recent evaluation reports and studies concerning various aspects of the US food aid programme.

Title I programme food aid   US programme food aid is highly concentrated geographically and provided to countries with a high priority in US foreign policy. The top five recipients received 44% of total programme food aid in FY 1988, with an average programme size of $89 million. Over half, in value terms, was supplied to countries in the Asia and Near East regions.

The main findings of a 1989 study (Bremer-Fox and Bailey, 1989) were that programme food aid appeared to have a generally positive impact at the macroeconomic and sectoral levels in recipient countries and should therefore be continued as a useful component of US assistance programmes to promote economic development, particularly in the food and agriculture sector. However, experience in using programme food aid to promote policy reform appears to have been mixed. The study found that, while programme food aid generally worked well, the grant component should be increased and the funds generated from food aid sales used to achieve greater short-term impact on the poor, thereby giving better support to structural adjustment and legislative reform.

The study stressed that food aid was, first and foremost, a resource transfer. It identified four ways by which programme food aid had the potential to increase incomes and reduce poverty: (i) transferring resources; (ii) stimulating policy reform; (iii) supporting investment in agricultural development; and (iv) directing benefits to the poor. The analysis concluded that, given its current design, programme food aid was unlikely to have an immediate or direct benefit for the poor because in general it did not increase the supply of food or its availability to them in the short term. It might have an indirect and long-term impact through promoting growth-supporting policies and agricultural programmes, but these measures were highly imperfect means of increasing the real incomes and consumption of the poor, and could even affect them negatively in the short term. Food aid could potentially bring greater short-term benefits to the poor if some of the local currency resources generated from food aid sales were redirected to support income transfer programmes, an approach that was rarely used at present.

At the macroeconomic level, the study concluded that programme food aid had largely served as balance of payments support and had generally financed imports that would probably have taken place in any case. In general, therefore, it had not added to the food supply available for consumption. Resources generated by programme food aid had had a generally positive effect on the allocation of resources by governments for development, primarily by encouraging funding of agricultural and rural development programmes.

Title II project food aid The three most prominent uses of Title II food aid for development have been: maternal and child health (MCH) supplementary feeding; school feeding; and FFW programmes. A guide has been published by AID on the design of food-aided development projects (Bryson *et al.*, 1991).

MCH supplementary feeding programmes were studied by Mora *et al.* (1990). From 1979 to 1989, according to the study, Title II non-emergency food aid reached an annual average of over 11 million beneficiaries in 39 developing countries through such programmes, which were implemented by US PVOs. US food aid also contributed to MCH programmes supported by WFP. The study noted that although, with the exception of WFP, it was the largest food-aided programme of its kind, US food aid reached only a small fraction of mothers and children suffering from persistent nutrition problems.

The main finding was that MCH feeding programmes can be effective in improving the dietary intake and nutritional status of recipients. In general, evaluations have not been adequately designed, however, to demonstrate their nutritional impact. Such programmes have increased the demand for, and use of, health services, improved nutrition knowledge, and served to transfer income to the poor. They continue to be needed, especially where malnutrition and chronic or seasonal household food insecurity affect large portions of the populations, as in sub-Saharan Africa. The study noted, however, that the number of beneficiaries of such programmes in that region declined by over half from 1983 to 1989, while those in Asia substantially increased.

Among the study's main technical and operational recommendations for future MCH feeding programmes were the incorporation of micro-nutrient supplementation; plans for the phasing-out of aid and handing over to recipient governments and beneficiary communities; and plans for sustaining health and nutrition benefits. The study recommended revision of AID policy and operational support for MCH feeding programmes by: shifting the emphasis from overall coverage to quality and effectiveness by delivering a better package of assistance to core beneficiary groups; focusing on both pregnant and lactating women and children under three years of age; using alternative approaches and institutions to reach vulnerable populations beyond the reach of the government delivery system; integrating MCH feeding into other development activities, such as income generation and community development projects, to ensure their sustainability; placing more emphasis on operational research; encouraging a more extensive but judicious use of monetization of the food aid provided; and developing training for strengthening institutional capacity, especially in beneficiary countries.

School feeding programmes supported by US food aid have in general three stated objectives: (i) increased enrolment and attendance; (ii) improved nutritional status; and (iii) improved cognitive or academic performance. Levinger (1986) found that evaluations were inconclusive on enrolment and attendance, mainly because there have been no baseline data, enrolment rates based on solid demographic data have not been used, information is lacking on the many variables that influence school attendance, and studies do not report changes over a long enough period of time. However, teachers have observed a positive impact in terms of attendance and performance. School feeding programmes may be most effective where poverty and deprivation are particularly acute, where attendance is not already high and where children come from rural, relatively poor, backgrounds. Several studies have pointed to the need for regularity of food supplies and have emphasized the importance of ensuring continuity of supplies from other sources when aid comes to an end.

Nutritional status can influence school attendance and performance. Studies have suggested, however, that other factors exert as much of an influence on school performance as feeding programmes. Nevertheless, the importance of improving nutrition should not be underestimated. A more integrated effort in addition to school feeding is required in programmes to improve school attendance and performance in order to remove the negative effects of interaction between acute malnutrition, hunger and the home environment. School feeding programmes seem to work best in poor, stable, rural areas. They seem to be less effective where there is great need for child labour as a contribution to the income of poor households. Alternative project designs that stress the income-transfer effect of school feeding programmes might counteract this negative effect.

Food-for-work (FFW) has been widely used in the Title II project food aid programme. A review by Bryson and others (1990) noted that, in FY 1989, over 148,000 tons of commodities, valued at $41 million and representing 15% of the Title II development budget, were used for FFW. Two-thirds went to Asia, the Middle East and North Africa, 16% to Latin America and 18% to sub-Saharan Africa.

The review observed that PVOs and WFP use FFW in development projects and emergency operations as a mode of food aid delivery that requires work from the recipient in return for the food received. It is regarded as an effective way to reach the truly needy in poor households and communities in food-deficit areas. FFW can bring development and welfare benefits and can provide relief in times of disaster. It may also draw labour away from other work, however, which can have negative effects.

Bryson and her colleagues found that FFW was successful in reaching poor areas and people, including women. FFW provided a useful device for identifying the needy in emergency situations as they were only ones who would work for food. Opportunities to achieve development results were created but regulations, administrative procedures and commodity management were not always helpful. Development benefits were significantly improved when food was combined with other resources (tools, materials, technical and administrative supervision) and when FFW activities were coordinated with the development programme of the recipient government.

The review recommended using FFW in conjunction with other Title II activities, for example with MCH supplementary feeding programmes, to provide sustainability through the creation of employment, income and assets, and as a means of targeting benefits on the poor. The study also recommended that, in using FFW, priority should be placed on preparedness for food emergencies, especially in Africa; increasing food availability in food-deficit areas; supporting public works and other asset creation activities in deprived communities; assisting relief and reconstruction following emergencies; alleviating the negative effects of structural adjustment on the poor; and addressing women's needs for jobs, training and opportunities to participate in enterprises that provide longer-term income and employment.

Targeted consumer food subsidies: An AID-sponsored workshop was held in November 1989 on targeted consumer food subsidies and the role of US food aid in Africa (Rubey *et al.*, 1991). The workshop concluded that targeted subsidies can cost-effectively ensure that low-income households have access to food. Food aid, in the form of either commodities or local currencies generated from food aid sales, has traditionally been used to supplement income through MCH and FFW programmes. However, food aid can also be used in targeted schemes that provide subsidized food, such as food stamp programmes, fair-price shops or programmes that subsidize the price of only those foods that self-target on the poor. Schemes where only food staples consumed primarily by the poor were subsidized have worked within the domestic food market, minimizing the cost of targeting and offering a means of reaching the poorest households without disrupting supply to the rest of the population.

The workshop concluded that self-targeted schemes were most likely to succeed when: (i) significant differences in food preferences existed between poor and wealthier households; (ii) a food commodity preferred by the poor passed through central points in the marketing chain, making it easier to apply the subsidy; (iii) there was no political opposition to using less preferred food for subsidizing consumption by the poor; and (iv) the subsidized food was not purchased for animal feed or industrial processing.

Title III programmes   It is too early to assess the impact of the Title III food aid programmes designed under the new legislation. A brief description of a sample of these programmes gives an indication of their scope and objective.

A Title III agreement signed with Honduras supports strengthened agricultural policy reforms. Balance of payments support is supplied for food purchases without increasing the country's severe foreign debt burden, thereby allowing scarce foreign exchange to be used for other imports needed to spur economic growth. Agricultural sector reform measures agreed upon include a redefinition of land tenure policies, continued liberalization of agricultural prices and trade, increased access to production inputs and services through the private sector, and promotion of higher levels of exports by investing local currency generated from food aid sales. A targeted food aid programme provides a safety net to mitigate the adverse social effects of the economic adjustment programme. Maternal/child and single mothers food coupon programmes are to be expanded to increase attendance at health centres and help reduce drop-out and repetition rates in primary schools.

A Title III agreement has been signed with Kenya with the goal of increasing agricultural productivity and net farm incomes, in co-ordination with a World Bank agricultural sector adjustment loan and a cereal sector reform programme supported by the European Community. A more efficient national maize and bean marketing system is being developed that will provide greater price incentives to producers. Budget support will be provided from food aid sales for improving rural roads, thereby reducing marketing costs.

In Mozambique, a Title III agreement has been signed to improve food security, expand the participation of the private sector in the economy and ensure access to food for the most vulnerable groups. A well targeted and integrated safety net programme is being developed. Competitive markets are being strengthened and trade liberalized. The efficiency of public sector management of food assistance programmes is being improved. The government's direct role in the importation, processing, marketing and rationing of essential food items is to be reduced. A common set of principles for improving the developmental effectiveness of local currency generated from the sale of food aid will be developed.

US PVOs and co-operatives   PVOs and co-operatives are seen as having an important role to play in the implementation of the new US food aid legislation. Accordingly, between $10 million and $13.5 million in cash will be made available to them each year under Title II to establish new food aid programmes and to meet administrative, transport and distribution costs. They are also eligible for support from local currency proceeds generated from food aid sales under Title III.

A Food Aid Consultative Group established under the new legislation will include a representative of each US PVO and co-operative participating in the Title II programme as well as representatives of indigenous non-governmental organizations. AID has provided funding to Food Aid Management, a consortium of five of the major PVOs involved in the programme, to promote the adoption of common policies and management standards for food aid programming, to develop basic food aid management systems, to design training programmes, to provide a forum for discussions on management concerns and generally to facilitate collaborative activities among PVOs.

AID recognizes the significant role that PVOs and co-operatives play in providing humanitarian and development assistance to the developing world. US PVO humanitarian activities originated over a century ago in response to natural disasters. With their ability to respond quickly and effectively, PVOs have become key actors in disaster relief. Their efforts have also broadened to include programmes aimed at addressing the root causes of hunger, poverty and vulnerability to disasters, and hence longer-term development.

In 1989, 13 PVOs and co-operatives operating in 34 countries received 770,000 tons of US food aid commodities valued at $210 million for development projects. Over 85% was channelled through the two largest PVOs, Co-operative for American Relief Everywhere (CARE) and Catholic Relief Services (CRS). These and other PVOs also provide essential non-food inputs for food-aided projects. They also play an important advocacy role in the public debate and with the media concerning US food aid and other foreign assistance.

A report to Congress by the US General Accounting Office (1990) on non-emergency food aid provided through PVOs and co-operatives addressed two important issues: (i) whether PVOs were less willing than in the past to sponsor non-emergency projects, particularly in Africa; and (ii) the problems encountered by PVOs in implementing them. The report found that PVOs continued to have a strong commitment to the non-emergency, Title II programme. While the volume of food aid provided by PVOs world-wide under that programme was about the same in 1989 as it was in 1986, there had been a drop of about 10% in the aid to Africa, where needs were perceived to be growing. Furthermore, PVOs had changed the ways they used Title II commodities in Africa. While fewer PVO requests were being made for traditional MCH supplementary and school feeding projects, more were being made for FFW programmes. In addition, significantly more food aid was requested for sale.

Among the reasons given for these trends were that PVOs and recipient governments now emphasized community-based development projects, rather than charitable relief; the high operating costs of MCH projects; the limited technical, managerial and operational capacities of local organizations to implement effective health and educational projects; and the inconclusive or negative results of many MCH projects, which gave the impression that they were ineffective in reaching their objective of improving nutritional status.

About a third of the value of US food aid for the PVO programmes in Africa was sold in FY 1990 compared with 14% in 1987. According to AID and PVO officials, factors contributing to this increase have included: weak transportation, health and education infrastructure, making projects involving direct food distribution more difficult and expensive, and hence less attractive, to implement; use of sales proceeds to buy domesticly produced foods, thereby reducing inland transport and storage costs and encouraging increased local production and offsetting operating costs; and the emergence of new PVOs requesting Title II commodities to generate local currencies for development projects rather than to distribute food directly to needy people. The report recommended that the adequacy of PVOs' financial and management systems be considered when reviewing their requests to sell Title II commodities and that, if necessary, sufficient sales proceeds should be set aside for improving these systems.

Emergency assistance As with other donors, much of US emergency food aid went to sub-Saharan Africa during the 1980s. An evaluation of the US response to the African famine in 1984–6 noted that it was larger than that of any other donor and represented the concerted effort of numerous government agencies, PVOs, businesses and the general public (Wood *et al.*, 1986). The evaluation report pointed out that resolving Africa's food problems would require a long-term development effort.

The report found that successful emergency food aid distribution was achieved by PVOs, the private sector and regional and local governments, much of whose attention was focused on removing logistical constraints. All distribution modes, including FFW, sales and general distribution, were used. Sales were effective, especially in urban areas, where commercial markets were used to monetize emergency food assistance.

Recipient governments could be effective in co-ordinating an emergency food aid response, but most had limited capabilities. Strengthening those capabilities, especially in chronically drought-affected countries, helped foster government commitment to deal with food emergencies.

Fully effective co-ordination among donors was not achieved in all cases, but where it was, the impact of emergency food assistance programmes was enhanced. Donor co-ordination was most effective if begun early, when donors were collectively involved in identifying and assessing needs. Donor co-ordination was maximized when the government of the affected country was the principal co-ordinating agent at the central, regional and local levels.

The evaluation found that the private sector played an effective role, principally in logistics. Its contribution could be expanded, thereby easing the burden on public sector institutions and increasing the impact of emergency food aid operations. Increased authority to contract for private sector resources and more experience in using them would increase the contribution of the private sector to emergency food relief efforts.

Effective targeting through improved information and early warning systems was

essential for effective emergency operations. Without adequate and accurate information, neither the government nor donors were willing to act decisively. Traditional
coping mechanisms greatly reduced suffering, saved many lives, extended emergency
food distribution over time and to others, and mitigated the negative effects of distribution shortfalls. Better information about these coping mechanisms would, therefore, assist in the design and implementation of emergency food aid operations.

The evaluation emphasized the links between emergency food aid and development.
Lack of adequate income was at the root of both underdevelopment and food emergencies. Development programmes were often not aimed at increasing the economic well-
being of groups most vulnerable to drought. When drought occurred, the income of
these groups collapsed, leading to famine and the need for emergency food aid.

Flexible food aid Four mechanisms have been used with the aim of increasing the
effectiveness and flexibility of US food aid: counterpart funds in Title I programmes,
monetization in Title II and Section 416 programmes, trilateral transactions and food
auctions.
Counterpart funds have been generated from the sale of Title I commodities, and have
been placed in special accounts in the recipient countries. They may be owned by the
benefiting government or by the US: in either case, the US has retained control over
their use. It was in the Marshall Plan that the counterpart fund concept became widely
known and the issues associated with it began to occupy widespread attention. The
concept was attractive. Providing food aid met a genuine human need. Counterpart
funds provided resources to help a country become independent of aid. Donor
influence over their use increased the possibility of their being invested productively.

A recent review of the literature on the developmental impact of counterpart funds
(Bruton and Hill, 1991) concluded that their effectiveness depended heavily on the circumstances in the recipient country at the particular time. They could increase or
decrease the money supply; affect resource allocation within government budgets, and
between the public and private sectors; and influence government policy choices.
Where recipient governments and donors agreed, counterpart funds could be used to
support policy objectives and change. Where there was disagreement, the review concluded that counterpart funds probably played little role in attempts by donors to
impose their views through conditionality. The real transfer of aid took place when
the food commodities were provided, not when the counterpart funds were used.
Counterpart funds could play a role, however, if their existence led to continued
discussion between recipient and donor so that some enhanced understanding of
development was achieved by both.

These conclusions are consistent with several aspects of current AID policy on
counterpart funds. This policy does not require that counterpart funds be generated
in all countries but only when required by statute or when deemed to be desirable by
the AID country mission. Current AID policy also imposes more rigorous accountability standards for managing local currency. The literature review questions
whether this will increase the benefits of generating and programming counterpart
funds, while involving greater administrative costs. The review found very few
instances where counterpart funds had been destabilizing and inflationary, and concluded that these concerns were rarely important.
Monetization of Title II and Section 416 commodities has become an important way
of helping PVOs and co-operatives meet the local currency costs of development projects and food distribution. A recent study (Pines, 1990) noted that monetization had
totalled more than $39 million in FY 1990. Several factors had slowed the monetization

process, however, including the costs and time required for project preparation, the absence of clear initial guidance and delays in approval. A field manual on monetization has now been issued. AID country missions and US embassies have supported PVOs in identifying opportunities for monetization. Pines' study found that, while evidence supported optimistic conclusions about monetization, some problems and issues remained, including protecting the proceeds against loss of value caused by devaluation and inflation, the risk of dependence on monetization, and the high administrative costs of preparing and implementing major programmes involving the sale of food aid commodities. It concluded that monetization alone could not satisfy the financial needs of PVOs and co-operatives working in development. Dollar as well as local currency costs had to be met. Although a useful tool, monetization proved to be an important, but limited, means of financing development assistance.

Trilateral food aid transactions have been implemented whereby a food commodity (e.g. wheat) provided by the US to one developing country (e.g. Zimbabwe) has been exchanged for a locally produced food (e.g. white maize) not produced in the US, which has been used as food aid in another developing country (e.g. Zambia). A study of trilateral transactions carried out in the mid-1980s (Ronco, 1988) concluded that they could be at least as timely as the provision of food aid through bilateral transactions. They might be slower, however, where the logistics were complicated and food had to be transported over long distances by road. The cost of trilateral transactions varied considerably. The transactions examined were all related to emergency operations. The study suggested, however, that they could effectively support policy dialogue and complement production-oriented project assistance where local currencies were generated from food aid sales.

The dangers of trilateral operations reinforcing high-cost, inefficient parastatals with a monopoly on grains trading to the detriment of private traders were recognized. Any negative impact on commercial trade was found to be marginal, however, as the quantities involved were small. These transactions could support market development by assisting developing countries to market their surpluses and thereby increase their purchasing power to buy additional commodities. Trilateral transactions also allowed developing countries on both the supplying and receiving sides to benefit in the context of South-South trading arrangements.

Food auctions have been used in African countries with varying degrees of success. AID is seeking ways of using US food aid to support liberalization of grain markets, including channelling food aid commodities through private sector outlets. One mechanism has been to sell the commodities to private traders through oral auctions or sealed bids.

Investigation of the African experience with food aid auctions has provided several lessons (Bremer-Fox *et al.*, 1990). Auctions can be used with success to sell food aid commodities. They offer a promising mechanism for transferring such commodities into private marketing channels. However, governments and traders in developing countries have relatively little experience with auctions. Substantial care and attention must therefore be devoted to the design of auctions and follow-up procedures if serious problems are to be avoided. Furthermore, auctions cannot be conducted successfully in all situations; negotiated sales may therefore have to be used in specific cases to move food aid commodities into private channels.

Factors to be taken into consideration in designing and implementing food aid auctions include choosing commodities with a strong and competitive market; understanding the local market structure; obtaining full government support; and establishing well-defined financial and pricing procedures. The timing of auctions is likely to have an important impact on the outcome, given the weakness and volatility of food markets in Africa. Holding auctions when the market is already well provisioned should be avoided as demand would be weak, local currency generation reduced and private marketing channels disrupted. These negative effects might be reduced by holding a number of smaller auctions and by announcing auctions in advance so that traders can adjust their buying and selling plans accordingly. This approach might involve substantial storage costs, however, which might exceed the costs to the government and private traders of immediate sales.

Domestic economy and commercial trade The effects of US food aid on its own domestic economy and commercial trade have been the subject of controversial debate over many years.

The domestic effects of the US food aid in wheat over the period 1986/87 – 1988/89 have recently been analysed using different assumptions about the degree to which food aid displaces commercial exports (Price *et al.*, 1990). The domestic effects of the food aid programmes depend primarily on their influence on prices, which in turn is affected by the amount of aid provided and the overriding supply and demand conditions. The effect of food aid on prices is greater in times of tight supply than in periods of surplus. The extent to which food aid displaces commercial exports also plays a role. When food aid is mostly additional to what exports would have been in any case, the impact is greatest.

The study showed that the effects of food aid, and the resulting price increases, were felt differently by producers, marketers, consumers and taxpayers. Wheat producers benefited from higher farm income; maize producers benefited from greater demand for their product as the amount of wheat available for feed diminished. Marketers and processors were adversely affected by higher wheat prices to the extent that they could not pass them on to consumers. Exporters and the US merchant marine benefited from higher shipments and revenues. Consumers may have faced slightly higher retail prices for wheat products, but there were no overall inflationary effects. Under reasonable assumptions concerning the commercial displacement effect of food aid, taxpayers paid more to provide food aid than when aid was not extended (as they do for any foreign assistance). However, the domestic price effects and resultant government savings mitigated the taxpayer's net commodity cost; in effect, the total domestic costs of providing food aid were lower than the direct budget costs.

The commercial trade effects of US food aid remain unclear, even after almost 40 years of experience and many studies and reports. A recent review of the evidence (Nathan Associates Inc., 1990) explored the short-term impact and found that food aid generally displaced commercial imports substantially in countries where it accounted for a relatively minor share of total food availability. The impact on commercial imports, positive or negative, was relatively minor in countries where food aid was a major source of both imports and total grain availability. The review suggested that more study was necessary, however, before definitive conclusions could be made.

A second major conclusion of the study was that the short-term impact of food aid on commercial imports depended both on the design of the food aid programme and the structure of food markets in recipient countries, which were influenced by domestic policy. Programmes that provided food aid through channels that did not directly compete with commercial markets, and provided a net increase in consumption by low-income consumers, were less likely to displace commercial imports than programmes that closely resembled commercial imports in their design and operation. Food aid programmes operating outside commercial channels generally provided food at below market prices. They had the potential to increase demand through income transfer and price effects.

These findings suggest that Title I programme food aid, which is sold for local currency, is more likely to substitute for commercial imports than Title II project food aid targeted on the poor through non-commercial channels, such as MCH supplementary feeding and FFW programmes. Programme food aid is more likely to add to commercial imports when sold at subsidized prices. Without concessional financing, however, subsidized sales programmes are less likely to translate into increased commercial imports over the longer term.

Future Directions

Prospects for future US food aid must take into account significant international and domestic changes that have occurred in the recent past. Internationally, the end of the cold war period and the reordering of East-West relationships could have a strong positive effect on all development assistance, including food aid, through the 'peace dividend' resulting from large reductions in military expenditures, including military aid. For some countries, on the other hand, a diminished foreign policy stake could lead to a decrease in food aid and other forms of assistance.

Domesticly, the multiple constituencies and objectives of US food aid have given it a broad base of support. To what extent will the balance of interests and concerns be influenced by recent major world events and by domestic considerations? How will the new legislation affect the traditional relationship between agricultural, foreign policy, international development and humanitarian constituencies and interests that has been the hallmark of US food aid over the past 40 years? Will food aid continue to be treated separately from other forms of foreign assistance, or will it be brought within the totality of US foreign economic aid?

The new food aid legislation calls on the US President to make increased food aid contributions to meet new food aid requirements. The strong humanitarian impulse of food aid is likely to remain, but in an era when development agencies are required to do more with fewer resources, and each element of the US aid programme must achieve maximum developmental impact, how will food aid fare in the competition for aid resources?

A major factor that could influence future US food aid policy is the GATT Uruguay Round of agricultural trade negotiations. It has been argued that the single most important step that can be taken to provide global food security is the reform of the world agricultural trading system. The US has proposed a post-Uruguay Round food aid regime that would have two main elements: (i) the establishment of mechanisms to ensure that the implementation of a Uruguay Round agreement would not adversely affect the food aid needs of developing countries; and (ii) a mechanism to avoid any circumvention of disciplines on export subsidies under the guise of food aid. The US has proposed that the contracting parties work within the context of the Committee on Food Aid Policies and Programmes, the Food Aid Committee and the Consultative Subcommittee on Surplus Disposal to develop mutually acceptable criteria for providing food aid, to review food aid uses and disciplines and to reinforce the system of usual marketing requirements. It has also proposed that the level of food aid requirements projected periodically by the CFA be reviewed, and that a new Food Aid Convention be initiated to establish a level of food aid commitments sufficient to meet the legitimate needs of developing countries in the post-Uruguay Round period.

Another factor will be performance attained under the new food aid legislation. Provision has been written into the 1990 Act for an independent evaluation of the activities carried out under each of the three titles of the food aid programme 'not later than two years after the date of the enactment of this Act'. The US Comptroller General, whose basic responsibility is to serve Congress by conducting reviews of federal programmes, will prepare and submit a report on the results of the evaluations to the Committees on Foreign Affairs and on Agriculture of the House of Representatives and the Committee on Agriculture, Nutrition and Forestry of the Senate.

The new legislation emphasizes the role of food aid in enhancing food security and combating hunger and malnutrition. It also gives policy priority to privatization. Experience in these fields is recent and limited. The legislation calls for food aid to be co-ordinated and integrated into US development assistance objectives and programmes and with the overall development strategies of recipient countries. Special emphasis is to be placed on, and funds devoted to, activities that will increase the nutritional impact of the food aid programmes and their effects on child survival programmes and projects in least developed countries by improving their design and implementation. Africa will be a focus of attention owing to its special and urgent problems. But successful use of food aid in that region has been limited, and US PVOs have met with significant problems.

The priorities given to food aid in the new legislation will call for effective co-ordination both in the US and in the developing countries. How will Title I food aid programmes with market development objectives, that are supplied through government channels, relate to Title III programmes designed to privatize agricultural marketing and trade? How will food aid provided under the different titles be co-ordinated in the same country? Arrangements will be needed in the recipient countries to ensure that food aid flows from all sources are co-ordinated and that the skills, experience and resources of all donors and agencies are combined within an integrated country programme of assistance for the benefit of poor, food-insecure people.

By the beginning of the 1990s, the US had started to reshape its economic assistance programme to respond to the demands of a new era and to lay the foundations of a new partnership for development. In September 1990, a new AID mission statement was issued, pledging assistance to developing countries 'to realize their full national potential through the development of open and democratic societies and the dynamism of free markets and individual initiative'. US development assistance would be guided by six principles: support for free markets and broad-based economic growth; concern for individuals and the development of their economic and social well-being; support for democracy; encouragement of responsible environmental policies and prudent management of natural resources; support for lasting solutions to transnational problems; and provision of humanitarian assistance to those who suffer from natural or man-made disasters. Food aid integrated with other forms of US assistance was seen as having an important role to play in supporting these principles. With the new Clinton Administration, further redefinition of goals and of the means of attaining them can be expected.

References

Bremer-Fox, Jennifer and Bailey, Laura (1989). *The Development Impact of U.S. Program Food Assistance: Evidence from the A.I.D. Evaluation Literature*. Washington, D.C., Robert R. Nathan Associates, Inc. for A.I.D., August.

Bremer-Fox, Jennifer *et al.* (1990). *Experience with Auctions of Food Aid Commodities in Africa*. Washington, D.C., Nathan Associates, Inc., for A.I.D., March.

Bruton, Henry and Hill, Catherine (1991). *The Developmental Impact of Counterpart Funds. A Review of the Literature.* Washington, D.C., A.I.D., February.

Bryson, Judy *et al.* (1991). *Project Food Aid. User's Guide for the Design of Food-aided Development Projects.* Washington, D.C., A.I.D., May.

Bryson, Judy *et al.* (1990). *Food for Work: A Review of the 1980s with Recommendations for the 1990s.* Washington, D.C., A.I.D., February.

Levinger, Beryl (1986). *School Feeding Programs in Developing Countries: An Analysis of Actual and Potential Impact.* Washington, D.C., A.I.D. Evaluation Special Study No. 30, January.

Mora, Jose O. *et al.* (1990). *The Effectiveness of Maternal and Child Health (MCH) Supplementary Feeding Programs. An Analysis of Performance in the 1980s and Potential Role in the 1990s.* Washington, D.C., Logical Technical Services Corporation for A.I.D., September.

Nathan Associates, Inc. (1990). *Food Aid Impacts on Commercial Trade. A Review of Evidence.* Washington, D.C., A.I.D., October.

Pines, James M. (1990). *Monetization Comes of Age. A Review of U.S. Government, PVOs and Cooperatives Experience.* Washington, D.C., A.I.D., June.

Price, J. Michael *et al.* (1990). *The Domestic Effects of U.S. Overseas Wheat Aid.* Washington, D.C., US Department of Agriculture, May.

Ronco Consulting Corporation (1988). *Trilateral Food Aid Transactions: U.S.G. Experience in the 1980s.* Washington, D.C., March.

Rubey, Lawrence M. *et al.* (1991). *Targeted Consumer Food Subsidies and the Role of United States Food Aid Programming in Africa.* Washington, D.C., A.I.D., January.

United States General Accounting Office (1990). *Foreign Assistance: Non-Emergency Food Aid Provided through Private Voluntary Organizations.* Report to Congressional Requesters, GAO/NSIAD-90-179, Washington, D.C., July.

Wood, Dennis H. *et al.* (1986). *The U.S. Response to the African Famine, 1984–86. Vol. 1. An Evaluation of the Emergency Food Assistance Program: Synthesis Report.* Washington, D.C., Program Evaluation Report No. 16, A.I.D., November.

Appendix Table 17.1 *US: Cereal food aid deliveries ('000 tons – in grain equivalent)*

	1987	1988	1989	1990	1991	1987–91 Average
Total:	7613.2	7420.0	5958.7	7641.0	7156.3	7157.8
By food aid channel:						
– Bilateral	7095.9	6569.6	5495.0	7050.7	6370.9	6516.5
– Gvt-to-Gvt	6484.3	5619.3	4621.6	5873.2	5506.4	5621.0
– through NGOs	611.6	950.3	873.3	1177.5	864.5	895.5
– Multilateral	517.3	850.4	463.7	590.3	785.3	641.4
By food aid category:						
– Emergency Relief	368.8	773.8	520.0	778.6	1030.5	694.3
– Project	1480.4	1833.2	1232.5	1206.4	940.3	1338.5
– Agr./Rural Development	294.9	525.1	284.2	277.6	158.8	308.1
– Nutrition Intervention	593.6	792.3	380.4	266.9	291.0	464.8
– Food Reserve	–	11.2	3.0	–	13.3	5.5
– Other Development Project	591.9	504.7	564.9	661.9	477.2	560.1
– Non-project (Programme)	5764.1	4813.0	4206.1	5656.1	5185.6	5125.0
By region:						
– Sub-Saharan Africa	1442.9	1571.4	1082.5	1134.0	1521.3	1350.4
– North Africa/Mid-East	2323.2	1564.6	1913.1	2541.7	2346.6	2137.8
– Asia and Pacific	1802.3	2351.7	1368.5	1162.8	1232.6	1583.6
– Latin America and Caribbean	2044.1	1932.4	1583.1	1854.3	1555.5	1793.9
– Europe	0.7	–	11.5	948.2	500.3	292.1

Source: WFP/INTERFAIS Database

Appendix Table 17.2 *US: Non-cereal food aid deliveries ('000 tons)*

	1987	1988	1989	1990	1991	1987–91 Average
Total:	813.3	944.7	526.1	627.0	411.1	664.4
By food aid channel:						
– Bilateral	720.3	882.2	481.2	577.9	350.9	602.6
– Gvt-to-Gvt	559.9	755.8	392.1	437.5	193.6	467.8
– through NGOs	160.4	126.4	89.5	140.4	157.3	134.8
– Multilateral	93.0	62.5	44.5	49.1	60.2	61.9
By food aid category:						
– Emergency Relief	82.4	78.0	59.3	73.3	105.9	79.8
– Project	284.8	236.2	126.0	121.1	132.2	180.1
– Agr./Rural Development	44.8	58.2	30.9	35.7	37.3	41.4
– Nutrition Intervention	149.2	133.3	33.5	32.8	34.0	76.6
– Other Development Project	90.7	44.7	61.6	52.6	60.9	62.1
– Non-project (Programme)	446.2	630.5	340.8	432.6	173.0	404.6
By region:						
– Sub-Saharan Africa	149.6	118.5	100.2	88.8	104.4	112.3
– North Africa/Mid-East	106.1	145.5	92.5	61.6	63.7	93.9
– Asia and Pacific	284.1	479.4	239.4	287.1	116.3	281.2
– Latin America and Caribbean	272.2	201.4	89.4	112.1	116.2	158.3
– Europe	1.2	–	4.5	77.5	10.5	18.7

Source: ibid.

Appendix Figure 17.1 US food aid levels 1955–89

Source: Economic Research Service, US Department of Agriculture

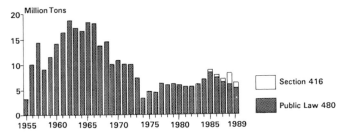

Appendix Figure 17.2 US food aid and total agricultural exports 1955–88

Source: ibid.

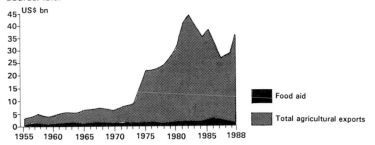

Appendix Figure 17.3 US and global cereal food aid: 1970/71–1988/89 (July/June)

Source: Donors, IWC, WFP/INTERFAIS

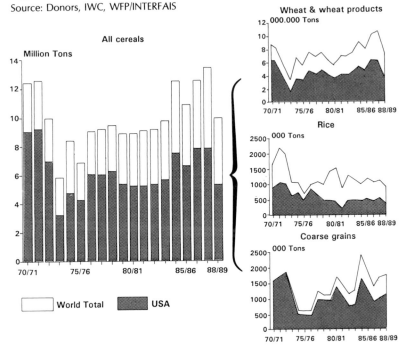

Appendix Figure 17.4 US and global non-cereal food aid: 1977–88 (left)
Source: Donors, WFP/INTERFAIS (left)

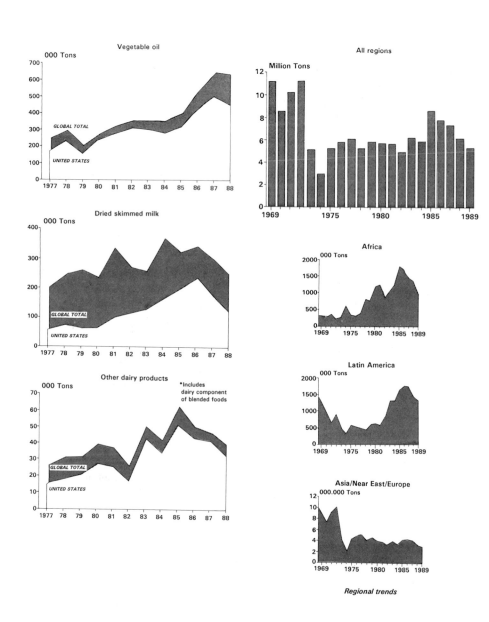

Appendix Figure 17.5 US food aid by region: 1969–89 (right)
Source: A.I.D. (right)

Index

exports, 1, 63, 77–80 *passim*, 90, 100, 111, 131, 133, 134, 143, 195, 221, 227, 232, 233, 237; earnings, 41, 78, 111, 120, 132–5 *passim*
extension, 65, 85, 104, 115, 137, 139, 178, 180
Ezekiel, M., 61

fair-price shops, 58, 64, 69, 70, 227
family planning, 99, 178
famine, 2, 5, 7, 41, 45, 51, 57, 60, 69, 126, 140, 150, 173, 215, 216, 218, 222, 229, 230
FAO, 1, 4, 5, 61, 83, 93, 115, 116, 125, 135, 136, 138, 140, 159, 179, 183, 189
feed, livestock, 70, 104–5, 215, 227
fertilizers, 42, 43, 79, 112, 196, 200, 215
Finland, 3, 7, 33, 35
fish, 71, 101, 134, 135, 157, 158, 169, 196, 202, 203, 208
fisheries, 46, 48, 49, 66
financial assistance, 8, 11, 13, 14, 16, 24, 30, 41, 59, 72, 115, 116, 166, 173, 175, 179–81 *passim*, 185, 194, 197, 198, 204, 205, 210–12 *passim*
flexibility, 14, 16, 24, 25, 80, 193, 197, 198, 210, 219, 230–2
floods, 41, 42, 47, 50, 94, 101; protection, 11, 46, 48, 49, 51
Food Aid Conventions, 3, 5, 8, 16, 23, 143, 144, 146, 157, 159, 161, 165, 167–9 *passim*, 177, 178, 183, 185, 192, 197, 200, 202, 203, 208, 211, 221–2, 233
food coupon/stamp programmes, 94, 227
Food-for-Work, 2, 11–12, 30, 113, 149, 150, 171, 178, 180, 184, 195, 198, 212, 223, 226–9 *passim, see also under individual countries*
foreign exchange, 2, 14, 61, 79, 80, 101, 111, 131, 133–7 *passim*, 140, 149, 150, 152, 218, 227
foreign policy, 16, 216, 217, 224, 233
forestry, 64–5, 68, 71, 79, 81–2, 100, 124, 136
fortified foods, 61, 213, 224
France, 35, 34, 53, 86, 87, 96, 97, 101, 106, 111, 114, 141
fruit, dried, 146, 147
fuel, 15, 71, 81, 114, 124, 137
fumigation, 91

G24, 172
GATT, 152, 233
Germany, 14, 16–23, *passim*, 33, 34, 37, 38, 46, 53, 54, 73, 74, 86, 87, 96, 97, 107, 114, 115, 117, 136, 147, 177–88; administration, 17, 18, 181–4; agriculture, 172, 177–9, *passim*, 184; and EC aid, 181, 185; BALM, 182, 183; bilateral programme, 179, 180, 184–5, 187, 188; BMZ, 179, 181–2, 185; emergency aid, 179, 180, 183, 187, 188; GTZ, 182–4 *passim*; NGOs, 177, 183, 185–6; ODA, 177, 183, 186
Germany, East, 186
Ghana, 159, 211
grains, 14, 22, 41, 42, 57–63 *passim*, 68, 70, 72, 93, 105, 134, 160, 161, 189, 202, 221, 222; International Grains Agreement, 144
grants, 1, 2, 4, 6, 8, 18, 27, 30, 59, 91, 100, 102, 151, 159, 166, 170, 200–3 *passim*, 205, 217, 219, 222, 224
Greece, 35, 86
Green Revolution, 9, 57, 58, 61, 71, 77, 222
groundnuts, 111
growth, 10, 26, 42, 58, 72, 78, 89, 100, 105, 110, 131–3 *passim*, 140
Guatemala, 94, 184
guidelines, 7, 30–1, 143–4, 157, 178–81 *passim*, 192, 207, 233, 234
Gulf crisis, 100

habits, food, 14, 15, 29, 92, 173, 179, 198, 203, 227
Haiti, 184
handling costs, 25, 46, 80–1, 84, 91, 110, 113, 114, 116, 146, 204
Hay, R., 12
health care, 12, 13, 46, 60, 64, 65, 71, 78, 81, 83–5 *passim*, 89, 92–5 *passim*, 104, 105, 110, 114–16

passim, 121, 133, 172, 181, 184, 185, 211, 225, 227, 229; MCH, 2, 12, 67, 83, 92, 93, 103, 121, 126, 225–9 *passim*
high yielding varieties, 41–3, *passim*, 61, 71, 78, 85
Hill, Catherine, 230
Honduras, 9–11, 13–15 *passim*, 35, 36, 88–97, 179, 184, 227; administration, 91, 95; agriculture, 89–93 *passim*; COHASA, 90–2 *passim*, 95; emergency aid, 94, 96, 97; FFW, 89, 92–3, programme aid, 91–2, 96, 97; project aid, 89, 92–3, 96, 97; SECPLAN, 90–6 *passim*
housing, 60, 64, 68, 104, 136
humanitarian factors, 8, 16, 18, 26, 47, 145, 172, 182, 189, 207, 211, 228, 233
hunger, 7, 11, 41, 51, 59–61 *passim*, 71, 179, 186, 191, 197, 207, 216–19 *passim*, 226, 228, 234

immunization, 67, 83, 93, 132
imports, commercial, 2, 5, 15, 41, 61–3, 78–80 *passim*, 111, 122, 131, 132, 135–8 *passim*, 180, 193–5 *passim*, 218, 225, 227, 232–3
income, 11, 12, 15, 67–9 *passim*, 71, 77, 80, 89, 91–4, 103–5, 224–7 *passim*, 230; transfer, 2, 46, 47, 49, 64, 94, 104, 205, 225, 226, 233
India, 5, 8–11, 13–15, 34–6 *passim*, 53, 56–74, 135, 171, 172, 195; administration, 70; agriculture, 57, 58, 60, 69, 71; as donor, 71; emergency aid, 61, 68–70, 73, 74; Employment Guarantee Schemes, 68–9; fair-price shops, 58, 64, 68, 70; FFW, 63–4, 68, 70; ICDS, 66–7, 71; NDDB, 65, 66; Operation Flood, 65; programme aid, 57, 59–61, 73, 74; project aid, 57, 61–70 *passim*, 73, 74
Indonesia, 8, 148, 184, 203
industry/industrialization, 42, 71, 78, 89, 110, 132, 134
inflation, 58, 60, 90, 208, 219, 230, 231
infrastructure, 11, 13, 15, 26, 42, 48, 58, 65, 68, 82, 92, 95, 101, 103, 104, 114–15, 121, 123–4, 128, 133, 149, 161, 197, 201
integration, of food aid, 14, 23–5 *passim*, 51, 52, 72, 89, 96, 101–3, 105, 113, 131, 145, 157, 162, 166, 174, 179, 186, 189, 192, 198, 217, 219
interest rates, 111, 133, 208
International Development Association, 30 n1, 110, 115
International Emergency Food Reserve, 3, 13, 25–6, 28–9, 31, 71, 143, 144, 147, 148, 158, 159, 165, 170, 177, 185, 194, 196, 200–2 *passim*, 204, 208, 211, 223, 224; Immediate Response Account, 3, 7, 25, 29
International Finance Corporation, 136
International Food Policy Research Institute, 44, 46, 99
International Fund for Agricultural Development, 135
International Labour Organization, 82, 136, 140
International Monetary Fund, 58, 100, 179
investment, 11, 42, 52, 58, 59, 61, 78, 82, 90, 100, 101, 139, 186, 225, 227
Iraq, 7
irrigation, 11, 42, 43, 46, 49, 58, 60, 61, 65, 68–71 *passim*, 78–9, 82, 85, 99, 100, 104, 112–13, 134, 137
Islamic Development Bank, 79
Italy, 33, 34, 101, 106, 107, 117, 141, 142

Jamaica, 159
Japan, 3, 7, 16–23 *passim*, 33, 34, 37, 38, 53, 85, 86, 111, 117, 121, 122, 129, 141, 147, 200–6; administration, 17, 18, 201–2; bilateral programme, 201–4 *passim*, 206; emergency aid, 206; NGOs, 201, 203, 204; ODA, 200, 202, 204; triangular transactions, 85, 202, 203, 205

Kampuchea, 7, 20, 151, 152, 211
Kenya, 8, 184, 203, 227
Konandreas, Panos, 223,
Korea, Republic of, 205,
Kuwait, 35

labour, 10, 42, 68, 113–15 *passim*, 136, 226